Ethics
and the
Environment

edited by
Donald Scherer
Thomas Attig
Bowling Green State University

PRENTICE-HALL, INC., Englewood Cliffs, New Jersey 07632

Library of Congress Cataloging in Publication Data

Main entry under title:
Ethics and the environment.

  Bibliography:
  1. Environmental policy—Addresses, essays, lectures.
2. Environmental policy—Moral and ethical aspects—
Addresses, essays, lectures. 3. Environmental policy—
United States—Addresses, essays, lectures. 4. Environ-
mental policy—United States —Moral and ethical aspects—
Addresses, essays, lectures. I. Scherer, Donald.
II. Attig, Thomas (date)
HC79.E5E75 1983   179   82-20502
ISBN 0-13-290163-3

Editorial/production supervision and by F. Hubert
Cover design: Wanda Lubelska
Manufacturing buyer: Harry P. Baisley

Printed in the United States of America

10 9 8 7 6 5 4 3 2 1

ISBN 0-13-290163-3

Prentice-Hall International, Inc., *London*
Prentice-Hall of Australia Pty. Limited, *Sydney*
Editora Prentice-Hall do Brasil, Ltda., *Rio de Janeiro*
Prentice-Hall Canada Inc., *Toronto*
Prentice-Hall of India Private Limited, *New Delhi*
Prentice-Hall of Japan, Inc., *Tokyo*
Prentice-Hall of Southeast Asia Pte. Ltd., *Singapore*
Whitehall Books Limited, *Wellington, New Zealand*

Contents

Preface

The rich and growing literature on ethics and the environment has not to date received the wider circulation it deserves. The timeliness of this collection is a function both of the new activity in the area of environmental ethics and of the urgency and pervasiveness of the ethical problems themselves.

Ethics and the Environment is ideally suited for use as a text in courses on contemporary moral problems. The collection may also be considered the first anthology suited for use in a course devoted exclusively to environmental ethics. The range of materials encompasses many problem areas as well as the variety of positions taken within contemporary philosophical literature on the environment. The literature on the meaning of an environmental ethic and the rethinking of ethics implied by the incorporation of environmental values is widely sampled in the first half of the book. In the second half, selections focus on three areas: (1) land use and property rights, (2) the use of cost-benefit analysis for deciding how the environment may be treated, and (3) the values reflected in natural and social environments managed according to alternative models of decision-making.

The editors wish to take this opportunity to thank the reviewers of the manuscript for their helpful suggestions and to encourage users of this book to share with them their responses to it.

PART ONE
DEFINING AN ENVIRONMENTAL ETHIC

INTRODUCTION

An ethic is a statement of the most fundamental principles of conduct. It is an attempt to answer the question of what is right and wrong in a systematic way. "People ought always to seek pleasure and avoid pain"; "Treat humanity, whether in your own person or in others, always as an end and never as a means only." The *systematic* character of principles such as these becomes clear when we see that they could be applied to any proposed action; for instance, one could compare the merits of two different actions by comparing how much pleasure and pain each is likely to produce. The importance of calling such injunctions *principles* is twofold: They seem to provide reasons (or justifications) for courses of action, and they have the intuitive feel of geometric axioms, so that while they can serve as reasons, no further reasons seem needed to justify them.

But what is an *environmental* ethic? It is easy to think of an environmental ethic as an ordinary ethic applied to situations in which facts about the environment are important. If, for example, people are to be treated as ends and an energy crisis makes gas expensive or scarce, what action should be taken to see that no one runs roughshod over the poor or unfortunate? Environmental ethics, however, is more than a specialized ethic. It is emerging not simply as a field in which traditional principles are applied to situations of resource depletion and pollution, but rather as one in which a dominating question is whether an enhanced understanding of ecosystems will entail the *transformation* of fundamental ethical principles, not just new applications.

Much of the inspiration for the emergence of an environmental ethic in the 1970s has come from the work of Aldo Leopold who, discontented with traditional ways of thinking, urged us to "think like a mountain." In most traditional ethical systems, human beings are given the central position. The assumption is that the nonhuman world—the environment—is material to be used by humans as they see fit. Where human beings may have duties to respect one another, they have no duties to respect the environment, or elements within it, for its or their own sake. Human rights to appropriate and use the nonhuman world are limited only by whatever duties people may have to respect other human users of that world. This definition of right conduct, which acknowledges only instrumental value in the environment, is reinforced in definitions of humankind as independent of and set over the environment within which it lives. Humans are conceived as controllers, dominators, and manipulators of a sphere of being with which they have no intimate relationship. In turn, the environment is defined in terms of the opportunities (resources) it presents to human beings and the obstacles (pollution) human beings create to the satisfaction of their wants and needs. Leopold's exhortation to "think like a mountain" may be seen as a call to uproot this traditional framework. It suggests that we must see the attempt to define a distinctively environmental ethic as a struggle against a culturally entrenched paradigm. Such a paradigm is more than a definition or set of definitions; rather, it is a way of thinking that encompasses much more than definitions: it includes examples or models, metaphors and images which reinforce the definitions, justifications which focus on the examples as the norms, and explanations which "explain away" the inconsistencies and left-overs that do not fit neatly into the scheme. Thus a way of thinking is pervasive, and since it has been developed to fit, it is coherent, self-reinforcing, and not easily attacked.

Writers on environmental ethics have challenged the traditional human-centered paradigm by asking whether the environment has more than instrumental value and how humanity might be more intimately related to its environment. The question has proved intriguing and its answer elusive for three reasons: (1) The currently prominent idea that human beings are somehow the sole source or locus of value is vague and ambiguous. What does it mean? In what sense, if any, is it true? (2) The idea that there might be some intrinsic value in the existence of some state of the environment is indefinite and controversial in that it does not tell us which state or what value. (3) The relationship between the human species and the environment has proved to be much richer—and much more complex—than might have been supposed. Many writers have suggested that, indeed, in one way or another, human beings cannot be defined independently of the environment in which they live.

The nine selections that follow address the conceptual issue of whether (and how) the character of an ethic must be redefined in the light of environmental considerations. Leopold suggests that the integrity, stability, and beauty of the environment are values worth preserving. He expresses the hope that we are on the verge of a cultural revolution, a revolution that will lead us from thinking of the environment in terms of its usefulness to loving the environment. Speaking as an agent for that change, he invites us to consider the earth as an organism.

The next voice is that of W. H. Murdy, a biologist sympathetic to environmental concerns but convinced that human beings ought to pursue their own interests, not the interests of other species. Murdy agrees that nonhuman species have intrinsic value, but since each species should pursue its self-interest, humans should pursue their intrinsic value even if it conflicts with other species' interests. Murdy sees the human domination of the planet as an evolutionary development: the cultural ability to pass knowledge on to new generations increases a species' power because new generations need not discover everything new. Human interests seem appropriately dominant to Murdy because of their cultural development. Thus, Murdy agrees with the current paradigm.

Mark Sagoff, in his essay "On Preserving the Natural Environment," can be read as agreeing with Murdy or as suggesting a fundamental challenge to his view. Read as agreeing with Murdy, Sagoff seems to say that our history and culture lead us to see expressive qualities as actually, if metaphorically, in the natural environment. The value in the environment derives from human beings finding expressive qualities in nature. But is this all Sagoff is saying? Additionally, Sagoff seems to suggest that who we are is defined by our heritage, and that heritage, history, and culture in turn can be defined only in terms of the expressive qualities of nature. Thus he argues that human self-definition is impossible except in relation to nature.

Another alternative to Murdy's anthropocentrism is offered by Kenneth Goodpaster. He denies that human beings are the sole source of value yet recognizes that human beings are valuing creatures and thus sufficient for the existence of value. But he asks, "Are they necessary?" He holds that things have value for any creatures that have interests and urges, against several prominent philosophers, that all living things have interests. According to Goodpaster, neither self-conscious rationality nor sentience is required for having interests. Whereas Murdy argues that each species should pursue its own interests, Goodpaster argues that the interests of other species have intrinsic value worthy of human respect and consideration.

Holmes Rolston considers two answers to the question of whether there is an ecological ethic. There might be an ethic with the aim of homeostasis—that is, the aim of maintaining presently functioning ecosystems. Such an ethic could be interpreted as working from the maxim, "Make human interests perpetually pursuable." While such an ethic contains implications for the rights of *future* human beings (rights, in part, opposed to those of present human beings), it remains human-centered. We might, within the framework of that ethic, attribute value to nonhuman beings only insofar as their survival would be conducive to the well-being of humans. This homeostatic ethic is in accord with Murdy's anthropocentrism. Rolston, however, conceives another sort of ecological ethic: he suggests that an ecological understanding implies seeing human beings and the environment as interacting, rather than as separate, entities. Whereas Sagoff suggests that human self-definition builds on a culture's relation to its natural environment, Rolston underscores the ecological inseparability of humans and their environment. Rolston's ecological views also contrast with Goodpaster's view that value can be defined in terms of interests. In his lyrical presentation, Rolston tries to evoke the concept of human beings as one intrinsic part of a vast ecological order and urges us to see the value of human life as emerging from the ecological setting.

Another attempt to move beyond an anthropocentric ethic has taken sentience as a defining characteristic of a valuing thing. In the nineteenth century, Jeremy Bentham urged that the capacity to feel pain is, alone or with the capacity to feel pleasure, the characteristic which makes a creature worthy of moral consideration. In the 1970s Peter Singer has revived and updated this argument. The contemporary version of this argument seems to have two foundations: (1) it is always wrong to bring about unnecessary (unjustified) pain, and (2) the conditions under which animals have come to be raised for food since the 1950s, and the ways in which animals are sometimes used as subjects of experiments involve unnecessary, unjustified pain. No one questions the vast increase in animal pain and anxiety factory farming has produced; no one denies that animals have been subjected to pain in experiments not always for the sake of human health, but sometimes simply for the sake of human curiosity. Yet J. Baird Callicott argues that the moral significance of pain is overrated, that pain should be viewed as part of a desirable warning system. Moreover, he suggests that what happens to populations of domesticated animals is itself of little ecological (and ultimately ethical) relevance because such species are themselves the products of selective breeding by human beings. He sees the evolution of domesticated species much less naturalistically than Murdy. But Callicott does not fall back into anthropocentrism and individualism. Instead, he appeals to an ecological understanding of populations, species, and the biotic community to defend a range of holistic values. The value of the integrity of the ecosystem leads Callicott to ascribe value to individuals only as the individuals participate in stable wholes. Gone is Goodpaster's view that having interests makes individuals morally significant. But what room, we might ask, is left for the concept of individual rights? Is too much sacrificed for the values Callicott commends?

Donald Scherer's article, "Anthropocentrism, Atomism and Environmental Ethics," presents an alternative to Callicott's holism. Scherer attempts to preserve a notion of individual rights by jettisoning all considerations of self-interest. He suggests developing an ethic that respects the capacities of individuals, populations, species, and ecosystems to flourish. But he tries to divorce such an ethic from the holism Callicott endorses by stressing flourishing, whether in individuals or the ecosystem, as fundamentally valuable. Where Callicott suggests that deliberate sacrifice of individuals may be required to preserve ecosystems, does Scherer argue convincingly that essential conflicts are largely avoidable?

John Rodman articulates four clusters of value on which human concern about the environment is based. He characterizes what he calls conservationism, preservationism, moral extensionism, and ecological sensibility. He traces the historical development of attitudes toward the environment. In characterizing ecological sensibility, Rodman proposes evaluating prospective actions both in terms of a principle of respect for anything that has a capacity for internal self-direction and in light of a cluster of Leopoldian qualities worth maintaining.

When environmental ethics is conceived, as in these selections, as focused on defining what it is, the discussion quickly focuses on these questions: "How should we think?" "What values and attitudes should shape the concepts through which we define ourselves and the world in which we live?" The fundamental premise of this approach is that some ways of thinking are better than others, and that typical ways of thinking about the human-environment relationship are and have been mistaken. But there is a major difficulty confronting those who attempt to articulate an environmental ethic in this way. The further such thinkers diverge from the established paradigm, the harder it is for them to find ways of expressing what they mean. They are forced to communicate with a language permeated by the paradigm they are attempting to undermine. Inasmuch as the paradigm has many aspects and implications, and many sources contributing to it, the fact that different thinkers start from different vantage points and attempt to articulate an environmental ethic in different, though not unrelated, terms, is not surprising.

The Land Ethic

Aldo Leopold

When god-like Odysseus returned from the wars in Troy, he hanged all on one rope a dozen slave-girls of his household whom he suspected of misbehavior during his absence.

This hanging involved no question of propriety. The girls were property. The disposal of property was then, as now, a matter of expediency, not of right and wrong.

Concepts of right and wrong were not lacking from Odysseus' Greece: witness the fidelity of his wife through the long years before at last his black-prowed galleys clove the wine-dark seas for home. The ethical structure of that day covered wives, but had not yet been extended to human chattels. During the three thousand years which have since elapsed, ethical criteria have been extended to many fields of conduct, with corresponding shrinkages in those judged by expediency only.

THE ETHICAL SEQUENCE

This extension of ethics, so far studied only by philosophers, is actually a process in ecological evolution. Its sequences may be described in ecological as well as in philosophical terms. An ethic, ecologically, is a limitation on freedom of action in the struggle for existence. An ethic, philosophically, is a differentiation of social from anti-social conduct. These are two definitions of one thing. The thing has its origin in the tendency of interdependent individuals or groups to evolve modes of co-operation. The ecologist calls these symbioses. Politics and economics are advanced symbioses in which the original free-for-all competition has been replaced, in part, by co-operative mechanisms with an ethical content.

The complexity of co-operative mechanisms has increased with population density, and with the efficiency of tools. It was simpler, for example, to define the anti-social uses of sticks and stones in the days of the mastodons than of bullets and billboards in the age of motors.

The first ethics dealt with the relation between individuals; the Mosaic Decalogue is an example. Later accretions dealt with the relation between the individual and society. The Golden Rule tries to integrate the individual to society; democracy to integrate social organization to the individual.

There is as yet no ethic dealing with man's relation to land and to the animals and plants which grow upon it. Land, like Odysseus' slave-girls, is still property. The land-relation is still strictly economic, entailing privileges but not obligations.

Source: From *A Sand County Almanac, with other essays on conservation from Round River* by Aldo Leopold. Copyright © 1949, 1953, 1966, renewed 1977, 1981 by Oxford University Press, Inc. Reprinted by permission.

The extension of ethics to this third element in human environment is, if I read the evidence correctly, an evolutionary possibility and an ecological necessity. It is the third step in a sequence. The first two have already been taken. Individual thinkers since the days of Ezekiel and Isaiah have asserted that the despoliation of land is not only inexpedient but wrong. Society, however, has not yet affirmed their belief. I regard the present conservation movement as the embryo of such an affirmation.

An ethic may be regarded as a mode of guidance for meeting ecological situations so new or intricate, or involving such deferred reactions, that the path of social expediency is not discernible to the average individual. Animal instincts are modes of guidance for the individual in meeting such situations. Ethics are possibly a kind of community instinct in-the-making.

THE COMMUNITY CONCEPT

All ethics so far evolved rest upon a single premise: that the individual is a member of a community of interdependent parts. His instincts prompt him to compete for his place in that community, but his ethics prompt him also to co-operate (perhaps in order that there may be a place to compete for).

The land ethic simply enlarges the boundaries of the community to include soils, waters, plants, and animals, or collectively, the land.

This sounds simple: do we not already sing our love for and obligation to the land of the free and the home of the brave? Yes, but just what and whom do we love? Certainly not the soil, which we are sending helter-skelter downriver. Certainly not the waters, which we assume have no function except to turn turbines, float barges, and carry off sewage. Certainly not the plants, of which we exterminate whole communities without batting an eye. Certainly not the animals, of which we have already extirpated many of the largest and most beautiful species. A land ethic of course cannot prevent the alteration, management, and use of these 'resources,' but it does affirm their right to continued existence, and, at least in spots, their continued existence in a natural state.

In short, a land ethic changes the role of *Homo sapiens* from conqueror of the land-community to plain member and citizen of it. It implies respect for his fellow-members, and also respect for the community as such.

*   *   *

THE OUTLOOK

It is inconceivable to me that an ethical relation to land can exist without love, respect, and admiration for land, and a high regard for its value. By value, I of course mean something far broader than mere economic value; I mean value in the philosophical sense.

Perhaps the most serious obstacle impeding the evolution of a land ethic is the fact that our educational and economic system is headed away from, rather than toward, an intense consciousness of land. Your true modern is separated from the land by many middlemen, and by innumerable physical gadgets. He has no vital relation to it; to him it is the space between cities on which crops grow. Turn him loose for a day on the land, and if the spot does not happen to be a golf links or a 'scenic' area, he is bored stiff. If crops could be raised by hydroponics instead of farming, it would suit him very well. Synthetic substitutes for wood, leather, wool, and other natural land products suit him better than the originals. In short, land is something he has 'outgrown.'

Almost equally serious as an obstacle to a land ethic is the attitude of the farmer for whom the land is still an adversary, or a taskmaster that keeps him in slavery. Theoretically, the mechanization of farming ought to cut the farmer's chains, but whether it really does is debatable.

One of the requisites for an ecological comprehension of land is an understanding of ecology, and this is by no means co-extensive with 'education'; in fact, much higher education seems deliberately to avoid ecological concepts. An understanding of ecology does not necessarily originate in courses bearing ecological labels; it is quite as likely to be labeled geography, botany, agronomy, history, or economics. This is as it should be, but whatever the label, ecological training is scarce.

The case for a land ethic would appear hopeless but for the minority which is in obvious revolt against these 'modern' trends.

The 'key-log' which must be moved to release the evolutionary process for an ethic is simply this: quit thinking about decent land-use as solely an economic problem. Examine each question in terms of what is ethically and esthetically right, as well as what is economically expedient. A thing is right when it tends to preserve the integrity, stability, and beauty of the biotic community. It is wrong when it tends otherwise.

It of course goes without saying that economic feasibility limits the tether of what can or cannot be done for land. It always has and it always will. The fallacy the economic determinists have tied around our collective neck, and which we now need to cast off, is the belief that economics determines *all* land-use. This is simply not true. An innumerable host of actions and attitudes, comprising perhaps the bulk of all land relations, is determined by the land-users' tastes and predilections, rather than by his purse. The bulk of all land relations hinges on investments of time, forethought, skill, and faith rather than on investments of cash. As a land-user thinketh, so is he.

I have purposely presented the land ethic as a product of social evolution because nothing so important as an ethic is ever 'written.' Only the most superficial student of history supposes that Moses 'wrote' the Decalogue; it evolved in the minds of a thinking community, and Moses wrote a tentative summary of it for a 'seminar.' I say tentative because evolution never stops.

The evolution of a land ethic is an intellectual as well as emotional process. Conservation is paved with good intentions which prove to be futile, or even dangerous, because they are devoid of critical understanding either of the land, or of economic land-use. I think it is a truism that as the ethical frontier advances from the individual to the community, its intellectual content increases.

The mechanism of operation is the same for any ethic: social approbation for right actions; social disapproval for wrong actions.

By and large, our present problem is one of attitudes and implements. We are remodeling the Alhambra with a steam-shovel, and we are proud of our yardage. We shall hardly relinquish the shovel, which after all has many good points, but we are in need of gentler and more objective criteria for its successful use.

* * *

Conservation as a Moral Issue

Aldo Leopold

Thus far we have considered the problem of conservation of land purely as an economic issue. A false front of exclusively economic determinism is so habitual to Americans in discussing public questions that one must speak in the language of compound interest to get a hearing. In my opinion, however, one can not round out a real understanding of the situation in the Southwest without likewise considering its moral aspects.

In past and more outspoken days conservation was put in terms of decency rather than dollars. Who can not feel the moral scorn and contempt for poor craftsmanship in the voice of Ezekiel when he asks: *Seemeth it a small thing unto you to have fed upon good pasture, but ye must tread down with your feet the residue of your pasture? And to have drunk of the clear waters, but ye must foul the residue with your feet?*

In these two sentences may be found an epitome of the moral question involved. Ezekiel seems to scorn waste, pollution, and unnecessary damage as something unworthy—as something damaging not only to the reputation of the waster, but to the self-respect of the craft and the society of which he is a member. We might even draw from his words a broader concept—that the privilege of possessing the earth entails the responsibility of passing it on, the better for our use, not only to immediate posterity, but to the Unknown Future, the nature of which is not given us to know. It is possible that Ezekiel respected the soil, not only as a craftsman respects his material, but as a moral being respects a living thing.

Many of the world's most penetrating minds have regarded our so-called "inanimate nature" as a living thing, and probably many of us who have neither the time nor the ability to reason out conclusions on such

Source: From "Some Fundamentals of Conservation in the Southwest," *Environmental Ethics,* 1, no. 2 (Summer 1979), 131–41.

matters by logical processes have felt intuitively that there existed between man and the earth a closer and deeper relation than would necessarily follow the mechanistic conception of the earth as our physical provider and abiding place.

Of course, in discussing such matters we are beset on all sides with the pitfalls of language. The very words *living thing* have an inherited and arbitrary meaning derived not from reality, but from human perceptions of human affairs. But we must use them for better or for worse.

A good expression of this conception of an organized animate nature is given by the Russian philosopher Onpensky, who presents the following analogy:

> Were we to observe, from the inside, one cubic centimetre of the human body, knowing nothing of the existence of the entire body and of man himself, then the phenomena going on in this little cube of flesh would seem like elemental phenomena in inanimate nature.

He then states that it is at least not impossible to regard the earth's parts—soil, mountains, rivers, atmosphere, etc.—as organs, of parts of organs, or a coordinated whole, each part with a definite function. And, if we could see this whole, as a whole, through a great period of time, we might perceive not only organs with coordinated functions, but possibly also that process of consumption and replacement which in biology we call the metabolism, or growth. In such a case we would have all the visible attributes of a living thing, which we do not now realize to be such because it is too big, and its life processes too slow. And there would also follow that invisible attribute—a soul, or consciousness—which not only Onpensky, but many philosophers of all ages, ascribe to all living things and aggregations thereof, including the "dead" earth.

There is not much discrepancy, except in language, between this conception of a living earth, and the conception of a dead earth, with enormously slow, intricate, and interrelated functions among its parts, as given us by physics, chemistry, and geology. The essential thing for present purposes is that both admit the interdependent functions of the elements. But "anything indivisible is a living being," says Onpensky. Possibly, in our intuitive perceptions, which may be truer than our science and less impeded by words than our philosophies, we realize the indivisibility of the earth—its soil, mountains, rivers, forests, climate, plants, and animals, and respect it collectively not only as a useful servant but as a living being, vastly less alive than ourselves in degree, but vastly greater than ourselves in time and space—a being that was old when the morning stars sang together, and, when the last of us has been gathered unto his fathers, will still be young.

Philosophy, then, suggests one reason why we can not destroy the earth with moral impunity; namely, that the "dead" earth is an organism possessing a certain kind and degree of life, which we intuitively respect as such. Possibly, to most men of affairs, this reason is too intangible to either accept or reject as a guide to human conduct. But philosophy also offers another and more easily debatable question: was the earth made for man's use, or has man merely the privilege of temporarily possessing an earth made for other and inscrutable purposes? The question of what he can properly do with it must necessarily be affected by this question.

Most religions, insofar as I know, are premised squarely on the assumption that man is the end and purpose of creation, and that not only the dead earth, but all creatures thereon, exist solely for his use. The mechanistic or scientific philosophy does not start with this as a premise, but ends with it as a conclusion and hence may be placed in the same category for the purpose in hand. This high opinion of his own importance in the universe Jeanette Marks stigmatizes as "the great human impertinence." John Muir, in defense of rattlesnakes, protests: " . . . as if nothing that does not obviously make for the benefit of man had any right to exist; as if our ways were God's ways." But the noblest expression of this anthropomorphism is Bryant's "Thanatopsis":

> . . . The hills
> Rock-ribbed and ancient as the sun,—the vales
> Stretching in pensive quietness between;
> The venerable woods—rivers that move
> In majesty, and the complaining brooks
> That make the meadows green, and, poured round all
> Old oceans gray and melancholy waste,—
> *Are but the solemn decorations all*
> *Of the great tomb of man.*

Since most of mankind today profess either one of the anthropomorphic religions or the scientific school of thought which is likewise anthropomorphic, I will not dispute the point. It just occurs to me, however, in answer to the scientists, that God started his show a good many million years before he had any men for audience—a sad waste of both actors and music—and in answer to both, that it is just barely possible that God himself likes to hear birds sing and see flowers grow. But here again we encounter the insufficiency of words as symbols for realities.

Granting that the earth is for man—there is still a question: what man? Did not the cliff dwellers who tilled and irrigated these our valleys think that they were the pinnacle of creation—that these valleys were made for them? Undoubtedly. And then the Pueblos? Yes. And then the Spaniards? Not only thought so, but said so. And now we Americans? Ours beyond a doubt! (How happy a definition is that one of Hadley's which states, "Truth is that which prevails in the long run"!)

Five races—five cultures—have flourished here. We may truthfully say of our four predecessors that they left the earth alive, undamaged. Is it possibly a proper question for us to consider what the sixth shall say about us? If we are logically anthropomorphic, yes. We and

> . . . all that tread
> The globe are but a handful to the tribes
> That slumber in its bosom. Take the wings

Of morning; pierce the Barcan wilderness
Or lose thyself in the continuous woods
Where rolls the Oregon, and hears no sound
Save his own dashings—yet the dead are there,
And millions in those solitudes, since first
The flight of years began, have laid them down
In their last sleep.

And so, in time, shall we. And if there be, indeed, a special nobility inherent in the human race—a special cosmic value, distinctive from and superi-
or to all other life—by what token shall it be manifest?

By a society decently respectful of its own and all other life, capable of
inhabiting the earth without defiling it? Or by a society like that of John
Burrough's potato bug, which exterminated the potato, and thereby exterminated itself? As one or the other shall we be judged in "the derisive
silence of eternity."

Anthropocentrism: A Modern Version

W. H. Murdy

The capacity of man to affect the environment beyond himself is an evolutionary emergent, continuous with the much more limited ability of other
organisms to affect the environment beyond themselves. It enables man to
modify environments to suit his needs, which is a root cause of both his
biological success and ecological problems. It also enables man to enhance
values beyond himself, and this is a major feature of the new anthropocentrism expressed in this article.

PRE-DARWINIAN ANTHROPOCENTRISM

Socrates, in a dialogue with Euthydemus (1), is reported to have said:

> Tell me, Euthydemus, has it ever occurred to you to reflect on the care the
> gods have taken to furnish man with what he needs? . . . Now, seeing that we
> need food, think how they make the earth to yield it, and provide to that end
> appropriate seasons which furnish in abundance the diverse things that min-
> ister not only to our wants but to our enjoyment.

The idea that nature was created to benefit man was a popular belief
throughout Western history and was still very much alive in the 19th cen-

Source: Reprinted by permission of the author and *Science*, vol. 187 (March 1975), 1168–72.
Copyright 1975 by the American Association for the Advancement of Science.

tury. Cuvier, "father" of comparative anatomy and paleontology, "could think of no better reason for the existence of fishes . . . than that they provided food for man" *(2)*, and Lyell, a leading geologist of the 19th century, in his early years, believed that domestic animals had been expressly designed for man's use. He writes *(3):*

> The power bestowed on the horse, the dog, the ox, the sheep, the cat, and many species of domestic fowls, of supporting almost every climate, was given expressly to enable them to follow man throughout all parts of the globe in order that we might obtain their services, and they our protection.

DARWINIAN ANTHROPOCENTRISM

Charles Darwin, in *The Origin of Species*, provided sufficient evidence to finally inter the idea that nature exists to serve man. According to William Paley, 18th-century exponent of natural theology, the rattlesnake's rattle was expressly designed to give warning to its prey. Darwin *(4*, p. 196) asserts that "natural selection cannot possibly produce any modification in a species exclusively for the good of another species" and makes the following declaration:

> If it could be proved that any part of the structure of any one species had been formed for the exclusive good of another species it would annihilate my theory, for such could not have been produced through natural selection.

Species exist as ends in themselves. They do not exist for the exclusive benefit of any other species. The purpose of a species, in biological terms, is to survive to reproduce. Potter *(5*, p. 16) writes: "All successful living organisms behave purposefully in terms of their own or their species survival." Species that failed to do so became extinct.

A MODERN VIEW OF ANTHROPOCENTRISM

To be anthropocentric is to affirm that mankind is to be valued more highly than other things in nature—by man. By the same logic, spiders are to be valued more highly than other things in nature—by spiders. It is proper for men to be anthropocentric and for spiders to be arachnocentric. This goes for all other living species. The following statement by Simpson *(6) expresses the modern version of anthropocentrism:*

> Man is the highest animal. The fact that he alone is capable of making such judgment is in itself part of the evidence that this decision is correct. And even if he were the lowest animal, the anthropocentric point of view would still be manifestly the only proper one to adopt for consideration of his place in the scheme of things and when seeking a guide on which to base his actions and his evaluations of them.

Anthropocentrism is a pejorative in many of the articles which deal with the so-called "ecological crisis." Lynn White (7), in his widely quoted article, "The historical roots of our ecological crisis," upbraids Christianity for being the most anthropocentric religion the world has seen:

> Christianity, in absolute contrast to ancient paganism and Asia's religions (except perhaps Zoroastrianism), not only established a dualism of man and nature but also insisted that it is God's will that man exploit nature for his proper ends.

White is right to remind us of how tragically myopic has been our exploitation of nature. However, he is wrong to infer that it is somehow wrong for man to exploit nature for "his proper ends." We must exploit nature to live. The problem lies in our difficulty to distinguish between "proper ends," which are progressive and promote human values, and "improper ends," which are retrogressive and destructive of human values.

Another attitude toward nature that eschews anthropocentrism is the "Franciscan" belief in the fundamental equality of all life. In this view, man is merely one of several million different species comprising a "democracy of all God's creatures" (7). Jordan (8) states: "The time will come when civilized man will feel that the rights of all living creatures on earth are as sacred as his own." Julian Huxley (9) expresses a similar opinion: "In ethical terms, the golden rule applies to man's relations with nature as well as to relations between human beings."

If we affirm that all species have "equal rights," or, that the rights of man are not of greater value than the rights of other species, how should it affect our behavior toward nature? The golden rule, "As ye would that men should do to you, do ye to them likewise," is a moral axiom which requires reciprocity among ethicizing beings. How does such a principle apply to nonethicizing forms of life which cannot reciprocate? The callous, wanton destruction of life is surely not a proper end for man, but what about our destruction of pathogenic bacteria, in order that we might remain healthy, or our destruction of plant and animal life, in order that we might be nourished? To affirm that men, dogs, and cats have more rights than plants, insects, and bacteria is a belief that species do not have equal rights. If, however, we believe in the equality of all species, none should be genetically manipulated or killed for the exclusive benefit of another.

To ascribe value to things of nature as they benefit man is to regard them as instruments to man's survival or well-being. This is an anthropocentric point of view. As knowledge of our dependent relationships with nature grows, we place instrumental value on an ever greater variety of things. Phytoplankton of the oceans becomes valuable when we recognize the key role of these organisms in providing the earth's free oxygen. Continued growth of knowledge may lead to an awareness that no event in nature is without some effect on the whole of which we are a part and therefore we should value all items in nature. Basic to the kind of anthropocentrism expounded in this article is the recognition that an individual's well-being depends on the well-being of both its social group and ecological support system.

Birch contends that to evaluate things of nature in terms of instrumental value, regardless of how enlightened our evaluation might be, will not provide us with a "valid ethic of nature." He writes *(10):* "Conservation will rest on very uncertain foundations unless it comes to be based on a view that living creatures besides man have intrinsic worth. Unless they have, there seems no sound reason for conservation other than to suit the purposes of man, and these changes from time to time and place to place." To have a "valid ethic of nature," according to Birch, we must affirm "the intrinsic value of every item in creation."

An anthropocentric attitude toward nature does not require that man be the source of all value, nor does it exclude a belief that things of nature have intrinsic value. According to Laszlo *(11,* p. 105): "There is nothing in all the realms of natural systems which would be value-free when looked at from the vantage point of the systems themselves." Whitehead *(12,* p. 93) writes: "The element of value, of being valuable, of having value, of being an end in itself, of being something which is for its own sake, must not be omitted in any account of an event as the most concrete actual something."

I may affirm that every species has intrinsic value, but I will behave as though I value my own survival and that of my species more highly than the survival of other animals or plants. I may assert that a lettuce plant has intrinsic value, yet I will eat it before it has reproduced itself because I value my own nutritional well-being above the survival of the lettuce plant. Birch *(10)* writes: "Man left only with his self-interest, however enlightened, will not provide sufficient motivation for ecological survival." Even this statement can be interpreted in terms of instrumental value, that is, man should acknowledge the intrinsic value of things; otherwise he will not have sufficient motivation for ecological survival, which I assume includes human survival individually and as a species.

MAN'S PLACE IN NATURE

Whitehead *(12,* p. 94) writes:

> That which endures is limited, obstructive, intolerant, infecting its environment with its own aspects. But it is not self-sufficient. The aspects of all things enter into its very nature. It is only itself as drawing together into its own limitation the larger whole in which it finds itself. Conversely it is only itself by lending its aspects to this same environment in which it finds itself.

Ecologists have a saying: "You cannot do just one thing." Many of our actions, motivated by a desire to improve the quality of human life, have, to our detriment, caused unexpected consequences because we failed to recognize the essential interrelatedness of all things. "Man's first realization that he was not identical with nature" was a crucial step in evolution, writes

Bohm *(13)*, "because it made possible a kind of autonomy in his thinking, which allowed him to go beyond the immediately given limits of nature, first in his imagination, and ultimately in his practical work." Realization that our freedom of choice is "bounded by the limits of compatibility with the dynamic structure of the whole" *(11*, p. 75) and must "remain within the limits of natural systems values" *(11*, p. 107) is yet another crucial step in evolution. "Not until man accepts his dependency on nature and puts himself in place as part of it," writes Iltis *(14)*, "not until then does man put man first. This is the greatest paradox of human ecology."

A human being is both a hierarchical system (composed of subsystems such as organs, cells, and enzyme systems) and a component of supra-individual, hierarchical systems (populations, species, ecosystems, cultural systems). Man is therefore a set within a hierarchical system of sets. "In hierarchies a given set must be described not only for itself but in terms both of what is within it, and what it is within" *(15)*. Because science up to now has been strongly reductionist, we know more about the systems that make up our bodies and our cells than we do about those that transcend our individual lives—the evolutionary, ecologic, and social "wholes" of which we are "parts."

In an evolutionary sense, the life that animates us has existed in an unbroken line of descent, in numerous forms adapted to myriad environments, since life first appeared on earth some 3 billion years ago. Before life, our ancestry extends back through billions of years of molecular change to the nuclei of former stars. Here the elements necessary for life were built up from hydrogen, the simplest and most abundant element in the universe. Beyond primordial hydrogen, our ancestral roots become lost in a profound mystery—the beginning of things, the origin of the universe of matter, energy, space, and time.

In an ecologic sense, our existence depends upon the proper functioning of the earth's present ecosystem. In the course of cosmic evolution the forces of matter and energy produced a planet fit to support life. In the course of biologic evolution, the activities of living things produced an environment fit to support human life. The day-to-day maintenance of our "life-support system" depends on the functional interaction of countless, interdependent biotic and physicochemical factors. The movement of ocean currents and the activity of soil microbes are as essential to our existence as the oxygen we breathe.

In a social sense, we are as much a product of our culture as of our genes. "We are not ourselves only," writes Wells *(16)*, "We are also part of human experience and thought." We possess no greater innate intelligence, artistic skill, or emotional feeling than did our prehistoric predecessors, who painted vivid images on cave walls over 30,000 years ago. We are different from Cro-Magnon man because we are heirs to a greater store of knowledge collected by the human species over thousands of years of cultural evolution. In large measure, our personalities are determined by a collective consciousness which we can contribute to and which is itself evolving.

CULTURE, KNOWLEDGE, AND POWER

Once the evolutionary process produced a species with culture, it was inevitable that knowledge of nature would accrue to such a species at an accelerating pace. Culture represents a unique way of acquiring, storing, and transmitting knowledge about the world. Knowledge acquired by one generation may be transmitted to succeeding generations by the agency of social learning. While each newborn person must acquire cultural knowledge anew, the amount of cultural knowledge available to the social group tends to grow in a cumulative fashion. "Cultures may die," writes Hawkins (17), "as cells may; but death is not built into them, as it is into multicellular animals. And through cultures learning becomes cumulative, evolutionary."

A species that can learn from the experiences of its predecessors can, potentially, build new knowledge upon an ever-expanding base. Cumulative knowledge provides man, the cultural species, with ever-increasing power to exploit nature and, as a result, he is a great biological success. The human species successfully occupies a greater variety of habitats, over a greater geographic range, with greater numbers, than any other species. Man is recognized as the latest dominant type in a succession of dominant types which emerged during the process of evolution, and represents the first time a species, and not a group of species, has achieved world dominance.

In acquiring his present position of dominance, the human species has radically reshaped the face of nature. "Whole landscapes are now occupied by man-dominated (and in part man-created) faunas and floras" (18). For the first time in earth's evolution, one species can genetically manipulate other species to their detriment, but to its own advantage. Darwin (4, p. 46) remarks:

> One of the most remarkable features in our domesticated races is that we see in them adaptation, not indeed to the animal's or plant's own good, but to man's use or fancy.

Maize (Zea mays) is a species which was molded into an artifact by our prehistoric ancestors. It is unable to survive in nature without man's intervention. Maize was the agricultural base of the great pre-Columbian civilizations of the New World. European colonists encountered it almost everywhere in America, but they found it only in cultivation. The "ear" or pistillate inflorescence of maize was modified by prehistoric man into a botanical monstrosity. There is "no natural way by which the grains can be detached from the cob, escape from the husks, and be dispersed." When the entire ear falls to the ground, "the germinating grains produce a compact cluster of seedlings, none of which has much chance to survive" (19).

Man's ability to exploit nature has been limited by the amount of energy available to the species. For most of human history, energy for man's activities came exclusively from the consumption of plants and animals. "The earliest culture systems developed techniques of hunting, fishing, trapping, collecting, gathering, etc. as means of exploiting the plant and animal resources of nature" (20, p. 371). The first quantum jump in the energy resources for culture building took place with the domestication of plants and animals. White asserts that a few thousand years after this event, "the great civilizations of antiquity . . . came quickly into being." The second quantum jump in the amount of energy available to man was the tapping of fossil fuel deposits of coal, oil, and natural gas. "The consequences of the fuel revolution," writes White (20, p. 373), "were in general much like those of the agricultural revolution: an increase in population, larger political units, bigger cities, an accumulation of wealth, a rapid development of the arts and sciences, in short, a rapid and extensive advance of culture as a whole."

Creation of the Cathedral of Chartres or the Declaration of Independence required the existence of civilizations based on artificial ecosystems. Natural ecosystems have intrinsic value, but the realization of value in human evolution, a proper end for man, has depended upon their replacement by artificial systems, which produce more energy.

* * *

PARTICIPATION IN OUR OWN EVOLUTION

If all of man's actions were determined, he could not hope to constructively affect the course of human evolution by conscious intent, even if he were to conclude that its direction is inimical to personal freedom and human values. He could only hope to "fathom the direction of the process" in order to "make it less painful by accepting it rather than fighting it" (20, p. 355). In this view, since man cannot direct change toward human purposes, his only recourse is to endlessly adjust human purposes to accommodate purposeless change.

The dismal portrayal of man as a passive entity in an evolutionary drama totally dominated by the environment is only one side of the evolutionary process. Evolution is more than the molding of entities by their surroundings. It also involves the ability of entities to interact with, adapt to, and change environments in creative, intelligent, and novel ways.

Man, because of his power of projection, has greater potential for affecting his own evolution than any other species. He is the only species, as far as is known, with the capacity to project purposes (goal-ideas), which arise in his mind from hopes, fantasies, and dreams about the future, and then proceed to work toward their realization. Birch (21) writes: "Possibilities are unseen realities. So far as our human lives are concerned they are potent causes that guide and transform our lives." Thus, the image of the future that man adopts is not merely an illusion, but an element in the chain of causality.

Birth, death, and reproduction are common to all life, but man, because he is capable of reflection and of planning his own actions, does not blindly respond to nature like other organisms; he assimilates and transforms nature and invests it with a meaning and intelligible moral value (*22*, p. 40). "We cannot recapture the animal security of instinct," writes Teilhard de Chardin (*22*, p. 44). "Because, in becoming men, we have acquired the power of looking to the future and assessing the value of things. We cannot do nothing, since our very refusal to decide is a decision in itself."

FAITH IN THE POTENTIALITIES OF MANKIND

Man is not the measure of all things. He is not the center of the universe, nor the source of all value, nor the culmination of terrestrial evolution. Nevertheless, he is "the present crest of the evolutionary wave" (*22*, p. 237), the entity in which the evolutionary trends of greater organizational complexity and greater consciousness have their most advanced development. It is in human evolution that the higher values of truth, justice, love, and beauty have their greatest expression. Further progress toward the realization of higher states of these values, if it is to occur at all, must develop in and through man. He is the key not only to his own survival, but to the survival and furtherance of values of cosmic significance.

In order to influence evolution in wise and responsible ways, we must strive for an even fuller understanding of our relationship to greater wholes—society, nature, and ultimately to the primary source of order and value in the world. Personal identification with greater wholes is essential to the discovery of our own wholeness. An entity is only itself, according to Whitehead, "as drawing together into its own limitations the larger whole in which it finds itself. Conversely it is only itself by lending its aspects to this same environment in which it finds itself" (*12*, p. 94).

Effective participation in our own evolution requires not only that we establish a harmonious relationship to larger wholes, but, in addition, that we affirm the human phenomenon to be a vitally significant process in its own right and our individual selves to be holistic centers "of spontaneity and self-creation contributing distinctively to the world" (*23*).

Teilhard de Chardin (*22*, p. 296) saw, as a possibility, "mankind falling suddenly out of love with its own destiny. This disenchantment would be conceivable, and indeed inevitable," he writes, "if as a result of growing reflection we came to believe that our end could only be collective death in an hermetically sealed world." Boulding (*24*) concurs: "An ideology which states that the world is essentially meaningless but that we ought to strive, suffer and fight for it is unlikely to be powerful because of the essential contradictions among its components. If an interpretation of history says the world is meaningless, then our value system is likely to be pure hedonism—'Eat, drink, and be merry, for tomorrow we die'—or else one of apathy or stoic resignation."

Unbridled self-indulgence on the part of one generation without regard to future ones is the modus operandi of biological evolution and may be regarded as rational behavior. Heilbroner (*25*) asks: "On what private, 'rational' considerations, after all, should we make sacrifices now to ease the lot of generations whom we will never live to see?" If man, with his extraordinary power to multiply, consume, and pollute, seeks only to maximize short-term gain, global disaster will result in the very near future. The only possible answer to the above question, according to Heilbroner, "lies in our capacity to form a collective bond of identity with future generations." To do so is to affirm that the human enterprise has value which transcends our individual lives.

An anthropocentric faith in mankind affirms that we are not isolated monads acting out absurd roles within a meaningless context, but that we are essential elements of a meaningful whole and that our individual acts are vitally significant to the self-actualization of the process of human evolution itself and to the enhancement of value in the world.

SUMMARY

Anthropocentrism is proposed as a valid and necessary point of view for mankind to adopt for consideration of his place in nature. Our current ecological problems do not stem from an anthropocentric attitude per se, but from one too narrowly conceived. Anthropocentrism is consistent with a philosophy that affirms the essential interrelatedness of things and that values all items in nature since no event is without some effect on wholes of which we are parts. The ecological crisis is viewed as an inevitable crisis in human evolution. Through cultures knowledge becomes cumulative. A crisis occurs when our knowledge of nature, which determines our power to exploit nature, exceeds our knowledge of how to use knowledge for our own survival and for improvement in the quality of our lives. An anthropocentric belief in the value, meaningfulness, and creative potential of the human phenomenon is considered a necessary motivating factor to participatory evolution which, in turn, may be requisite to the future survival of the human species and its cultural values.

REFERENCES

1. XENOPHON, *Memorabilia and Oeconomicus* (Harvard University Press, Cambridge, Mass., 1959), p. 299.
2. G. G. SIMPSON, *This View of Life* (Harcourt, Brace & World, New York, 1964), p. 101.
3. C. LYELL, *Principles of Geology* (Kay, Jun, and Brother, Philadelphia, 1837), vol. 1, p. 512.
4. C. DARWIN, *The Origin of Species* (Doubleday, Garden City, N.Y., 1872 ed).
5. V. R. POTTER, *Bioethics* (Prentice-Hall, Englewood Cliffs, N.J., 1971).
6. G. G. SIMPSON, *The Meaning of Evolution* (Yale University Press, New Haven, Conn., 1949), p. 286.
7. L. WHITE, JR. *Science* **155,** 1205. (1967).
8. D. S. JORDAN, QUOTED IN H. M. SMITH, *Biologist* **52,** 56 (1970).
9. J. HUXLEY, *The Human Crisis* (University of Washington Press, Seattle, 1963), p. 24.
10. C. BIRCH, *Zygon* **8,** 255 (1973).

11. E. LASZLO, *The Systems View of the World* (Braziller, New York, 1972).
12. A. N. WHITEHEAD, *Science and the Modern World* (Macmillan, New York, 1925).
13. D. BOHM, *The Van Leer Jerusalem Foundation Series* (Humanities Press, New York, 1973), p. 18.
14. H. H. ILTIS, *BioScience* **20,** 820 (1970).
15. C. GROBSTEIN, IN *Hierarchy Theory.* H. H. Pattee, ed. (Braziller, New York, 1973), p. 31.
16. H. G. WELLS, IN *Living Philosophies* (Simon & Schuster, New York, 1931), p. 83.
17. D. HAWKINS, *The Language of Nature* (Freeman, San Francisco, 1964), p. 276.
18. E. ANDERSON, *Smithsonian Institution Annual Reports* (1956), p. 461.
19. P. WEATHERWAX, *Indian Corn in Old America* (Macmillan, New York, 1954), p. 179.
20. L. WHITE, *The Science of Culture* (Farrar & Straus, New York, 1949), pp. 371–373.
21. C. BIRCH, *Journal of the American Academy of Religion* **40,** 158 (1972).
22. P. TEILHARD DE CHARDIN, *The Future of Man* (Harper & Row, New York, 1964).
23. I. G. BARBOUR, *Issues in Science and Religion* (Prentice-Hall, Englewood Cliffs, N.J., 1966), p. 131.
24. K. E. BOULDING, *The Meaning of the Twentieth Century* (Harper & Row, New York, 1965), p. 163.
25. R. L. HEILBRONER. *An Inquiry into the Human Prospect* (Norton, New York, 1974), p. 115.

On Preserving the Natural Environment

Mark Sagoff

A NONUTILITARIAN RATIONALE FOR PRESERVING THE NATURAL ENVIRONMENT

A

Even if nature in the rough were beautiful, this would not be an adequate reason to protect it from development, for no one has shown that beauty has any value other than the pleasure it produces, and there is usually more pleasure in exploiting a natural environment than in leaving it alone. Nor has anyone shown that pleasure taken in beauty is better than less expensive enjoyments; indeed, it is difficult to know what "better" in this context could mean. The truth is often heard that to value a woman because of her good looks is to trivialize her, to ignore her more important qualities, and to regard her only as an object of use. It is likewise true of the environment.

Source: Reprinted by permission of The Yale Law Journal Company and Fred B. Rothman & Company from *The Yale Law Journal,* Vol. 84, No. 2 (1974), pp. 245–252, 264–267.

We regard nature only as a source of recreation if we do not see the difference between a wilderness and a pretty garden. We know the difference. Let us say what it is. The respect, reverence, and benevolence many of us feel toward nature and attribute to its beauty in fact is felt for its expressive qualities. A wild area may be powerful, majestic, free; an animal may express courage, innocence, purpose, and strength. As a nation we value these qualities: the obligation toward nature is an obligation toward them.

Suppose a big company proposes to build a ski resort on a mountain top in a national park; suppose, too, it intends to construct an access highway through an untouched forest. Let us assume, moreover, that the economic benefits of this proposal are great compared to the needed investment. The benefits, of course, would extend to wildlife and to the park itself. The denizens of the forest, for example, would be fed balanced meals by the management, and their cubs, or whatever, would be checked regularly by veterinarians; the bears would sleep on foam rubber all winter in quality-controlled dens, clown with the visitors, or possibly ski themselves. The developer will be quick to point out that without proper landscaping the terrain is rough, violent, and hostile. It is not really decorative; it is not quite beautiful. Artists usually provide relief to their landscapes by including some sign of human habitation—you can pick out a country lane or church spire in the distance. A landscape as vast as a national park, however, requires more than a country road to make it beautiful; it takes a six lane highway to do the job. Few people go to church who also ski; but the rough terrain could be relieved by the graceful arches of a popular hamburger stand. And it will not cost the taxpayer a cent.

What can the environmentalist say? He can argue that the mountain will lose its fierceness, power and integrity. The wildlife will no longer be wild; it will forfeit its freedom and strength. There is no reason to think, however, that the animals value these qualities. Certainly very few people wish to confront nature on its own terms. They want an air-conditioned motel; they are glad to see the forest from a gondola after a drink. So what if they do not feel its cool hostility. Now environmentalists might begin to worry that they alone cherish the fierceness and power of nature and its integrity, or that only they and a few others value independence, power, endurance, sureness, and freedom as these are expressed by natural objects. The environmentalist will then despairingly point out that the development of a wild area, though increasing its amenity, destroys many of its expressive qualities. A protectionist policy reflects a concern with these qualities. It is justified by them and it may take on some of these qualities itself.

Let us suppose that the developer replies to this argument in the following way. A highway and a ski resort, he contends, are themselves symbols of power and freedom, not indeed the same kind of power and freedom that nature exemplifies, but the kind Americans really want. If someone reads our national literature, he might get the idea that the qualities of character Americans respect and seek are those expressed by objects in the natural environment: but this is the merest sentiment. Times have changed and the qualities we now value are symbolized by a fast pizza and a stick shift. A few snobs read books, and disagree about their meaning, but for the rest of us, who prefer magazines and watch television, the message is clear. The freshness and purity thought to be exemplified by a mountain stream now have a brand of mentholated cigarette as their symbol, and it is no longer a bear but a beverage which is wild and free. Power, as we now understand it, has nothing to do with nature. It is expressed by a hair tonic, perhaps, or by a detergent, or by a lot of engine under the hood. A century ago, natural objects were cheaper, and we could afford to use them as symbols. Now they are becoming scarce, and so we should accept a less expensive brand. Developed areas can take on the expressive function of untouched environments; the highway can replace the waterfall in our affection; the motel can take the place of the mountain.

The benefits of new symbols greatly outweigh the costs. Artificial trees can be advertised as symbols of life and integrity, and strip mines may be promoted as geological wonders—the view of the earth from the inside. Pollution exists only because we call it so; people would enjoy it if it were described as progress. The point is that we must stop attending to the literature, music, and art, written for an earlier century, which found in nature, then cheaper to preserve, the examples of important qualities. We should now believe our advertisers instead. When we realize that freedom comes with the right breakfast food, we will see that it costs much less than we expect (about 42 cents a day) to be free. From a cost-benefit standpoint you can't beat this. There is no reason that a ski lodge cannot be accepted as a symbol of all that we value. It is already. We can have our development and our aesthetic enjoyment, too.

The developer need not reply to the environmentalist in such an uncompromising manner; he could also answer in a softer way. He could agree with the environmentalist that nature does possess important aesthetic qualities, that it expresses freedom, purpose, and strength, for example, and that natural objects are more appropriate paradigms of these qualities than are breakfast foods and kitchen appliances. Accordingly, he might concede that the country has some stake in preserving or at least respecting the expressive qualities of nature, even if he is not sure what this stake may be. The developer might declare his willingness, then, to protect the aesthetic qualities of the environment as he understands them and wherever they do not simply prevent development. He might promise, for example, not to domesticate wildlife; either the animals will die or have enough room to preserve their strength and independence by fending for themselves. He might also decide not to build a pleasure palace for rich people whose only need is to amuse themselves. Nature should not be an idle spectacle; therefore he will build an arduous ski area where people will have to confront the mountain somewhat on its own terms and do rather more for their pleasure than throw a beer can out a car window. Visitors would come, then, with respect for the mountain, not to disgrace it after it has been subdued by machinery, but themselves to conquer it. In these and other ways, the developer could compromise with the environmentalist. But he must know how to determine the aesthetic qualities of various

environments. He wants to understand why these qualities are so important, especially since they are often the ones which make nature least pleas-
ant, and he needs to understand how to preserve them in a development.
The problem of the symbolic aspect of nature is an important one, and it
should be stated clearly and correctly.

The following pages attempt to explain the aesthetic value of natural
environments. We consider only the expressive qualities of these environments and not their beauty, considered formally, or their amenity, about
which enough has been said. We begin, then, by defining the expression
"aesthetic quality." An "aesthetic quality" is any quality named in a metaphorical way. The distinction between the nonaesthetic and the aesthetic
and the distinction between the literal and the metaphorical coincide. The
distinction between the objective and the subjective is logically independent
of the other distinctions: thus, a metaphorical or aesthetic quality can be
objective as well. A brook, for example, may be "laughing" and "wet" in
exactly the same way. Once we have these distinctions properly before us,
we can understand the definition of "expression": if an object *expresses* a
quality, that quality is metaphorical, the object possesses the quality, and
the object exemplifies the quality.[1] Thus objects are examples or paradigms
of the qualities they express. Now, paradigms have a cognitive function;
they provide samples by which we learn to recognize given qualities.
Change the paradigms of "freedom" and you change your understanding
of what it is to be free. Thus, the question of substituting one symbol for
another, and therefore one paradigm for another, is a very tricky one. It
involves a change in the objects we recognize as having the quality; in other
words, it changes the quality itself.

After we establish all this, we move on to determine the aesthetic
qualities of nature and the natural environments to which they belong. The
criterion here is our cultural history, not our advertising, and the reason is
not hard to find. The business of the arts is to provide expressive objects
and to represent other objects as expressive; therefore, art objects are
themselves paradigms of aesthetic qualities and they represent other objects as paradigms. Just as the sciences have the function of describing the
theoretical properties of things, so the arts determine, by way of providing
crucial examples, aesthetic qualities. The arts, no less than the sciences
describe a way the world is. This is the cognitive function of art.

Having said this much, we defend it against one objection, *viz.*,
disagreements about the aesthetic properties of objects of art and nature
seem to show that these properties are not objective, but belong to the
subject's response. This objection is not compelling; after all there can be
disagreement as well about commonsense and theoretical properties. The
important thing is that we have conditions for determining at least in
principle when a description—aesthetic, commonsensical, or theoretical—
is true or false. These conditions will be stated for the aesthetic description
of nature and art.

---

[1]*See* N. Goodman, *Languages of Art* 68 (1968) ("metaphorical possession is not literal
possession; but possession is actual whether literal or metaphorical").

B

An "aesthetic quality" is any quality named by a metaphorical predicate. Here are some predicates: "is laughing," "is sad," "is empty," "is free." Each of these can be used in a metaphorical and in a literal sense. When we attach the predicate "is laughing" to the subject "Mary," the predicate is used literally. Attaching it to the subject "the brook" gives us a metaphorical description. There are occasions in which a term can be predicated of an object both literally and metaphorically; then we have to determine by the context which is meant. To say that Mary is empty, for example, may characterize her personality (the metaphorical use) or assert that she has not eaten anything (her stomach is literally empty)—and one description may be true while the other is false. The difference between the metaphorical and the literal use of predicates is a matter of conventionality: the literal is the more usual, habitual, or familiar use. As a rule, metaphorical terms are transferred from their routine or literal realm of application—say, sentient beings—and applied to objects which they do not conventionally describe. Thus, when we say that a river is happy or that a mountain is hostile, we do not mean that either has feelings; we are using predicates that habitually describe sentient beings to describe inanimate things. A family of predicates has been transferred from a conventional to a less conventional realm. This is the characteristic of metaphor. A predicate which is used in a metaphorical way describes a metaphorical quality. And whether we say "metaphorical quality" or "aesthetic quality" we are talking about the same thing.

The aesthetic qualities of nature are not just those qualities which are described in metaphorical terms. These terms, or predicates, very often have human beings in their literal realm or extension. When we find nature to express a metaphorical quality—*e.g.,* freedom—it is often a quality which we literally may possess. Thus there is a connection between the ways we describe and therefore understand and experience nature and the ways we describe, understand, and experience ourselves.

In spite of the fact that the aesthetic is easily defined, as we have defined it, without any reference to the subjective, people have thought that aesthetic judgments must be or usually are subjective—and this is a mistake. Aesthetic qualities can be objective. The statement that a mountain is hostile or noble is as much a factual description as the statement that it is tall and in Spain. This is not to say, of course, that mountains are *literally* hostile or noble. On the contrary, they do not have feelings nor descend from noble blood: rather, the terms "hostile" and "noble" are used as they apply to inanimate objects and not as they apply to human beings. This use of these predicates is unconventional, of course, but not arbitrary; it is unusual, but still true or false. Metaphorical properties are not routinely ascribed to mountains, but they are correctly or incorrectly ascribed to mountains; they are actual properties nonetheless.

Why have people thought otherwise? Why is it common to believe that aesthetic descriptions are not objective but express only a subjective response? The reasons seem to be three. First, some people have thought that the aesthetic value of nature and art consists in the production or transmission of emotion in or to an audience. On this theory, a river is "happy" insofar as it causes those who see it to feel happy merely by seeing it, and a painting is "sad" insofar as it makes those who perceive it feel sad. The receipt of these emotions, on this view, explains part of the purpose of art. This theory does make aesthetic judgments subjective. Neither the mountain nor the canvas would be the logical subject of the emotional qualities. They would cause these qualities, and the subject would be the spectator himself. Second, some people have also believed that the sadness and the happiness belong as properties neither to the object nor to the subject but to a special kind of subjective or "phenomenal" entity that exists "in" experience or "in" the imagination. If this view can be understood at all, it also seems to make aesthetic qualities depend upon subjective response. Finally, the fact that people disagree concerning the aesthetic qualities they find in things also suggests that these qualities may belong or be logically tied to the subject more than to the object of experience. Since aesthetic descriptions are by definition unconventional, however, disagreement of this sort is to be expected. Nevertheless, it does raise the question whether principles for resolving such disagreements can be found.

Because these "reasons" for believing that aesthetic judgments are subjective are so widely held and respected, we shall pause to refute them. In doing so, we do not prove that aesthetic judgments and qualities are factual—only that certain reasons for believing otherwise are false. The argument for thinking that they are factual will be given later. Throughout the discussion, we shall use examples drawn from nature and from art. There is no difference between them in respect to the theory advanced here, and sometimes a painting is a less unwieldy example of a principle than is a forest or a mountain.

The belief that the function of art consists primarily in the production of emotion, although it is popular, is ludicrous. Of all art, soap operas, on such a view, become the most important, but even they are outdistanced by a roller coaster, a Baptist revival, or even a good family fight. The fact is that only preadolescents have energy for emotional thrills, and this explains their interest in hard rock; you appreciate peace and quiet after 25. Accordingly, it is hard to understand why an object that stimulates emotion is *valuable;* it would seem to be the very thing to avoid. Empathy with others, of course, is sometimes morally desirable, but for this art is no help to us. The variety of emotions with which people respond to well known works suggests that they use the occasion to feel whatever is in their own hearts and not the hearts of others. Accordingly, there can be therapy in this sort of response—we all like a good ghost story—but there is no understanding of the value of art.

It is not hard to refute the view that nature and art function aesthetically to cause pleasures and emotions in us. We need only to distinguish the emotional quality of the spectator from the emotional quality of the work. In order to recognize the passionateness of the painting the perceiver need no more become passionate than to recognize the colors of the painting he need turn red and green. This is not to deny, by the way, that the experience of a painting or of nature is emotional: we can feel *that* the painting is passionate just as we can feel *that* a person in a metaphorical sense is warm. To do this we need not ourselves become passionate or warm. We can act in the context of cognition rather than that of stimulus and response.

Of all theories of art which make it the cause of a feeling, the most heady, no doubt, is the "Formalist" thesis that "there is a particular kind of emotion provoked by works of visual art, and this . . . emotion is called the aesthetic emotion."[2] While the Formalists did not extend this hypothesis to nature, we could easily do so by holding that nature, too, proffers a special "aesthetic emotion." Clive Bell, the most vocal of the Formalists, announced that "to appreciate a work of art we need bring with us nothing from life, no knowledge of its ideas or affairs, no familiarity with its emotions."[3] Art, then, is supposed to be entertainment for the senses, when the mind is empty. But what is this "particular emotion" and why is it valuable? Needless to say, the emotion is defined in terms of the "significant form" of the painting, and vice versa, thus describing a circle, which also provokes an emotion. It need not detain us that Bell characterizes aesthetic pleasure as an ecstasy or as an exaltation, for this is said by the drunkard about alcohol, the seducer about fornication, the addict about heroin, the miser about money. They are all voluptuaries, each praising the consciousness-expanding properties of his drug. And there is no evidence that the aesthete is in fact any better for his pleasures than if he had sniffed the paint instead of looked at it. Nor need it bother us that the Formalist view makes most art before Cezanne inconsequential. Objections such as these are too easy to make, but they do teach us to avoid one perspective.

The purpose of art is not to give us a special tingle. That is the purpose of a massage. Nature and art are not mere stimuli to which we respond with an emotion or a feeling of pleasure; they contain symbols which our perception and our tradition allow us to recognize and understand.

C

Earlier this century, conservationist groups argued with some success that governments should protect the national environment from excessive exploitation in order to safeguard and, by proper planning, to increase the benefits nature offers man. These conservationists wished to save the goose—but primarily for the sake of the golden egg. Today, environmentalists have come to see the inappropriateness and futility of this kind of argument. The argument is inappropriate because it distracts attention from the real motivation of the ecology movement, which is not to derive economic or recreational benefit from nature so much as to respect it for what it is and therefore to preserve it for its own sake. And the argument is futile, as we have said, because utility is generally to be gained by changing

---

[2]C. Bell, *Art* 6–7 (1958).
[3]*Id.* at 25.

natural environments, not by preserving them. Accordingly, a different and, indeed, a nonutilitarian rationale is needed to support protectionist policies. This paper proposes such a rationale.

Our proposal is this: We have an obligation to protect natural environments insofar as we respect the qualities they express. We have seen that these qualities do actually belong to some environments, which are their paradigms; and the discovery or identification of these qualities is effected in our language and by our arts. Preserving an environment may be compared to maintaining an institution, for symbols are to values as institutions are to our legal and political life. The obligation to preserve nature, then, is an obligation to our cultural tradition, to the values which we have cherished and in terms of which nature and this nation are still to be described. It is difficult and indeed unnecessary to argue that fulfilling this obligation to our national values, to our history, and, therefore, to ourselves confers any kind of benefit; perhaps fulfilling a responsibility is itself a benefit, but this view requires not that we define "responsibility" in terms of "benefits," as the utilitarian does, but that we define "benefits" in terms of "responsibilities." In any case, preservation of the qualities, and accordingly the values, that this nation, as a nation, has considered peculiarly its own—and these are the qualities of nature—certainly obliges us to do otherwise than follow our pleasure and our profit. Consequently, there may be reason to think that fidelity to our historic values imposes both a "benefit" and a "cost."[4]

What are the legal implications of this rationale for preserving the national environment? Can a citizen claim interest in the monuments of his nation's culture and history as such? Can he, more generally, assert legal membership in a cultural as well as political union? We believe that he can. Everyone allows that citizens have the right to vote, based on the Constitution; surely they have a right to participate in the *culture* of the nation as well. A political community does not develop independently of a cultural one, and unless people have a way of protecting their cultural as well as their political and legal institutions, eventually they may lose all of them. Now, participation in a culture must mean at least two things: individuals may contribute to it by entering the sciences or the arts, and they may become familiar with it through acquaintance with the great monuments and achievements of their nation's past. This means, of course, that people should be able to go to the National Gallery, for example, and not have Muzak piped at them, for Muzak expresses competing and distracting properties. People have a right, moreover, at least to ensure the existence of places like Sequoia National Park and to go there if they can, without

---

[4]About this problem Reinhold Niebuhr wrote: "The real question is whether a religion or a culture is capable of interpreting life in a dimension sufficiently profound to understand and anticipate the sorrows and pains which may result from a virtuous regard for our responsibility; and to achieve a serenity within sorrow and pain which is something less but also something more than 'happiness.' Our difficulty as a nation is that we must now learn that prosperity is not simply coordinated to virtue, that virtue is not simply coordinated to historic destiny, and that happiness is no simple possibility of human experience." R. Niebuhr, *The Irony of American History* 54 (1952).

having to do the usual battle with automobiles. They can demand that the mountains be left as a symbol of the sublime, a quality which is extremely important in our cultural history, rather than be turned into an expression of the soft life, which is not. The protection of the symbols—the institutions as we have said—of our cultural tradition is a condition for the maintenance of other traditions—particularly, the legal and political tradition to which our culture gives life. Accordingly, we need to respect these symbols as well as, and on the same grounds as we respect our legal and political rights. The safeguards appropriate to environmental policy, then, are not to be found in administrative codes and procedures only; we need restraints of a more dramatic and decisive kind. These must be as strong as those which protect our most fundamental rights. If restraints on the exploitation of our environment are to be adequate, then, they must be found in the Constitution itself, either as a forthright basis for statutory action[5]—placing certain national paradigms in trust,[6] for example—or simply as the national guarantor of those structures and relations necessary to maintain the American nation.[7]

To say that an environmental policy can be based on the Constitution[8] does not require, of course, a constitutional passage or article which directly concerns the environment; rather the argument would rest on the concept of nationhood, the structure created by the Constitution as a single instrument functioning in all of its parts. It is reasonable to think that cultural traditions and values constitute a condition—at least a causal one—of our political and legal freedom; and therefore insofar as the Constitution safeguards our nation as a political entity, it must safeguard our cultural integrity as well. Citizenship, then, can be seen to involve not only legal and political but also cultural rights and responsibilities. This possibility requires a legal argument and legal argument is not offered here. But here is a suggestion for someone else to argue. The right to cherish traditional national symbols, the right to preserve in the environment the qualities we associate with our character as a people, belongs to us as Americans. The concept of nationhood implies this right; and for this reason, it is constitutionally based.

But nothing is sacred; everything changes. It is just that changes which inhibit us from sharing our common heritage should not come at the whim of the developer. Nor should they depend on the conflicting interests of outdoors-people who like to hike and swim. Far different issues are at stake. They go to our sense of ourselves as a national community. Given this fact, it is satisfying to ground the protection of the environment on our

[5]This, instead of the well-worn Commerce Clause. After all, it is the fact that the eagle soars in the mind's eye, and not that he may fly across state lines, which is important.

[6]*Cf.* Nantucket Islands Trust Bill, S.3536 & H.R. 15081, 93rd Cong., 2d Sess. (1974).

[7]*See* C. Black, Jr., *Structure and Relationship in Constitutional Law* (1969).

[8]Even if such a rationale were held to provide the power by which Congress creates such trusts rather than implying the limitation itself, the recognition of this view would act as a check on governmental action. For example, public, rather than private access, is implicit; standing to sue is granted citizens once such a constitutional right has been accorded judicial recognition; interference with the protection of paradigms can be enjoined.

most national legal institution. The right of our citizens to their history, to the signs and symbols of their culture, and therefore to some means of protecting and using their surroundings in a way consistent with their values is as important as the right to an equally apportioned franchise[9] or to participation in a party primary.[10] These rights are not to be denied on economic grounds. One sees too much withdrawal, aloofness, and exile in our society not to know that. As the right of the people to membership in our culture is recognized and defined, our people will become more aware and take more advantage of their membership. If with flexible constitutional structures at hand, we nonetheless forsake our national paradigms, we will not only lose once-cherished objects; we will sacrifice the values these objects express. These are the values by which we describe our national character and purpose; they are the qualities which we associate with our nation, our environment, and with the Constitution itself.[11]

[9]*Reynolds* v. *Sims*, 377 U.S. 533 (1964).
[10]*Smith* v. *Allwright*, 321 U.S. 649 (1944).

[11]One afternoon last fall I was on my way to my class in constitutional law. I was going to lead a discussion of certain technicalities having to do with the application of the Fourteenth Amendment, as implemented by acts of Congress, to voting and other rights. My head was full of section numbers in the Federal Revised Statutes. I fear I was mumbling to myself, a practice I cannot recommend to those who hold reputation dear.

I happened to look up—all the way up, over the tops of the red stone buildings into the sky as the Indians of Connecticut must have seen it before the white settlers came, with the great autumnal castles of clouds as far as imagination could reach. And somehow, very suddenly, all this illimitable expansiveness and lofty freedom connected within me with the words I was tracing from the Fourteenth Amendment through the statute books—"privileges or immunities of citizens," "due process of law," "equal protection of the laws." And I was caught for a moment by the feeling of a Commonwealth in which these words had not the narrow, culture-bound, relative meaning we are able to give them in a "real" world, but were grown to the vastness that is germinal within them. C. Black, Jr., *The Occasions of Justice: Essays Mostly on Law* 29–30 (1963).

On Being Morally Considerable

Kenneth E. Goodpaster

A thing is right when it tends to preserve the integrity, stability, and beauty of the biotic community. It is wrong when it tends otherwise.

—Aldo Leopold

What follows is a preliminary inquiry into a question which needs more elaborate treatment than an essay can provide. The question can be and

Source: Reprinted with deletions by permission of the author and *The Journal of Philosophy*, LXXV, no. 6 (1978), 308–25.

has been addressed in different rhetorical formats, but perhaps G. J. Warnock's formulation of it[1] is the best to start with:

> Let us consider the question to whom principles of morality apply from, so to speak, the other end—from the standpoint not of the agent, but of the "patient." What, we may ask here, is the condition of moral *relevance?* What is the condition of having a claim to be *considered,* by rational agents to whom moral principles apply? (148)

* * *

Modern moral philosophy has taken ethical egoism as its principle foil for developing what can fairly be called a *humanistic* perspective on value and obligation. That is, both Kantian and Humean approaches to ethics tend to view the philosophical challenge as that of providing an epistemological and motivational generalization of an agent's natural self-interested concern. Because of this preoccupation with moral "take-off," however, too little critical thought has been devoted to the flight and its destination. One result might be a certain feeling of impotence in the minds of many moral philosophers when faced with the sorts of issues . . . that question the breadth of the moral enterprise more than its departure point. To be sure, questions of conservation, preservation of the environment, and technology assessment *can* be approached simply as application questions, e.g., "How shall we evaluate the alternatives available to us instrumentally in relation to humanistic satisfactions?" But there is something distressingly uncritical in this way of framing such issues—distressingly uncritical in the way that deciding foreign policy solely in terms of "the national interest" is uncritical. Or at least, so I think.

It seems to me that we should not only wonder about, but actually follow "the road not taken into the wood." Neither rationality nor the capacity to experience pleasure and pain seem to me necessary (even though they may be sufficient) conditions on moral considerability. And only our hedonistic and concentric forms of ethical reflection keep us from acknowledging this fact. Nothing short of the condition of *being alive* seems to me to be a plausible and nonarbitrary criterion. What is more, this criterion, if taken seriously, could admit of application to entities and systems of entities heretofore unimagined as claimants on our moral attention (such as the biosystem itself). Some may be inclined to take such implications as a *reductio* of the move "beyond humanism." I am beginning to be persuaded, however, that such implications may provide both a meaningful ethical vision and the hope of a more adequate action guide for the long-term future. Paradigms are crucial components in knowledge—but they can conceal as much as they reveal. Our paradigms of moral considerability are individual persons and their joys and sorrows. I want to venture the belief

---

[1]*The Object of Morality* (New York: Methuen, 1971); parenthetical page references to Warnock will be to this book.

that the universe of moral consideration is more complex than these paradigms allow.

My strategy, now that my cards are on the table, will be to spell out a few rules of the game . . . and then to examine the "hands" of several respected philosophers whose arguments seem to count against casting the moral net as widely as I am inclined to. . . . In concluding . . . I will discuss several objections and touch on further questions needing attention.

The first (of four) distinctions that must be kept clear in addressing our question has already been alluded to. It is that between moral *rights* and moral *considerability*. My inclination is to construe the notion of rights as more specific than that of considerability, largely to avoid what seem to be unnecessary complications over the requirements for something's being an appropriate "bearer of rights." The concept of rights is used in wider and narrower senses, of course. Some authors (indeed, one whom we shall consider later in this paper) use it as roughly synonymous with Warnock's notion of "moral relevance." Others believe that being a bearer of rights involves the satisfaction of much more demanding requirements. The sentiments of John Passmore[2] are probably typical of this narrower view:

> The idea of "rights" is simply not applicable to what is non-human. . . . It is one thing to say that it is wrong to treat animals cruelly, quite another to say that animals have rights (116/7).

I doubt whether it is so clear that the class of rights-bearers is or ought to be restricted to human beings, but I propose to suspend this question entirely by framing the discussion in terms of the notion of moral considerability (following Warnock), except in contexts where there is reason to think the widest sense of "rights" is at work. Whether beings who deserve moral consideration in themselves, not simply by reason of their utility to human beings, also possess moral *rights* in some narrow sense is a question which will, therefore, remain open here—and it is a question the answer to which need not be determined in advance.

A second distinction is that between what might be called a *criterion of moral considerability* and a *criterion of moral significance*. The former represents the central quarry here, while the latter, which might easily get confused with the former, aims at governing *comparative* judgments of moral "weight" in cases of conflict. Whether a tree, say, deserves any moral consideration is a question that must be kept separate from the question of whether trees deserve more or less consideration than dogs, or dogs than human persons. We should not expect that the criterion for having "moral standing" at all will be the same as the criterion for adjudicating competing claims to priority among beings that merit that standing. In fact, it may well be an insufficient appreciation of this distinction which leads some to a preoccupation with rights in dealing with morality. I suspect that the real force of attributions of "rights" derives from comparative contexts, con-

---

[2] *Man's Responsibility for Nature* (New York: Scribner's, 1974).

texts in which moral considerability is presupposed and the issue of strength is crucial. Eventually, of course, the priority issues have to be dealt with for an operational ethical account—this much I have already acknowledged—but in the interests of clarity, I set them aside for now.

Another important distinction, the third, turns on the difference between questions of intelligibility and questions of normative substance. An adequate treatment of this difficult and complicated division would take us far afield,[3] but a few remarks are in order. It is tempting to assume, with Joel Feinberg,[4] that we can neatly separate such questions as

1. What sorts of beings can (logically) be *said* to deserve moral consideration?

from questions like

2. What sorts of beings do, as a matter of "ethical fact" deserve moral consideration?

But our confidence in the separation here wanes (perhaps more quickly than in other philosophical contexts where the conceptual/substantive distinction arises) when we reflect upon the apparent *flexibility* of our metamoral beliefs. One might argue plausibly, for example, that there were times and societies in which the moral standing of blacks was, as a matter of *conceptual analysis,* deniable. Examples could be multiplied to include women, children, fetuses, and various other instances of what might be called "metamoral disenfranchisement." I suspect that the lesson to be learned here is that, as William Frankena has pointed out,[5] metaethics is, and has always been, a partially normative discipline. Whether we are to take this to mean that it is really impossible ever to engage in morally neutral conceptual analysis in ethics is, of course, another question. In any case, it appears that, with respect to the issue at hand, keeping (1) and (2) apart will be difficult. At the very least, I think, we must be wary of arguments that purport to answer (2) *solely* on the basis of "ordinary language"-style answers to (1).

Though the focus of the present inquiry is more normative than conceptual [hence aimed more at (2) than at (1)], it remains what I called a "framework" inquiry nonetheless, since it prescinds from the question of relative weights (moral significance) of moral considerability claims.

Moreover—and this brings us to the fourth and last distinction—there is another respect in which the present inquiry involves framework questions rather than questions of application. There is clearly a sense in which we are subject to *thresholds* of moral sensitivity just as we are subject to

---

[3]Cf. R. M. Hare, "The Argument from Received Opinion," in *Essays on Philosophical Method* (New York: Macmillan, 1971), p. 117.

[4]"The Rights of Animals and Unborn Generations," in Blackstone, *Philosophy and Environmental Crisis* (University of Georgia, 1974), p. 43; parenthetical page references to Feinberg will be to this paper.

[5]"On Saying the Ethical Thing," in Goodpaster, ed., *Perspectives on Morality* (Notre Dame, Ind.: University Press, 1976), pp. 107–24.

thresholds of cognitive or perceptual sensitivity. Beyond such thresholds we are "morally blind" or suffer disintegrative consequences analogous to "information overload" in a computer. . . . Let us, then, say that the moral considerability of X is *operative* for an agent A if and only if the thorough acknowledgment of X by A is psychologically (and in general, causally) possible for A. If the moral considerability of X is defensible on all grounds independent of operativity, we shall say that it is *regulative*. An agent may, for example, have an obligation to grant regulative considerability to all living things, but be able psychologically and in terms of his own nutrition to grant operative consideration to a much smaller class of things (though note that capacities in this regard differ among persons and change over time).

Using all these distinctions, and the rough and ready terminology that they yield, we can now state the issue in (1) as a concern for a relatively substantive (vs. purely logical) criterion of moral considerability (vs. moral significance) of a regulative (vs. operative) sort. As far as I can see, X's being a living thing is both necessary and sufficient for moral considerability so understood, whatever may be the case for the moral *rights* that rational agents should acknowledge. Let us begin with Warnock's own answer to the question, now that the question has been clarified somewhat. In setting out his answer, Warnock argues (in my view, persuasively) against two more restrictive candidates. The first, what might be called the *Kantian principle*, amounts to little more than a reflection of the requirements of moral *agency* onto those of moral considerability:

3.   For X to deserve moral consideration from A, X must be a rational human person.

Observing that such a criterion of considerability eliminates children and mentally handicapped adults, among others, Warnock dismisses it as intolerably narrow.

The second candidate, actually a more generous variant of the first, sets the limits of moral considerability by disjoining "potentiality":

4.   For all A, X deserves moral consideration from A if and only if X is a rational human person or is a potential rational human person.

Warnock's reply to this suggestion is also persuasive. Infants and imbeciles are no doubt potentially rational, but this does not appear to be the reason why we should not maltreat them. And we would not say that an imbecile reasonably judged to be incurable would thereby reasonably be taken to have no moral claims (151). In short, it seems arbitrary to draw the boundary of moral *considerability* around rational human beings (actual or potential), however plausible it might be to draw the boundary of moral *responsibility* there.[6]

----

[6]Actually, it seems to me that we ought not to draw the boundary of moral responsibility just here. See my "Morality and Organizations," in *Proceedings of the Second National Conference on Business Ethics* (Waltham, Mass.: Bentley College, 1978).

Warnock then settles upon his own solution. The basis of moral claims, he says, may be put as follows:

> . . . just as liability to be judged as a moral agent follows from one's general capability of alleviating, by moral action, the ills of the predicament, and is for that reason confined to rational beings, so the condition of being a proper "beneficiary" of moral action is the capability of *suffering* the ills of the predicament—and for that reason is not confined to rational beings, nor even to potential members of that class (151).

The criterion of moral considerability then, is located in the *capacity to suffer:*

5. For all *A*, *X* deserves moral consideration from *A* if and only if *X* is capable of suffering pain (or experiencing enjoyment).

And the defense involves appeal to what Warnock considers to be (analytically) the *object* of the moral enterprise: amelioration of "the predicament."

*   *   *

W. K. Frankena, in a recent paper,[7] joins forces:

> Like Warnock, I believe that there are right and wrong ways to treat infants, animals, imbeciles, and idiots even if or even though (as the case may be) they are not persons or human beings—just because they are capable of pleasure and suffering, and not just because their lives happen to have some value to or for those who clearly are persons or human beings.

And Peter Singer[8] writes:

> If a being is not capable of suffering, or of experiencing enjoyment or happiness, there is nothing to be taken into account. This is why the limit of sentience (using the term as a convenient, if not strictly accurate, shorthand for the capacity to suffer or experience enjoyment or happiness) is the only defensible boundary of concern for the interests of others (154).

. . . although I acknowledge and even applaud the conviction expressed by these philosophers that the capacity to suffer (or perhaps better, *sentience*) is sufficient for moral considerability, I fail to understand their reasons for thinking such a criterion necessary. To be sure, there are hints at reasons in each case. Warnock implies that nonsentient beings could not be proper "beneficiaries" of moral action. Singer seems to think that beyond sentience "there is nothing to take into account." And Frankena suggests that nonsentient beings simply do not provide us with moral rea-

---

[7]"Ethics and the Environment," in K. E. Goodpaster and K. M. Sayre, eds., *Ethics and Problems of the 21st Century* (Notre Dame, Ind.: University Press, 1978).

[8]"All Animals Are Equal," in Tom Regan and Peter Singer, *Animal Rights and Human Obligations* (Englewood Cliffs, N.J.: Prentice-Hall, 1976). See p. 316.

sons for respecting them unless it be potentiality for sentience.[9] Yet it is so clear that there *is* something to take into account, something that is not merely "potential sentience" and which surely does qualify beings as beneficiaries and capable of harm—namely, *life*—that the hints provided seem to me to fall short of good reasons.

Biologically, it appears that sentience is an adaptive characteristic of living organisms that provides them with a better capacity to anticipate, and so avoid, threats to life. This at least suggests, though of course it does not prove, that the capacities to suffer and to enjoy are ancillary to something more important rather than tickets to considerability in their own right. In the words of one perceptive scientific observer:

> If we view pleasure as rooted in our sensory physiology, it is not difficult to see that our neurophysiological equipment must have evolved via variation and selective retention in such a way as to record a positive signal to adaptationally satisfactory conditions and a negative signal to adaptationally unsatisfactory conditions. . . . The pleasure signal is only an evolutionarily derived indicator, not the goal itself. It is the applause which signals a job well done, but not the actual completion of the job.[10]

Nor is it absurd to imagine that evolution might have resulted (indeed might still result?) in beings whose capacities to maintain, protect, and advance their lives did not depend upon mechanisms of pain and pleasure at all.

*   *   *

Joel Feinberg offers (51) what may be the clearest and most explicit case for a restrictive criterion on moral considerability (restrictive with respect to life). . . .

*   *   *

The central thesis defended by Feinberg is that a being cannot intelligibly be said to possess moral rights (read: deserve moral consideration) unless that being satisfies the "interest principle," and that only the subclass of humans and higher animals among living beings satisfies this principle:

> . . . the sorts of beings who can have rights are precisely those who have (or can have) interests. I have come to this tentative conclusion for two reasons:

[9]"I can see no reason, from the moral point of view, why we should respect something that is alive but has no conscious sentiency and so can experience no pleasure or pain, joy or suffering, unless perhaps it is potentially a consciously sentient being, as in the case of a fetus. Why, if leaves and trees have no capacity to feel pleasure or to suffer, should I tear no leaf from a tree? Why should I respect its location any more than that of a stone in my driveway, if no benefit or harm comes to any person or sentient being by my moving it?" ("Ethics and the Environment.")

[10]Mark W. Lipsey, "Value Science and Developing Society," paper delivered to the Society for Religion in Higher Education, Institute on Society, Technology and Values (July 15–August 4, 1973), p. 11.

(1) because a right holder must be capable of being represented and it is impossible to represent a being that has no interests, and (2) because a right holder must be capable of being a beneficiary in his own person, and a being without interests is a being that is incapable of being harmed or benefited, having no good or "sake" of its own (51).

Implicit in this passage are the following two arguments, interpreted in terms of moral considerability:

(A1) Only beings who can be represented can deserve moral consideration.
Only beings who have (or can have) interests can be represented.
Therefore, only beings who have (or can have) interests can deserve moral consideration.

(A2) Only beings capable of being beneficiaries can deserve moral consideration.
Only beings who have (or can have) interests are capable of being beneficiaries.
Therefore, only beings who have (or can have) interests can deserve moral consideration.

I suspect that these two arguments are at work between the lines in Warnock, Frankena, and Singer, though of course one can never be sure. In any case, I propose to consider them as the best defense of the sentience criterion in recent literature.

I am prepared to grant, with some reservations, the first premises in each of these obviously valid arguments. The second premises, though, are *both* importantly equivocal. To claim that only beings who have (or can have) interests can be represented might mean that "mere things" cannot be represented because they have nothing to represent, no "interests" as opposed to "usefulness" to defend or protect. Similarly, to claim that only beings who have (or can have) interests are capable of being beneficiaries might mean that "mere things" are incapable of being benefited or harmed—they have no "well-being" to be sought or acknowledged by rational moral agents. So construed, Feinberg seems to be right; but he also seems to be committed to allowing any *living* thing the status of moral considerability. For as he himself admits, even plants

> . . . are not "mere things"; they are vital objects with inherited biological propensities determining their natural growth. Moreover we do say that certain conditions are "good" or "bad" for plants, thereby suggesting that plants, unlike rocks, are capable of having a "good" (51).

But Feinberg pretty clearly wants to draw the nets tighter than this—and he does so by interpreting the notion of "interests" in the two second premises more narrowly. The contrast term he favors is not "mere things" but "mindless creatures." And he makes this move by insisting that "interests" logically presuppose *desires* or *wants* or *aims,* the equipment for which is not possessed by plants (nor, we might add, by many animals or even some humans?).

But why should we accept this shift in strength of the criterion? In doing so, we clearly abandon one sense in which living organisms like plants do have interests that can be represented. There is no absurdity in imagining the representation of the needs of a tree for sun and water in the face of a proposal to cut it down or pave its immediate radius for a parking lot. We might of course, on reflection, decide to go ahead and cut it down or do the paving, but there is hardly an intelligibility problem about representing the tree's interest in our deciding not to. In the face of their obvious tendencies to maintain and heal themselves, it is very difficult to reject the idea of interests on the part of trees (and plants generally) in remaining alive.[11]

Nor will it do to suggest, as Feinberg does, that the needs (interests) of living things like trees are not really their own but implicitly *ours:* "Plants may need things in order to discharge their functions, but their functions are assigned by human interests, not their own" (54). As if it were human interests that assigned to trees the tasks of growth or maintenance! The interests at stake are clearly those of the living things themselves, not simply those of the owners or users or other human persons involved. Indeed, there is a suggestion in this passage that, to be capable of being represented, an organism must *matter* to human beings somehow—a suggestion whose implications for human rights (disenfranchisement) let alone the rights of animals (inconsistently for Feinberg, I think)—are grim.

The truth seems to be that the "interests" that nonsentient beings share with sentient beings (over and against "mere things") are far more plausible as criteria of *considerability* than the "interests" that sentient beings share (over and against "mindless creatures"). This is not to say that interests construed in the latter way are morally irrelevant—for they may play a role as criteria of moral *significance*—but it is to say that psychological or hedonic capacities seem unnecessarily sophisticated when it comes to locating the minimal conditions for something's deserving to be valued for its own sake. Surprisingly, Feinberg's own reflections on "mere things" appear to support this very point:

> . . . mere things have no conative life: no conscious wishes, desires, and hopes; or urges and impulses; or unconscious drives, aims, and goals; or latent tendencies, direction of growth, and natural fulfillments. Interests must be compounded somehow out of conations; hence mere things have no interests (49).

Together with the acknowledgment, quoted earlier, that plants, for example, are not "mere things," such observations seem to undermine the interest principle in its more restrictive form. I conclude, with appropriate caution, that the interest principle either grows to fit what we might call a "life principle" or requires an arbitrary stipulation of psychological capacities (for desires, wants, etc.) which are neither warranted by (A1) and (A2) nor independently plausible.

*   *   *

[11]See Albert Szent-Gyorgyi, *The Living State* (New York: Academic Press, 1972), esp. chap. VI, "Vegetable Defense Systems."

Let us now turn to several objections that might be thought to render a "life principle" of moral considerability untenable quite independently of the adequacy or inadequacy of the sentience or interest principle.

* * *

(O1) Consideration of life can serve as a criterion only to the degree that life itself can be given a precise definition; and it can't.

(R1) I fail to see why a criterion of moral considerability must be strictly decidable in order to be tenable. Surely rationality, potential rationality, sentience, and the capacity for or possession of interests fare no better here. Moreover, there do seem to be empirically respectable accounts of the nature of living beings available which are not intolerably vague or open-textured:

> The typifying mark of a living system . . . appears to be its persistent state of low entropy, sustained by metabolic processes for accumulating energy, and maintained in equilibrium with its environment by homeostatic feedback processes.[12]

Granting the need for certain further qualifications, a definition such as this strikes me as not only plausible in its own right, but ethically illuminating, since it suggests that the core of moral concern lies in respect for self-sustaining organization and integration in the face of pressures toward high entropy.

(O2) If life, as understood in the previous response, is really taken as the key to moral considerability, then it is possible that larger systems besides our ordinarily understood "linear" extrapolations from human beings (e.g., animals, plants, etc.) might satisfy the conditions, such as the biosystem as a whole. This surely would be a *reductio* of the life principle.

(R2) At best, it would be a *reductio* of the life principle in this form or without qualification. But it seems to me that such (perhaps surprising) implications, if true, should be taken seriously. There is some evidence that the biosystem as a whole exhibits behavior approximating to the definition sketched above,[13] and I see no reason to deny it moral considerability on that account. Why should the universe of moral considerability map neatly onto our medium-sized framework of organisms?

(O3) There are severe epistemological problems about imputing interests, benefits, harms, etc. to nonsentient beings. What is it for a tree to have needs?

(R3) I am not convinced that the epistemological problems are more severe in this context than they would be in numerous others which the

---

[12]K. M. Sayre, *Cybernetics and the Philosophy of Mind* (New York: Humanities, 1976), p. 91.

[13]See J. Lovelock and S. Epton, "The Quest for Gaia," *The New Scientist,* 65 935 (February 6, 1975): 304–09.

objector would probably not find problematic. Christopher Stone has put this point nicely:

> I am sure I can judge with more certainty and meaningfulness whether and when my lawn wants (needs) water than the Attorney General can judge whether and when the United States wants (needs) to take an appeal from an adverse judgment by a lower court. The lawn tells me that it wants water by a certain dryness of the blades and soil—immediately obvious to the touch—the appearance of bald spots, yellowing, and a lack of springiness after being walked on; how does "the United States" communicate to the Attorney General? (24).

We make decisions in the interests of others or on behalf of others every day—"others" whose wants are far less verifiable than those of most living creatures.

(O4) Whatever the force of the previous objections, the clearest and most decisive refutation of the principle of respect for life is that one cannot *live* according to it, nor is there any indication in nature that we were intended to. We must eat, experiment to gain knowledge, protect ourselves from predation (macroscopic and microscopic), and in general deal with the overwhelming complexities of the moral life while remaining psychologically intact. To take seriously the criterion of considerability being defended, all these things must be seen as somehow morally wrong.

(R4) This objection . . . can be met, I think, by recalling the distinction made earlier between regulative and operative moral consideration. It seems to me that there clearly are limits to the operational character of respect for living things. We must eat, and usually this involves killing (though not always). We must have knowledge, and sometimes this involves experimentation with living things and killing (though not always). We must protect ourselves from predation and disease, and sometimes this involves killing (though not always). The regulative character of the moral consideration due to all living things asks, as far as I can see, for sensitivity and awareness, not for suicide (psychic or otherwise). But it is not vacuous, in that it does provide a *ceteris paribus* encouragement in the direction of nutritional, scientific, and medical practices of a genuinely life-respecting sort.

As for the implicit claim, in the objection, that since nature doesn't respect life, we needn't, there are two rejoinders. The first is that the premise is not so clearly true. Gratuitous killing in nature is rare indeed. The second, and more important, response is that the issue at hand has to do with the appropriate moral demands to be made on rational moral agents, not on beings who are not rational moral agents. Besides, this objection would tell equally against *any* criterion of moral considerability so far as I can see, if the suggestion is that nature is amoral.

*   *   *

Is There an Ecological Ethic?

Holmes Rolston III

The Ecological Conscience[1] is the arresting title of a representative environmental anthology. The puzzlement lies neither in the noun nor in the by now familiar modifier, but in their operation on each other. We are comfortable with a Christian or humanist ethic, but the moral noun does not regularly take a scientific adjective: a biological conscience, a geological conscience. . . .

The sense of anomaly will dissipate, though moral urgency may remain, if an environmental ethic proves to be only an ethic—utilitarian, hedonist, or whatever—*about* the environment, brought to it, informed concerning it, but not in principle ecologically formed or reformed. This would be like medical ethics, which is applied to but not derived from medical science. But we are sometimes promised more, a derivation in which the newest bioscience shapes (not to say, subverts) the ethic, a resurgent naturalistic ethics. "We must learn that nature includes an intrinsic value system," writes Ian McHarg.[2] A *Daedalus* collection is introduced with the same conviction: Environmental science "is the building of the structure of concepts and natural laws that will enable man to understand his place in nature. Such understanding must be one basis of the moral values that guide each human generation in exercising its stewardship over the earth. For this purpose ecology—the science of interactions among living things and their environments—is central."[3] We shall presently inquire into the claim that an ecological ultimacy lies in "The Balance of Nature: A Ground for Values." Just what sort of traffic is there here between science and morality?

The boundary between science and ethics is precise if we accept a pair of current (though not unargued) philosophical categories: the distinction between descriptive and prescriptive law. The former, in the indicative, marks the realm of science and history. The latter, including always an imperative, marks the realm of ethics. The route from one to the other, if any, is perhaps the most intransigent issue in moral philosophy. . . . No set of statements of fact by themselves entails any evaluative statement, except as some additional evaluative premise has been introduced. With careful analysis this evaluation will reappear, the ethics will separate out from the science. We shall press this logic on ecological ethics. Environmental sci-

[1]Robert Disch, ed., *The Ecological Conscience: Values for Survival* (Englewood Cliffs, N.J.: Prentice-Hall, 1970).

[2]Ian L. McHarg, "Values, Process, and Form," in Disch, p. 21.

[3]Roger Revelle and Hans H. Landsberg, eds., *America's Changing Environment* (Boston: Beacon Press, 1970), p. xxii.

Source: Reprinted by permission of the author and The University of Chicago Press from *Ethics* 85:2 (1975): 93–109.

ence describes what is the case. An ethic prescribes what ought to be. But an environmental ethic? If our categories hold, perhaps we have a muddle. Or perhaps a paradox that yields light on the linkage between facts and values.

We find representative spokesmen for ecological morality not of a single mind. But the multiple species can, we suggest, be classified in two genera, following two concepts that are offered as moral sources. *(A)* Prominent in, or underlying, those whom we hear first is the connection of homeostasis with morality. This issues largely in what we term an ethic that is secondarily ecological. *(B)* Beyond this, surpassing though not necessarily gainsaying it, is the discovery of a moral ought inherent in recognition of the holistic character of the ecosystem, issuing in an ethic that is primarily ecological.

But first, consider an analogue. When advised that we ought to obey the laws of health, we analyze the injunction. The laws of health are non-moral and operate inescapably on us. But, circumscribed by them, we have certain options: to employ them to our health, or to neglect them ("break them") to our hurt. Antecedent to the laws of health, the moral ought reappears in some such form as "You ought not to harm yourself." Similarly the laws of psychology, economics, history, the social sciences, and indeed all applied sciences describe what is (has been, or may be) the case; but in confrontation with human agency, they prescribe what the agent must do if he is to attain a desired end. They yield a technical ought related to an if-clause at the agent's option. So far they are nonmoral; they become moral only as a moral principle binds the agent to some end. This, in turn, is transmitted through natural law to a proximate moral ought. Let us map this as follows:

Technical Ought	**Natural Law**	**Antecedent If-Option**
You ought not to break the laws of health	for the laws of health describe the conditions of welfare	if you wish not to harm yourself.
Proximate Moral Ought	**Natural Law**	**Antecedent Moral Ought**
You ought not to break the laws of health	for the laws of health describe the conditions of welfare	and you ought not to harm yourself.

Allow for the moment that (in the absence of overriding considerations) prudence is a moral virtue. How far can ecological ethics transpose to an analogous format?

A

Perhaps the paramount law in ecological theory is that of homeostasis. In material, our planetary ecosystem is essentially closed, and life proceeds by recycling transformations. In energy, the system is open, with balanced solar input and output, the cycling being in energy subsystems of aggradation and degradation. Homeostasis, it should be noted, is at once an achievement and a tendency. Systems recycle, and there is energy balance; yet the systems are not static, but dynamic, as the forces that yield equilibrium are in flux, seeking equilibrium yet veering from it to bring counterforces into play. This perpetual stir, tending to and deviating from equilibrium, drives the evolutionary process.

1. How does this translate morally? Let us consider first a guarded translation. In "The Steady State: Physical Law and Moral Choice," Paul Sears writes: "Probably men will always differ as to what constitutes the good life. They need not differ as to what is necessary for the long survival of man on earth. Assuming that this is our wish, the conditions are clear enough. As living beings we must come to terms with the environment about us, learning to get along with the liberal budget at our disposal, promoting rather than disrupting those great cycles of nature—of water movement, energy flow, and material transformation that have made life itself possible. As a physical goal, we must seek to attain what I have called a steady state."[4] The title of the article indicates that this is a moral "must." To assess this argument, begin with the following:

Technical Ought	Ecological Law	Antecedent If-Option
You ought to recycle	for the life-supporting ecosystem recycles or perishes	if you wish to preserve human life.

When we replace the if-option by an antecedent moral ought, we convert the technical ought to a proximate moral ought. Thus the "must" in the citation is initially one of physical necessity describing our circumscription by ecological law, and subsequently it is one of moral necessity when this law is conjoined with the life-promoting ought.

Proximate Moral Ought	Ecological Law	Antecedent Moral Ought
you ought to recycle	for the life-supporting ecosystem recycles or perishes	and you ought to preserve human life.

The antecedent ought Sears takes, fairly enough, to be common to many if not all our moral systems. Notice the sense in which we can break ecological law. Spelling the conditions of stability and instability, homeostatic laws operate on us willy-nilly, but within a necessary obedience we have options, some of which represent enlightened obedience. To break an ecological law means, then, to disregard its implications in regard to an antecedent moral ought.

Thus far ecological morality is informed about the environment, conforming to it, but is not yet an ethic in which environmental science affects principles. Antecedent to ecological input, there is a classical ethical principle, "promoting human life," which, when ecologically tutored, better understands life's circulations, whether in homeostasis, or in DDT, or stron-

[4]Paul Shepard and Daniel McKinley, eds., *The Subversive Science* (Boston: Houghton Mifflin, 1969), p. 401.

tium 90. Values do not (have to) lie in the world but may be imposed on it, as man prudentially manages the world.

2. Much attention has focused on a 1968 address, "The Tragedy of the Commons," given by Garrett Hardin to the American Association for the Advancement of Science. Hardin's argument, recently expanded to book length, proposes an ecologically based "fundamental extension in morality."[5] While complex in its ramifications and deserving of detailed analysis, the essential ethic is simple, built on the model of a village commons. Used by the villagers to graze cattle, the commons is close to its carrying capacity. Any villager who does not increase his livestock will be disadvantaged in the market. Following self-interest, each increases his herd; and the commons is destroyed. Extended to the planet, seen as a homeostatic system of finite resources, the model's implication of impending tragedy is obvious. (The propriety of the extrapolation is arguable, but not at issue here.) The prescription of an ecological morality is "mutual coercion, mutually agreed on" in which we limit freedom to grow in order to stabilize the ecosystem to the mutual benefit of all.

To distill the ethics here is not difficult. We begin as before, with ecological law that yields options, which translate morally only with the addition of the life-promoting obligation.

Technical Ought	Ecological Law	Antecedent If-Option
We ought to stabilize the ecosystem thru mutually imposed limited growth	for the life-supporting ecosystem stabilizes at a finite carrying capacity or is destroyed	if we wish mutually to preserve human life.
Proximate Moral Ought	Ecological Law	Antecedent Moral Ought
We ought to stabilize the ecosystem thru mutually imposed self-limited growth	for the life-supporting ecosystem stabilizes at a finite carrying capacity or is destroyed	and we ought mutually to preserve human life.

To clarify the problem of mutual preservation, Hardin uses an essentially Hobbesian scheme. Every man is an ego set over against the community, acting in his own self-interest. But to check his neighbor's aggrandizement, he compromises and enters a social contract where, now acting in enlightened self-interest, he limits his own freedom to grow in return for a limitation of the encroaching freedom of his competitors. The result is surprisingly atomistic and anthropocentric, recalling the post-Darwinian biological model, lacking significant place for the mutal interdependence and symbiotic cooperation so prominent in recent ecology. In any event, it is clear enough that Hardin's environmental ethic is only a classical ethic applied in the matrix of ecological limitations.

*   *   *

3. Let us pass to a more venturesome translation of homeostasis into moral prescription, that of Thomas B. Colwell, Jr. "The balance of Nature

[5]Garrett Hardin, "The Tragedy of the Commons," *Science* 162 (1968): 1243–48.

provides an objective normative model which can be utilized as the ground of human value. . . . Nor does the balance of Nature serve as the source of all our values. It is only the *ground* of whatever other values we may develop. But these other values must be consistent with it. The balance of Nature is, in other words, a kind of ultimate value. . . . It is a *natural* norm, not a product of human convention or supernatural authority. It says in effect to man: 'This much at least you must do, this much you must be responsible for. You must at least develop and utilize energy systems which recycle their products back into Nature.' . . . Human values are founded in objectively determinable ecological relations with Nature. The ends which we propose must be such as to be compatible with the ecosystems of Nature."[6]

Morality and homeostasis are clearly blended here, but it is not so clear how we relate or disentangle them. Much is embedded in the meanings of "ground of human value," "ultimate value," the mixed moral and physical "must," and the identification of a moral norm with a natural limit. Let us mark out first a purely technical ought, followed by an antecedent moral ought which may convert to a proximate moral ought.

Technical Ought	Ecological Law	Antecedent If-Option
You ought to recycle	for the value-supporting ecosystem recycles or perishes	if you wish to preserve the ground of human value.
Proximate Moral Ought	**Ecological Law**	**Antecedent Moral Ought**
You ought to recycle	for the value-supporting ecosystem recycles or perishes	and you ought to preserve the ground of human value.

The simplest reading of Colwell is to hold, despite his exaggerated terms, that the "ground of human value" means only the limiting condition, itself value free, within which values are to be constructed. Homeostasis is not "an ultimate value," only a precondition of the value enterprise, necessary but not sufficient for value. . . . It is true, of course, that the means to any end can, in contexts of desperation and urgency, stand in short focus as ultimate values. Air, food, water, health, if we are deprived of them, become at once our concern. Call them ultimate values if you wish, but the ultimacy is instrumental, not intrinsic. We should think him immature whose principal goal was just to breathe, to eat, to drink, to be healthy— merely this and nothing more. We would judge a society stagnant whose ultimate goal was but to recycle. To say that the balance of nature is a ground for human values is not to draw any ethics from ecology, as may first appear, but only to recognize the necessary medium of ethical activity.

Thus far, ecological ethics reduces rather straightforwardly to the classical ethical query now advised of certain ecological boundaries. The stir is, to put it so, about the boundedness, not the morality. The ultimate science may well herald limits to growth; it challenges certain presumptions about rising standards of living, capitalism, progress, development, and so

[6]Thomas B. Colwell, Jr., "The Balance of Nature: A Ground for Human Values," *Main Currents in Modern Thought* 26 (1969): 50.

on; convinctions that, though deeply entrenched parameters of human value, are issues of what is, can, or will be the case, not of what ought to be. This realization of limits, dramatically shift ethical application though it may, can hardly be said to reform our ethical roots, for the reason that its scope remains (when optimistic) a maximizing of human values or (when pessimistic) human survival. All goods are human goods, with nature an accessory. There is no endorsement of any natural rightness, only the acceptance of the natural given. It is ecological secondarily, but primarily anthropological.

B

The claim that morality is a derivative of the holistic character of the ecosystem proves more radical, for the ecological perspective penetrates not only the secondary but also the primary qualities of the ethic. It is ecological in substance, not merely in accident; it is ecological per se, not just consequentially.

Return, for instance, to Colwell. He seems to mean more than the minimal interpretation just given him. The mood is that the ecological circumscription of value is not itself amoral or premoral, neatly articulated from morality. Construct values though man may, he operates in an environmental context where he must ground his values in ecosystemic obedience. This "must" is ecologically descriptive: certain laws in fact circumscribe him and embrace his value enterprises. And it is also morally prescriptive: given options within parameters of necessary obedience, he morally ought to promote homeostasis. But here, advancing on the preceding argument, the claim seems to be that following ecological nature is not merely a prudential means to moral and valuational ends independent of nature but is an end in itself; or, more accurately, it is within man's relatedness to his environment that all man's values are grounded and supported. In that construction of values, man doubtless exceeds any environmental prescription, but nevertheless his values remain environmental reciprocals. They complement a homeostatic world. His valuations, like his other perceptions and knowings, are interactionary, drawn from environmental transactions, not merely brought to it. In this environmental encounter, he finds homeostasis a key to all values—the precondition of values, if you will—but one which, for all that, informs and shapes his other values by making them relational, corporate, environmental. But we are passing over to moral endorsement of the ecosystemic character, and to a tenor of argument that others make clearer.

Perhaps the most provocative such affirmation is in a deservedly seminal essay, "The Land Ethic," by Aldo Leopold. He concludes, "A thing is right when it tends to preserve the integrity, stability, and beauty of the biotic community. It is wrong when it tends otherwise."[7] Leopold writes in

---

[7]Aldo Leopold, "The Land Ethic," in *A Sand County Almanac* (New York: Oxford University Press, 1949), pp. 201–26.

search of a morality of land use that escapes economic expediency. He too enjoins, proximately, recycling, but it is clear that his claim transcends the immediate context to teach that we morally ought to preserve the excellences of the ecosystem (or, more freely as we shall interpret him, to maximize the integrity, beauty, and stability of the ecosystem). He is seeking, as he says, to advance the ethical frontier from the merely interpersonal to the region of man in transaction with his environment.

Here the environmental perspective enters not simply at the level of the proximate ought which, environmentally informed and preceded by homocentrist moral principles, prescribes protection of the ecosystem. It acts at a higher level, as itself an antecedent ought, from which proximate oughts, such as the one earlier considered, about recycling, may be derived.

Proximate Moral Ought	Ecological Law	Antecedent Moral Ought
You ought to recycle	for recycling preserves the ecosystem	and you ought to preserve the integrity of the ecosystem.

Note how the antecedent parallels upper-level axioms in other systems (e.g., "You ought to maximize human good," or "You ought not to harm yourself or others," or "Love your neighbor as yourself"). Earlier, homeostatic connectedness did not really alter the moral focus; but here, in a shift of paradigms, the values hitherto reserved for man are reallocated to man in the environment.

Doubtless even Leopold's antecedent ought depends on a yet prior ought that one promote beauty and integrity, wherever he finds it. But this, like the injunction that one ought to promote the good, or that one ought to keep his promises, is so high level as to be, if not definitional or analytic, so general as to be virtually unarguable and therefore without any real theoretical content. Substantive values emerge only as something empirical is specified as the locus of value. In Leopold's case we have a feedback from ecological science which, prior to any effect on proximate moral oughts, informs the antecedent ought. There is a valuational element intrinsically related to the concepts utilized in ecological description. That is, the character of what is right in some basic sense, not just in application, is stated postecologically. Doubtless too, the natural course we choose to preserve is filtered through our concepts of beauty, stability, and integrity, concepts whose origins are not wholly clear and which are perhaps nonnatural. But, perspectival though this invariably is, what counts as beauty and integrity is not just brought to and imposed on the ecosystem but is discovered there. Let us map this as follows:

Proximate Moral Ought	Ecological Law	Antecedent Moral Ought	Ecosystemic Evaluation
You ought to recycle	for recycling preserves the integral ecosystem	and you ought to preserve the integrity of the ecosystem	for the integral ecosystem has value.

Our antecedent ought is not eco-free. Though preceding ecological law in the sense that, given this ought, one can transmit it via certain ecological laws to arrive at proximate oughts, it is itself a result of an ecosystemic appraisal.

This evaluation is not scientific description; hence not ecology per se, but metaecology. No amount of research can verify that the right is the optimum biotic community. Yet ecological description generates this evaluation of nature, endorsing the systemic rightness. The transition from "is" to "good" and thence to "ought" occurs here; we leave science to enter the domain of evaluation, from which an ethic follows. The injunction to recycle is technical, made under circumscription by ecological necessity and made moral only by the presence of an antecedent. The injunction to maximize the ecosystemic excellence is also ecologically derived but is an evaluative transition which is not made under necessity.

Our account initially suggests that ecological description is logically (if not chronologically) prior to the ecosystemic evaluation, the former generating the latter. But the connection of description with evaluation is more complex, for the description and evaluation to some extent arise together, and it is often difficult to say which is prior and which is subordinate. Ecological description finds unity, harmony, interdependence, stability, etc., and these are valuationally endorsed, yet they are found, to some extent, because we search with a disposition to value order, harmony, stability, unity. Still, the ecological description does not merely confirm these values, it informs them; and we find that the character, the empirical content, of order, harmony, stability is drawn from, no less than brought to, nature. In post-Darwinian nature, for instance, we looked for these values in vain, while with ecological description we now find them; yet the earlier data are not denied, only redescribed or set in a larger ecological context, and somewhere enroute our notions of harmony, stability, etc., have shifted too and we see beauty now where we could not see it before. What is ethically puzzling, and exciting, in the marriage and mutual transformation of ecological description and evaluation is that here an "ought" is not so much *derived* from an "is" as discovered simultaneously with it. As we progress from descriptions of fauna and flora, of cycles and pyramids, of stability and dynamism, on to intricacy, planetary opulence and interdependence, to unity and harmony with oppositions in counterpoint and synthesis, arriving at length at beauty and goodness, it is difficult to say where the natural facts leave off and where the natural values appear. For some observers at least, the sharp is/ought dichotomy is gone; the values seem to be there as soon as the facts are fully in, and both alike are properties of the system.

While it is frequently held that the basic criterion of the obligatory is the nonmoral value that is produced or sustained, there is novelty in what is taken as the nonmoral good—the ecosystem. Our ethical heritage largely attaches values and rights to persons, and if nonpersonal realms enter, they enter only as tributary to the personal. What is proposed here is a broadening of value, so that nature will cease to be merely "property" and become a commonwealth. The logic by which goodness is discovered or appreciated is notoriously evasive, and we can only reach it suggestively. "Ethics cannot be put into words," said Wittgenstein, such things *"make themselves manifest."*[8] We have a parallel, retrospectively, in the checkered advance of the ethical frontier recognizing intrinsic goodness, and accompanying rights, outside the self. If we now universalize "person," consider how slowly the circle has been enlarged fully to include aliens, strangers, infants, children, Negroes, Jews, slaves, women, Indians, prisoners, the elderly, the insane, the deformed, and even now we ponder the status of fetuses. Ecological ethics queries whether we ought again to universalize, recognizing the intrinsic value of every ecobiotic component.

Are there, first, existing ethical sentiments that are subecological, that is, which anticipate the ecological conscience, and on which we might build? Second, is the ecological evaluation authentic, or perhaps only a remodeled traditional humanist ethic? Lastly, what are the implications of maximizing the ecosystem, and what concept of nature warrants such evaluation?

1. Presumably the evaluation of a biotic community will rest partly on the worth of its elements, if not independently, then in matrix. We have a long-standing, if (in the West) rather philosophically neglected, tradition that grants some moral ought to the prevention of needless animal suffering: "A righteous man has regard for the life of his beasts" (Proverbs 12:10). Consider what we oddly call "humane" societies or laws against cockfighting, bear baiting, and (in our nation) bullfighting, and (in most states) steer busting. We prohibit a child's torture of a cat; we prosecute the rancher who carelessly lets horses starve. Even the hunter pursues a wounded deer. That one ought to prevent needless cruelty has no obvious ecological foundation, much less a natural one, but the initial point is that animals are so far endowed with a value that conveys something like rights, or at least obligates us.

More revelatory is the increasingly common claim that one ought not to destroy life, or species, needlessly, regardless of suffering. We prevent the wanton slaughter of eagles, whether they suffer or not. Even the zealous varmint hunter seems to need the rationalization that crows rob the cornfield. He must malign the coyote and wolf to slay them enthusiastically. He cannot kill just for fun. We abhor the oilspills that devastate birdlife. The Sierra Club defends the preservation of grizzlies or whooping cranes on many counts as means to larger ends—as useful components of the ecosystem, for scientific study, or for our children's enjoyment. (We shall return to the integrated character of such argument.) But sufficiently pressed, the defense is that one ought not to destroy a life form of beauty. Since ecosystems regularly eliminate species, this may be a nonecological ought. Yet it is not clearly so, for part of a species' evaluation arises as it is seen in environmental matrix. Meanwhile, we admit they should continue to exist, "as a matter of biotic right."[9]

---

[8]Ludwig Wittgenstein, *Tractatus Logico-Philosophicus,* trans. D. F. Pears and B. F. McGuiness (London: Routledge & Kegan Paul, 1969), 6:421, 522.

[9]Leopold, "The Land Ethic," p. 211.

* * *

This respect enlarges to the landscape. We preserve certain features of natural beauty—the Grand Canyon, or Rainbow Bridge, or the Everglades. Though it seems odd to accord them "rights" (for proposals to confer rights on some new entity always sound linguistically odd), we go so far as to say that, judged to be places of beauty or wonder, they ought to be preserved. Is this only as a means to an end, that we and others may enjoy them? The answer is complex. At least some argue that, as with persons, they are somehow violated, even prostituted, if treated merely as means; we enjoy them very largely for what they are in themselves. To select some landscapes is not to judge the omitted ones valueless. They may be sacrificed to higher values, or perhaps selected environments are judged sufficiently representative of more abundant ones. That we do preserve any landscape indicates our discovery of value there, with its accompanying ought. Nor are such environments only the hospitable ones. We are increasingly drawn to the beauty of wilderness, desert, tundra, the arctic, and the sea. Planetary forces ever reshape landscapes, of course, and former environments are now extinct; nevertheless, we find in extant landscapes an order of beauty that we are unwilling to destroy.

2. Do we perhaps have, even in this proposed primary ecological ethic, some eco-free ought? If Leopold's preserving the ecosystem is merely ancillary to human interests, the veiled antecedent ought is still that we ought to maximize human good. Were we so to maximize the ecosystem we should have a corporate anthropological egoism, "human chauvinism," not a planetary altruism. The optimum ecosystem would be but a prudential means to human welfare, and our antecedent ought would no longer be primarily ecological, but as before, simply a familiar one, incidentally ecological in its prudence.

Even when richly appreciative of nature's values, much ecological moralizing does in fact mix the biosystemic welfare with an appeal to human interests. Reminiscent of Leopold, Réné Dubos suggests extending the Decalogue with an eleventh commandment, "Thou shalt strive for environmental quality." The justification may have a "resources" cast. We preserve wilderness and the maximally diverse ecosystem for reasons scientific and aesthetic. Natural museums serve as laboratories. Useless species may later be found useful. Diversity insures stability, especially if we err and our monocultures trigger environmental upset. Wild beauty adds a spiritual quality to life. "Were it only for selfish reasons, therefore, we must maintain variety and harmony in nature. . . . Wilderness is not a luxury; it is a necessity for the protection of humanized nature and for the preservation of mental health."[10]

But the "were it only . . ." indicates that such reasons, if sufficient, are not ultimate. Deeper, nonselfish reasons respect "qualities inherent" in fauna, flora, landscape, "so as to foster their development." . . . "An enlightened anthropocentrism acknowledges that, in the long run, the

[10]Réné Dubos, *A God Within* (New York: Scribner's, 1972), pp. 166–67.

world's good always coincides with man's own most meaningful good. Man can manipulate nature to his best interests only if he first loves her for her own sake."[11]

This coincidence of human and ecosystemic interests, frequent in environmental thought, is ethically confusing but fertile. To reduce ecological concern merely to human interests does not really exhaust the moral temper here, and only as we appreciate this will we see the ethical perspective significantly altered. That alteration centers in the dissolution of any firm boundary between man and the world. Ecology does not know an encapsulated ego over against his environment. Listen, for instance, to Paul Shepard: "Ecological thinking, on the other hand, requires a kind of vision across boundaries. The epidermis of the skin is ecologically like a pond surface or a forest soil, not a shell so much as a delicate interpenetration. It reveals the self ennobled and extended, rather than threatened, as part of the landscape, because the beauty and complexity of nature are continuous with ourselves."[12] Man's vascular system includes arteries, veins, rivers, oceans, and air currents. . . . The self metabolically, if metaphorically, interpenetrates the ecosystem. The world is my body.

This mood frustrates and ultimately invalidates the effort to understand all ecological ethics as disguised human self-interest, for now, with the self expanded into the system, their interests merge. One may, from a limited perspective, maximize the systemic good to maximize human good, but one can hardly say that the former is only a means to the latter, since they both amount to the same thing differently described. We are acquainted with egoism, *égoïsme à deux, trois, quatres,* with familial and tribal egoism. But here is an *égoïsme à la système,* as the very etymology of "ecology" witnesses: the earth is one's household. In this planetary confraternity, there is a confluence of egoism and altruism. Or should we say that egoism is transformed into ecoism? To advocate the interests of the system as a means of promoting the interests of man (in an appeal to industry and to congressmen) is to operate with a limited understanding. If we wish, for rhetorical or pragmatic reasons, we may begin with maximizing human good. But when ecologically tutored, we see that this can be redescribed as maximizing the ecosystem. Our classical ought has been transformed, stretched, coextensively with an ecosystemic ought.

* * *

The human welfare which we find in the enriched ecosystem is no longer recognizable as that of anthropocentrism. Man judges the ecosystem as "good" or "bad" not in short anthropocentric focus, but with enlarged perspective where the integrity of other species enriches him. The moral posture here recalls more familiar (if frequently unsettled) ethical themes: that self-interest and benevolence are not necessarily incompatible, especially where one derives personal fulfillment from the welfare of others;

[11]Ibid., pp. 40–41, 45.
[12]Shepard and McKinley, *The Subversive Science,* p. 20.

that treating the object of ethical concern as an end in itself is uplifting; that one's own integrity is enhanced by recognition of other integrities.

3. This environmental ethic is subject both to limits and to development, and a fair appraisal ought to recognize both. As a partial ethical source, it does not displace functioning social-personal codes, but brings into the scope of ethical transaction a realm once regarded as intrinsically valueless and governed largely by expediency. The new ethical parameter is not absolute but relative to classical criteria. Such extension will amplify conflicts of value, for human goods must now coexist with environmental goods. In operational detail this will require a new casuistry. Mutually supportive though the human and the ecosystemic interests may be, conflicts between individuals and parties, the rights of the component members of the ecosystem, the gap between the real and the ideal, will provide abundant quandaries.

Further, interpreting charitably, we are not asked to idolize the whole except as it is understood as a cosmos in which the corporate vision surrounds and limits, but does not suppress the individual. The focus does not only enlarge from man to other ecosystemic members, but from individuals of whatever kind to the system. Values are sometimes personalized; here the community holds values. This is not, of course, without precedent, for we now grant values to states, nations, churches, trusts, corporations, and communities. And they hold these values because of their structure in which individuals are beneficiaries. It is similar with the ecosystem, only more so; for when we recall its diffusion of the boundary between the individual and the ecosystem, we cannot say whether value in the system or in the individual is logically prior.

Leopold and Shepard do not mean to deep freeze the present ecosystem. Despite their preservationist vocabulary, their care for the biosystemic welfare allows for "alteration, management, and use."[13] We are not committed to this as the best possible ecosystem; it may well be that the role of man—at once "citizen" and "king"—is to govern what has hitherto been the partial success of the evolutionary process. Though we revere the earth, we may yet "humanize" it, a point made forcefully by Réné Dubos.[14] This permits interference with and rearrangement of nature's spontaneous course. It enjoins domestication, for part of the natural richness is its potential in human life support. We recognize man's creativity, development, openness, and dynamism.

Species regularly enter and exit nature's theater; perhaps natural selection currently tests species for their capacity to coexist with man. Orogenic and erosional forces have produced perpetual environmental flux; man may well transform his environment. But this should complement the beauty, integrity, and stability of the planetary biosystem, not do violence to it. There ought to be some rational showing that the alteration is enriching; that values are sacrificed for greater ones. For this reason the

[13]Leopold, "The Land Ethic," p. 204.
[14]Dubos, *A God Within*, chap. 8.

right is not that which maintains the ecosystemic status quo, but that which preserves its beauty, stability, and integrity.

* * *

. . . After Darwin (through misunderstanding him, perhaps), the world of design collapsed, and nature, for all its law, seemed random, accidental, chaotic, blind, crude, an "odious scene of violence."[15] Environmental science has been resurveying the post-Darwinian natural jungle and has increasingly set its conflicts within a dynamic web of life. Nature's savagery is much less wanton and clumsy than formerly supposed, and we are invited to see the ecosystem not merely in awe, but in "love, respect, and admiration."[16] Ecological thinking "moves us to silent wonder and glad affirmation."[17] Oppositions remain in ecological models, but in counterpoint. The system resists the very life it supports; indeed it is by resistance not less than environmental conductivity that life is stimulated. The integrity of species and individual is a function of a field where fullness lies in interlocking predation and symbiosis, construction and destruction, aggradation and degradation. The planet that Darrow characterized, in the post-Darwinian heyday, as a miserable little "wart"[18] in the universe, eminently unsuited to life, especially human life, is now a sheltered oasis in space. Its harmony is often strange, and it is not surprising that in our immaturity we mistook it, yet it is an intricate and delicate harmony nevertheless.

Man, an insider, is not spared environmental pressures, yet, in the full ecosystemic context, his integrity is supported by and rises from transaction with his world and therefore requires a corresponding dignity in his world partner. Of late, the world has ceased to threaten, save as we violate it. How starkly this gainsays the alienation that characterizes modern literature, seeing nature as basically rudderless, antipathetical, in need of monitoring and repair. More typically modern man, for all his technological prowess, has found himself distanced from nature, increasingly competent and decreasingly confident, at once distinguished and aggrandized, yet afloat on and adrift in an indifferent, if not a hostile universe. His world is at best a huge filling station; at worst a prison, or "nothingness." Not so for ecological man; confronting his world with deference to a community of value in which he shares, he is at home again. . . .

. . . We must judge the worth of the extant ecosystem independently of its origins. To do otherwise would be to slip into the genetic fallacy. A person has rights for what he is, regardless of his ancestry; and it may well be that an ignoble evolutionary process has issued in a present ecosystem in

---

[15]John Stuart Mill, "Nature," in *Collected Works* (Toronto: University of Toronto Press, 1969), 10:398. The phrase characterizes Mill's estimate of nature.

[16]Leopold, "The Land Ethic," p. 223.

[17]Shepard and McKinley, *The Subversive Science*, p. 10.

[18]Clarence Darrow, *The Story of My Life* (New York: Scribner's, 1932), p. 417.

which we rightly rejoice. No one familiar with paleontology is likely to claim that the evolutionary sequence moves unfailingly and without loss toward an optimally beautiful and stable ecosystem. Yet many ecological mechanisms are also evolutionary, and the ecological reappraisal suggests as a next stage an evolutionary redescription, in which we think again whether evolutionary history, for all its groping, struggle, mutation, natural selection, randomness, and statistical movement, does not yield direction enough to ponder that nature has been enriching the ecosystem. The fossil record is all of ruins. We survey it first with a certain horror; but then out of the ruins emerges this integral ecosystem. He who can be persuaded of this latter truth will have an even more powerful ecological ethic, for the injunction to maximize the ecosystemic excellences will be an invitation to get in gear with the way the universe is operating. Linking his right to nature's processes, he will have, at length, an authentic naturalistic ethic.

* * *

Perhaps the cash value is the same whether our ethic is ecological in secondary or primary senses; yet in the latter I find appeal enough that it has my vote to be so if it can. To the one, man may be driven while he still fears the world that surrounds him. To the other, he can only be drawn in love.

Animal Liberation: A Triangular Affair

J. Baird Callicott

ENVIRONMENTAL ETHICS AND ANIMAL LIBERATION

Partly because it is so new to Western philosophy (or at least heretofore only scarcely represented) *environmental ethics* has no precisely fixed conventional definition in glossaries of philosophical terminology. Aldo Leopold, however, is universally recognized as the father or founding genius of recent environmental ethics. His "land ethic" has become a modern classic and may be treated as the standard example, the paradigm case, as it were, of what an environmental ethic is. *Environmental ethics* then can be defined ostensively by using Leopold's land ethic as the exemplary type. I do not mean to suggest that all environmental ethics should necessarily conform to Leopold's paradigm, but the extent to which an ethical system resembles Leopold's land ethic might be used, for want of anything better,

Source: Reprinted by permission of the author and *Environmental Ethics* 2, no. 4 (Winter 1980), 311–38.

as a criterion to measure the extent to which it is or is not of the environmental sort.

It is Leopold's opinion, and certainly an overall review of the prevailing traditions of Western ethics, both popular and philosophical, generally
confirms it, that traditional Western systems of ethics have not accorded
moral standing to nonhuman beings.[1] Animals and plants, soils and waters,
which Leopold includes in his community of ethical beneficiaries, have
traditionally enjoyed no moral standing, no rights, no respect, in sharp
contrast to human persons whose rights and interests ideally must be fairly
and equally considered if our actions are to be considered "ethical" or
"moral." One fundamental and novel feature of the Leopold land ethic,
therefore, is the extension of *direct* ethical considerability from people to
nonhuman natural entities.

At first glance, the recent ethical movement usually labeled "animal
liberation" or "animal rights" seems to be squarely and centrally a kind of
environmental ethics.[2] The more uncompromising among the animal liberationists have demanded equal moral consideration on behalf of cows,
pigs, chickens, and other apparently enslaved and oppressed nonhuman
animals.[3] The theoreticians of this new hyper-egalitarianism have coined
such terms as *speciesism* (on analogy with *racism* and *sexism*) and *human
chauvinism* (on analogy with *male chauvinism*), and have made animal liberation seem, perhaps not improperly, the next and most daring development
of political liberalism.[4] Aldo Leopold also draws upon metaphors of political liberalism when he tells us that his land ethic "changes the role of *Homo
sapiens* from conqueror of the land community to plain member and citizen
of it."[5] . . . As Leopold develops it, the land ethic is a cultural "evolutionary

[1]Aldo Leopold, *A Sand County Almanac* (New York: Oxford University Press, 1949), pp.
202–03.

[2]The tag "animal liberation" for this moral movement originates with Peter Singer,
whose book *Animal Liberation* (New York: New York Review, 1975) has been widely influential.
"Animal rights" have been most persistently and unequivocally championed by Tom Regan in
various articles, among them: "The Moral Basis of Vegetarianism," *Canadian Journal of Philosophy* 5 (1975). 181–214; "Exploring the Idea of Animal Rights" in *Animal Rights: A Symposium*,
eds. D. Patterson and R. Ryder (London: Centaur, 1979); "Animal Rights, Human Wrongs,"
Environmental Ethics 2 (1980): 99–120.

[3]Peter Singer and Tom Regan especially insist upon *equal* moral *consideration* for nonhuman animals. Equal moral *consideration* does not necessarily imply equal *treatment*, however,
as Singer insists.

[4]We have Richard Ryder to thank for coining the term *speciesism*. See his *Speciesism: The
Ethics of Vivisection* (Edinburgh: Scottish Society for the Prevention of Vivisection, 1974).
Richard Routley introduced the term *human chauvinism* in "Is There a Need for a New, an
Environmental Ethic?" *Proceedings of the Fifteenth World Congress of Philosophy* 1 (1973): 205–10.
Peter Singer ("All Animals Are Equal," in *Animal Rights and Human Obligations*, eds. Tom
Regan and Peter Singer [Englewood Cliffs, N.J.: Prentice-Hall, 1976], pp. 148–62) developed
the egalitarian comparison of speciesism with racism and sexism in detail. To extend the
political comparison further, animal liberation is also a reformist and activist movement. We
are urged to act, to become vegetarians, to boycott animal products, etc. The concluding
paragraph of Regan's "Animal Rights, Human Wrongs" (p. 120) is especially zealously
hortatory.

[5]Leopold, *Sand County Almanac*, p. 204.

possibility," the next "step in a sequence."[6] For Leopold, however, the next step is much more sweeping, much more inclusive than the animal liberationists envision, since it "enlarges the boundaries of the [moral] community to include soils, waters, [and] plants . . ." as well as animals.[7] The animal liberation movement *could* be construed as partitioning Leopold's perhaps undigestable and totally inclusive environmental ethic into a series of more assimilable stages: today animal rights, tomorrow equal rights for plants, and after that full moral standing for rocks, soil, and other earthy compounds, and perhaps sometime in the still more remote future, liberty and equality for water and other elementary bodies.

Put just this way, however, there is something jarring about such a graduated progression in the exfoliation of a more inclusive environmental ethic, something that seems absurd. A more or less reasonable case might be made for rights for some animals, but when we come to plants, soils, and waters, the frontier between plausibility and absurdity appears to have been crossed. Yet, there is no doubt that Leopold sincerely proposes that *land* (in his inclusive sense) be ethically regarded. The beech and chestnut, for example, have in his view as much "biotic right" to life as the wolf and the deer, and the effects of human actions on mountains and streams for Leopold is an ethical concern as genuine and serious as the comfort and longevity of brood hens.[8] In fact, Leopold to all appearances never considered the treatment of brood hens on a factory farm or steers in a feed lot to be a pressing moral issue. He seems much more concerned about the integrity of the farm *wood lot* and the effects of clear-cutting steep slopes on neighboring *streams*.

Animal liberationists put their ethic into practice (and display their devotion to it) by becoming vegetarians, and the moral complexities of vegetarianism have been thoroughly debated in the recent literature as an adjunct issue to animal rights.[9] (No one however has yet expressed, as among Butler's Erewhonians, qualms about eating plants, though such sentiments might be expected to be latently present, if the rights of plants are next to be defended.) Aldo Leopold, by contrast did not even condemn hunting animals, let alone eating them, nor did he personally abandon hunting, for which he had had an enthusiasm since boyhood, upon becoming convinced that his ethical responsibilities extended beyond the human sphere.[10] There are several interpretations for this behavioral peculiarity. One is that Leopold did not see that his land ethic actually ought to prohibit hunting, cruelly killing, and eating animals. A corollary of this interpreta-

---

[6]Ibid., p. 203.

[7]Ibid., p. 204.

[8]Ibid., p. 221 (trees); pp. 129–33 (mountains); p. 209 (streams).

[9]John Benson ("Duty and the Beast," *Philosophy* 53 [1978]: 547–48) confesses that in the course of considering issues raised by Singer et al. he was "obliged to change my own diet as a result." An elaborate critical discussion is Philip E. Devine's "The Moral Basis of Vegetarianism" (*Philosophy* 53 [1978]: 481–505).

[10]For a biography of Leopold including particular reference to Leopold's career as a "sportsman," see Susan L. Flander, *Thinking Like a Mountain* (Columbia: University of Missouri Press, 1974).

tion is that Leopold was so unperspicacious as deservedly to be thought stupid—a conclusion hardly comporting with the intellectual subtlety he usually evinces in most other respects. If not stupid, then perhaps Leopold was hypocritical. But if a hypocrite, we should expect him to conceal his proclivity for blood sports and flesh eating and to treat them as shameful vices to be indulged secretively. As it is, bound together between the same covers with "The Land Ethic" are his unabashed reminiscences of killing and consuming *game*.[11] This term (like *stock*) when used of animals, moreover, appears to be morally equivalent to referring to a sexually appealing young woman as a "piece" or to a strong, young black man as a "buck"—if animal rights, that is, are to be considered as on a par with women's rights and the rights of formerly enslaved races. A third interpretation of Leopold's approbation of regulated and disciplined sport hunting (and *a fortiori* meat eating) is that it is a form of human/animal behavior not inconsistent with the land ethic as he conceived it. A corollary of this interpretation is that Leopold's land ethic and the environmental ethic of the animal liberation movement rest upon very different theoretical foundations, and that they are thus two very different forms of environmental ethics.

The urgent concern of animal liberationists for the suffering of *domestic* animals, toward which Leopold manifests an attitude which can only be described as indifference, and the urgent concern of Leopold, on the other hand, for the disappearance of *species* of plants as well as animals and for soil erosion and stream pollution, appear to be symptoms not only of very different ethical perspectives, but profoundly different cosmic visions as well. The neat similarities, noted at the beginning of this discussion, between the environmental ethic of the animal liberation movement and the classical Leopold land ethic appear in light of these observations to be rather superficial and to conceal substrata of thought and value which are not at all similar. The theoretical foundations of the animal liberation movement and those of the Leopold land ethic may even turn out not to be companionable, complementary, or mutually consistent. The animal liberationists may thus find themselves not only engaged in controversy with the many conservative philosophers upholding *apartheid* between man and "beast," but also faced with an unexpected dissent from another, very different, system of environmental ethics.[12] Animal liberation and animal

[11]See especially, Leopold, *Sand County Almanac,* pp. 54–58; 62–66; 120–22; 149–54; 177–87.

[12]A most thorough and fully argued dissent is provided by John Rodman in "The Liberation of Nature," *Inquiry* 20 (1977): 83–131. It is surprising that Singer, whose book is the subject of Rodman's extensive critical review, or some of Singer's philosophical allies, have not replied to these very penetrating and provocative criticisms. Another less specifically targeted dissent is Paul Shepard's "Animal Rights and Human Rites" (*North American Review* 259 [1974]: 35–41). More recently Kenneth Goodpaster ("From Egoism to Environmentalism" in *Ethics and Problems of the 21st Century*, eds. K. Goodpaster and K. Sayre [Notre Dame: Notre Dame University Press, 1979], pp. 21–35) has expressed complaints about the animal liberation and animal rights movement in the name of environmental ethics. "The last thing we need," writes Goodpaster, "is simply another 'liberation movement'" (p. 29).

rights may well prove to be a triangular rather than, as it has so far been represented in the philosophical community, a polar controversy.

ETHICAL HUMANISM AND HUMANE MORALISM

The orthodox response of "ethical humanism" (as this philosophical perspective may be styled) to the suggestion that nonhuman animals should be accorded moral standing is that such animals are not worthy of this high perquisite. Only human beings are rational, or capable of having interests, or possess *self*-awareness, or have linguistic abilities, or can represent the future, it is variously argued.[13] These essential attributes taken singly or in various combinations make people somehow exclusively deserving of moral consideration. The so-called "lower animals," it is insisted, lack the crucial qualification for ethical considerability and so may be treated (albeit humanely, according to some, so as not to brutalize man) as things or means, not as persons or as ends.[14]

The theoreticians of the animal liberation movement ("humane moralists" as they may be called) typically reply as follows.[15] Not all human beings qualify as worthy of moral regard, according to the various criteria specified. Therefore, by parity of reasoning, human persons who do not so qualify as moral patients may be treated, as animals often are, as mere things or means (e.g., used in vivisection experiments, disposed of if their existence is inconvenient, eaten, hunted, etc., etc.). But the ethical humanists would be morally outraged if irrational and inarticulate infants, for example, were used in painful or lethal medical experiments, or if severely

[13]Singer, "All Animals Are Equal" (p. 159), uses the term *humanist* to convey a speciesist connotation. Rationality and future-conceiving capacities as criteria for rights holding have been newly revived by Michael E. Levin with specific reference to Singer in "Animal Rights Evaluated," *The Humanist* (July/August, 1977): 12; 14–15. John Passmore, in *Man's Responsibility for Nature* (New York: Scribner's, 1974), p. 116, has recently insisted upon having interests as a criterion for having rights and denied that nonhuman beings have interests. L. P. Francis and R. Norman ("Some Animals Are More Equal than Others," *Philosophy* 53 [1978]: 507–27) have argued, again with specific reference to animal liberationists, that linguistic abilities are requisite for moral status. H. J. McCloskey ("The Right to Life," *Mind* 84 [1975]: 410–13, and "Moral Rights and Animals," *Inquiry* 22 [1979]: 23–54), adapting an idea of Kant's, defends *autonomy* as the main ingredient of human nature which entitles human beings to rights. Michael Fox ("Animal Liberation: A Critique," *Ethics* 88 [1978]: 106–18) defends, among other exclusively human qualifications for rights holding, *self*-awareness. Richard A. Watson ("Self-Consciousness and the Rights of Nonhuman Animals and Nature," *Environmental Ethics* 1 [1979]: 99–129) also defends self-consciousness as a criterion for rights holding, but allows that some nonhuman animals also possess it.

[14]In addition to the historical figures, who are nicely summarized and anthologized in *Animal Rights and Human Obligations*, John Passmore has recently defended the reactionary notion that cruelty towards animals is morally reprehensible for reasons independent of any obligation or duties people have to animals as such (*Man's Responsibility*, p. 117).

[15]"Humane moralists" is perhaps a more historically accurate designation than "animal liberationists." John Rodman, "The Liberation of Nature" (pp. 88–89), has recently explored in a programmatic way the connection between the contemporary animal liberation/rights movements and the historical humane societies movement.

retarded people were hunted for pleasure. Thus, the double-dealing, the hypocrisy, of ethical humanism appears to be exposed.[16] Ethical humanism, though claiming to discriminate between worthy and unworthy ethical patients on the basis of objective criteria impartially applied, turns out after all, it seems, to be *speciesism,* a philosophically indefensible prejudice (analogous to racial prejudice) against animals. The tails side of this argument is that some animals, usually the "higher" lower animals (cetaceans, other primates, etc.), as ethological studies seem to indicate, may meet the criteria specified for moral worth, although the ethical humanists, even so, are not prepared to grant them full dignity and the rights of persons. In short, the ethical humanists' various criteria for moral standing do not include all or only human beings, humane moralists argue, although in practice ethical humanism wishes to make the class of morally considerable beings coextensive with the class of human beings.

The humane moralists, for their part, insist upon *sentience* (*sensibility* would have been a more precise word choice) as the only relevant capacity a being need possess to enjoy full moral standing. If animals, they argue, are conscious entities who, though deprived of reason, speech, forethought or even *self*-awareness (however that may be judged), are capable of suffering, then their suffering should be as much a matter of ethical concern as that of our fellow human beings, or strictly speaking, as our very own. What, after all, has rationality or any of the other allegedly uniquely human capacities to do with ethical standing? Why, in other words, should beings who reason or use speech (etc.) qualify for moral status, and those who do not fail to qualify?[17] Isn't this just like saying that only persons with white skin should be free, or that only persons who beget and not those who bear should own property? The criterion seems utterly unrelated to the benefit for which it selects. On the other hand, the capacity to suffer is, it seems, a more relevant criterion for moral standing because—as Bentham and Mill, notable among modern philosophers, and Epicurus, among the ancients, aver—pain is evil, and its opposite, pleasure and freedom from pain, good. As moral agents (and this seems axiomatic), we have a duty to behave in such a way that the effect of our actions is to promote and procure good, so far as possible, and to reduce and minimize evil. That would amount to an obligation to produce pleasure and reduce pain. Now pain is pain wherever and by whomever it is suffered. As a *moral* agent, I should not consider my pleasure and pain to be of greater consequence in determining a course of action than that of other persons. Thus, by the same token, if animals suffer pain—and among philosophers only strict Cartesians would deny that they do—then we are morally obliged to consider their suffering as much an evil to be minimized by conscientious moral agents as human

[16]Tom Regan styles more precise formulations of this argument, "the argument from marginal cases," in "An Examination and Defense of One Argument Concerning Animal Rights," *Inquiry* 22 (1979): 190. Regan directs our attention to Andrew Linzey, *Animal Rights* (London: SCM Press, 1976) as well as to Singer, *Animal Liberation,* for paradigmatic employment of this argument on behalf of moral standing for animals (p. 144).

[17]A particularly lucid advocacy of this notion may be found in Feinberg, "Human Duties and Animal Rights," especially p. 53ff.

suffering.[18] Certainly actions of ours which contribute to the suffering of animals, such as hunting them, butchering and eating them, experimenting on them, etc., are on these assumptions morally reprehensible. Hence, a person who regards himself or herself as not aiming in life to live most selfishly, conveniently, or profitably but rightly and in accord with practical principle, if convinced by these arguments, should, among other things, cease to eat the flesh of animals, to hunt them, to wear fur and leather clothing and bone ornaments and other articles made from the bodies of animals, to eat eggs and drink milk (if the animal producers of these commodities are retained under inhumane circumstances) and to patronize zoos (as sources of psychological if not physical torment of animals). On the other hand, since certain very simple animals are almost certainly insensible to pleasure and pain, they may and indeed should be treated as morally inconsequential. Nor is there any *moral* reason why trees should be respected or rivers or mountains or anything which is, though living or tributary to life process, unconscious. The humane moralists, like the moral humanists, draw a firm distinction between those beings worthy of moral consideration and those not. They simply insist upon a different but quite definite cut-off point on the spectrum of natural entities, and accompany their criterion with arguments to show that it is more ethically defensible (granting certain assumptions) and more consistently applicable than that of the moral humanists.[19]

THE FIRST PRINCIPLE OF THE LAND ETHIC

* * *

But what about the third (and certainly minority) party to the animal liberation debate? What sort of reasonable and coherent moral theory would at once urge that animals (and plants and soils and waters) be included in the same class with people as beings to whom ethical consideration is owed and yet not object to some of them being slaughtered (whether painlessly or not) and eaten, others hunted, trapped, and in various other ways seeming-

[18]Again, Feinberg in "Human Duties and Animal Rights" (pp. 57–59) expresses this point especially forcefully.

[19]John Rodman's comment in "The Liberation of Nature" (p. 91) is worth repeating here since it has to all appearances received so little attention elsewhere: "If it would seem arbitrary . . . to find one species claiming a monopoly on intrinsic value by virtue of its allegedly exclusive possession of reason, free will, soul, or some other occult quality, would it not seem almost as arbitrary to find that same species claiming a monopoly of intrinsic value for itself and those species most resembling it (e.g. in type of nervous system and behavior) by virtue of their common and allegedly exclusive possession of sentience [i.e., sensibility]?" Goodpaster ("From Egoism to Environmentalism," p. 29) remarks that in modern moral philosophy "a fixation on egoism and a consequent loyalty to a model of moral sentiment or reason which in essence generalizes or universalizes that egoism . . . makes it particularly inhospitable to our recent felt need for an environmental ethic. . . . For such an ethic does not readily admit of being reduced to 'humanism'—nor does it sit well with any class or generalization model of moral concern."

ly cruelly used? Aldo Leopold provides a concise statement of what might be called the categorical imperative or principal precept of the land ethic: "A thing is right when it tends to preserve the integrity, stability, and beauty of the biotic community. It is wrong when it tends otherwise."[20] What is especially noteworthy, and that to which attention should be directed in this proposition, is the idea that the good of the biotic *community* is the ultimate measure of the moral value, the rightness or wrongness, of actions. Thus, to hunt and kill a white-tailed deer in certain districts may not only be ethically permissible, it might actually be a moral requirement, necessary to protect the local environment, taken as a whole, from the disintegrating effects of a cervid population explosion. On the other hand, rare and endangered animals like the lynx should be especially nurtured and preserved. The lynx, cougar, and other wild feline predators, from the neo-Benthamite perspective (if consistently and evenhandedly applied) should be regarded as merciless, wanton, and incorrigible murderers of their fellow creatures, who not only kill, it should be added, but cruelly toy with their victims, thus increasing the measure of pain in the world. From the perspective of the land ethic, predators generally should be nurtured and preserved as critically important members of the biotic communities to which they are native. Certain plants, similarly, may be overwhelmingly important to the stability, integrity, and beauty of biotic communities, while some animals, such as domestic sheep (allowed perhaps by egalitarian and humane herdspersons to graze freely and to reproduce themselves without being harvested for lamb and mutton) could be a pestilential threat to the natural floral community of a given locale. Thus, the land ethic is logically coherent in demanding at once that moral consideration be given to plants as well as to animals and yet in permitting animals to be killed, trees felled, and so on. In every case the effect upon ecological systems is the decisive factor in the determination of the ethical quality of actions. . . .

THE LAND ETHIC AND THE ECOLOGICAL POINT OF VIEW

* * *

Since ecology focuses upon the relationships between and among things, it inclines its students toward a more holistic vision of the world. Before the rather recent emergence of ecology as a science the landscape appeared to be, one might say, a collection of objects, some of them alive, some conscious, but all the same, an aggregate, a plurality of separate individuals. With this "atomistic" representation of things it is no wonder that moral issues might be understood as competing and mutually contradictory clashes of the "rights" of separate individuals, each separately pursuing its "interests." Ecology has made it possible to apprehend the same landscape as an articulate unity (without the least hint of mysticism or ineffability). Ordinary organic bodies have articulated and discernible parts (limbs, vari-

[20]Leopold, *Sand County Almanac*, pp. 224–25.

ous organs, myriad cells); yet, because of the character of the network of relations among those parts, they form in a perfectly familiar sense a second-order whole. Ecology makes it possible to see land, similarly, as a unified system of integrally related parts, as, so to speak, a third-order organic whole.[21]

Another analogy that has helped ecologists to convey the particular holism which their science brings to reflective attention is that land is integrated as a human community is integrated. The various parts of the "biotic community" (individual animals and plants) depend upon one another *economically* so that the system as such acquires distinct characteristics of its own. Just as it is possible to characterize and define collectively peasant societies, agrarian communities, industrial complexes, capitalist, communist, and socialist economic systems, and so on, ecology characterizes and defines various biomes as desert, savanna, wetland, tundra, wood land, etc., communities, each with its particular "professions," "roles," or "niches."

Now we may think that among the duties we as moral agents have toward ourselves is the duty of self-preservation, which may be interpreted as a duty to maintain our own organic integrity. It is not uncommon in historical moral theory, further, to find that in addition to those peculiar responsibilities we have in relation both to ourselves and to other persons severally, we also have a duty to behave in ways that do not harm the fabric of society *per se*. The land ethic, in similar fashion, calls our attention to the recently discovered integrity—in other words, the unity—of the biota and posits duties binding upon moral agents in relation to that whole. Whatever the strictly formal logical connections between the concept of a social community and moral responsibility, there appears to be a strong psychological bond between that idea and conscience. Hence, the representation of the natural environment as, in Leopold's terms, "one humming community" (or, less consistently in his discussion, a third-order organic being) brings into play, whether rationally or not, those stirrings of conscience which we feel in relation to delicately complex, functioning social and organic systems.[22] . . .

. . . The more recent ecological perspective especially seems to be

[21]By "first," "second," and "third" order wholes I intend paradigmatically single-cell organisms, multicell organisms, and biocoenoses, respectively.

[22]"Some Fundamentals of Conservation in the Southwest," composed in the 1920s but unpublished until in 1979 (*Environmental Ethics* 1: 131–41), shows that the organic analogy, conceptually representing the nature of the whole resulting from ecological relationships, antedates the community analogy in Leopold's thinking, so far at least as its moral implications are concerned. "The Land Ethic" of *Sand County Almanac* employs almost exclusively the community analogy but a rereading of "The Land Ethic" in the light of "Some Fundamentals" reveals that Leopold did not entirely abandon the organic analogy in favor of the community analogy. For example, toward the end of "The Land Ethic" Leopold talks about "land health" and "land the collective organism" (p. 258). William Morton Wheeler, *Essays in Philosophical Biology* (New York: Russell and Russell, 1939), and Lewis Thomas, *Lives of a Cell* (New York: Viking Press, 1974), provide extended discussions of holistic approaches to social, ethical, and environmental problems. Kenneth Goodpaster, almost alone among academic philosophers, has explored the possibility of a holistic environmental ethical system in "From Egoism to Environmentalism."

ignored by humane moralists. The holistic outlook of ecology and the associated value premium conferred upon the biotic community, its beauty, integrity, and stability may simply not have penetrated the thinking of the animal liberationists, or it could be that to include it would involve an intolerable contradiction with the Benthamite foundations of their ethical theory. Bentham's view of the "interests of the community" was bluntly reductive. With his characteristic bluster, Bentham wrote, "The community is a fictitious *body* composed of the individual persons who are considered as constituting as it were its *members*. The interest of the community then is, what?—the sum of the interests of the several members who compose it."[23] . . . [But] the interests of a person are not those of his or her cells summed up and averaged out. Our organic health and well-being, for example, requires vigorous exercise and metabolic stimulation which cause stress and often pain to various parts of the body and a more rapid turnover in the life cycle of our individual cells. For the sake of the person taken as whole, some parts may be, as it were, unfairly sacrificed. On the level of social organization, the interests of society may not always coincide with the sum of the interests of its parts. Discipline, sacrifice, and individual restraint are often necessary in the social sphere to maintain social integrity as within the bodily organism. A society, indeed, is particularly vulnerable to disintegration when its members become preoccupied totally with their own particular interests, and ignore those distinct and independent interests of the community as a whole. One example, unfortunately, our own society, is altogether too close at hand to be examined with strict academic detachment. The United States seems to pursue uncritically a social policy of reductive utilitarianism, aimed at promoting the happiness of all its members severally. Each special interest accordingly clamors more loudly to be satisfied while the community as a whole becomes noticeably more and more infirm economically, environmentally, and politically.

* * *

ETHICAL HOLISM

Before we [turn to other issues], however, some points of interest remain to be considered on the matter of a holistic versus a reductive environmental ethic. To pit the one against the other as I have done without further qualification would be mistaken. A society is constituted by its members, an organic body by its cells, and the ecosystem by the plants, animals, minerals, fluids, and gases which compose it. One cannot affect a system as a whole without affecting at least some of its components. An environmental ethic which takes as its *summum bonum* the integrity, stability, and beauty of the biotic community is not conferring moral standing on something *else* besides plants, animals, soils, and waters. Rather, the former, the good of the community as a whole, serves as a standard for the assessment of the

[23]*An Introduction to the Principles of Morals and Legislation* (Oxford: Oxford University Press, 1823), chap. 1, sec. 4.

relative value and relative ordering of its constitutive parts and therefore provides a means of adjudicating the often mutually contradictory demands of the parts considered separately for *equal* consideration. If diversity does indeed contribute to stability (a classical "law" of ecology), then *specimens* of rare and endangered species, for example, have a *prima facie* claim to preferential consideration from the perspective of the land ethic. Animals of those species, which, like the honey bee, function in ways critically important to the economy of nature, moreover, would be granted a greater claim to moral attention than psychologically more complex and sensitive ones, say, rabbits and moles, which seem to be plentiful, globally distributed, reproductively efficient, and only routinely integrated into the natural economy. Animals and plants, mountains, rivers, seas, the atmosphere are the *immediate* practical beneficiaries of the land ethic. The well-being of the biotic community, the biosphere as a whole, cannot be logically separated from their survival and welfare.

Some suspicion may arise at this point that the land ethic is ultimately grounded in *human* interests, not in those of nonhuman natural entities. Just as we might prefer a sound and attractive house to one in the opposite condition so the "goodness" of a whole, stable, and beautiful environment seems rather to be of the instrumental, not the autochthonous, variety. The question of ultimate value is a very sticky one for environmental as well as for all ethics and cannot be fully addressed here. It is my view that there can be no value apart from an evaluator, that all value is as it were in the eye of the beholder. The value that is attributed to the ecosystem, therefore, is humanly dependent or (allowing that other living things may take a certain delight in the well-being of the whole of things, or that the gods may) at least dependent upon some variety of morally and aesthetically sensitive consciousness. Granting this, however, there is a further, very crucial distinction to be drawn. It is possible that while things may only have value because we (or someone) values them, they may nonetheless be valued for themselves as well as for the contribution they might make to the realization of our (or someone's) interests. Children are valued for themselves by most parents. Money, on the other hand, has only an instrumental or indirect value. Which sort of value has the health of the biotic community and its members severally for Leopold and the land ethic? It is especially difficult to separate these two general sorts of value, the one of moral significance, the other merely selfish, when something that may be valued in *both ways at once* is the subject of consideration. Are pets, for example, well-treated, like children, for the sake of themselves, or, like mechanical appliances, because of the sort of services they provide their owners? Is a healthy biotic community something we value because we are so utterly and (to the biologically well-informed) so obviously dependent upon it not only for our happiness but for our very survival, or may we also perceive it disinterestedly as having an independent worth? Leopold insists upon a noninstrumental value for the biotic community and *mutatis mutandis* for its constituents. According to Leopold, collective enlightened self-interest on the part of human beings does not go far enough; the land ethic in his opinion (and no doubt this reflects his own moral intuitions) requires "love, respect, and admiration for land, and a high regard for its value." The land ethic, in Leopold's view, creates "obligations over and above self-interest." And, "obligations have no meaning without conscience, and the problem we face is the extension of the social conscience from people to land."[24] If, in other words, any genuine ethic is possible, if it is possible to value *people* for the sake of themselves, then it is equally possible to value *land* in the same way.

Some indication of the genuinely biocentric value orientation of ethical environmentalism is indicated in what otherwise might appear to be gratuitous misanthropy. The biospheric perspective does not exempt *Homo sapiens* from moral evaluation in relation to the well-being of the community of nature taken as a whole. The preciousness of individual deer, as of any other specimen, is inversely proportional to the population of the species. Environmentalists, however reluctantly and painfully, do not omit to apply the same logic to their own kind. As omnivores, the population of human beings should, perhaps, be roughly twice that of bears, allowing for differences of size. A global population of more than four billion persons and showing no signs of an orderly decline presents an alarming prospect to humanists, but it is at present a global disaster (the more *per capita* prosperity, indeed, the more disastrous it appears) for the biotic community. If the land ethic were only a means of managing nature for the sake of man, misleadingly phrased in moral terminology, then man would be considered as having an ultimate value essentially different from that of his "resources." The extent of misanthropy in modern environmentalism thus may be taken as a measure of the degree to which it is biocentric. . . .

* * *

There is, however, a classical Western ethic, with the best philosophical credentials, which assumes a similar holistic posture (with respect to the social moral sphere). I have in mind Plato's moral and social philosophy. Indeed, two of the same analogies figuring in the conceptual foundations of the Leopold land ethic appear in Plato's value theory.[25] From the ecological perspective, according to Leopold as I have pointed out, land is like an organic body or like a human society. According to Plato, body, soul, and society have similar structures and corresponding virtues.[26] The

[24]Leopold, *Sand County Almanac*, pp. 223 and 209.

[25]In *Republic* 5 Plato directly says that "the best governed state most nearly resembles an organism" (462D) and that there is no "greater evil for a state than the thing that distracts it and makes it many instead of one, or a greater good than that which binds it together and makes it one" (462A). Goodpaster in "From Egoism to Environmentalism" (p. 30) has in a general way anticipated this connection: "The oft-repeated plea by some ecologists and environmentalists that our thinking needs to be less atomistic and more 'holistic' translates in the present context into a plea for a more embracing object of moral consideration. In a sense it represents a plea to return to the richer Greek conception of man by nature social and not intelligibly removable from his social and political context though it goes beyond the Greek conception in emphasizing that societies too need to be understood in a context, an ecological context, and that it is this larger whole that is the 'bearer of value.'"

[26]See especially *Republic* 4.444A–E.

goodness of each is a function of its structure or organization and the relative value of the parts or constituents of each is calculated according to the contribution made to the integrity, stability, and beauty of each whole.[27] In the *Republic*, Plato, in the very name of virtue and justice, is notorious for, among other things, requiring infanticide for a child whose only offense was being born without the sanction of the state, making presents to the enemy of guardians who allow themselves to be captured alive in combat, and radically restricting the practice of medicine to the dressing of wounds and the curing of seasonal maladies on the principle that the infirm and chronically ill not only lead miserable lives but contribute nothing to the good of the polity.[28] Plato, indeed, seems to regard individual human life and certainly human pain and suffering with complete indifference. On the other hand, he shrinks from nothing so long as it seems to him to be in the interest of the community. Among the apparently inhuman recommendations that he makes to better the community are a program of eugenics involving a phony lottery (so that those whose natural desires are frustrated, while breeding proceeds from the best stock as in a kennel or stable, will blame chance, not the design of the rulers), the destruction of the pair bond and nuclear family (in the interests of greater military and bureaucratic efficiency and group solidarity), and the utter abolition of private property.[29]

When challenged with the complaint that he is ignoring individual human happiness (and the happiness of those belonging to the most privileged class at that), he replies that it is the well-being of the community as a whole, not that of any person or special class at which his legislation aims.[30] This principle is readily accepted, first of all, in our attitude toward the body, he reminds us—the separate interests of the parts of which we acknowledge to be subordinate to the health and well-being of the whole—and secondly, assuming that we accept his faculty psychology, in our attitude toward the soul—whose multitude of desires must be disciplined, restrained, and, in the case of some, altogether repressed in the interest of personal virtue and a well-ordered and morally responsible life.

Given these formal similarities to Plato's moral philosophy, we may conclude that the land ethic—with its holistic good and its assignment of differential values to the several parts of the environment irrespective of their intelligence, sensibility, degree of complexity, or any other characteristic discernible in the parts concidered separarely—is somewhat foreign to modern systems of ethical philosophy, but perfectly familiar in the broader context of classical Western ethical philosophy. If, therefore, Pla-

---

[27]For a particularly clear statement by Plato of the idea that the goodness of anything is a matter of the fitting order of the parts in relation to respective wholes see *Gorgias* 503D–507A.

[28]Cf., *Republic* 5.461C (infanticide); 468A (disposition of captives); *Republic* 3.405D–406E (medicine).

[29]Cf., *Republic* 5.459A–460E (eugenics, nonfamily life and child rearing), *Republic* 3.416D–417B (private property).

[30]Cf., *Republic* 4.419A–421C and *Republic* 7.419D–521B.

to's system of public and private justice is properly an "ethical" system, then so is the land ethic in relation to environmental virtue and excellence.[31]

REAPPRAISING DOMESTICITY

Among the last philosophical remarks penned by Aldo Leopold before his untimely death in 1948 is the following: "Perhaps such a shift of values [as implied by the attempt to weld together the concepts of ethics and ecology] can be achieved by reappraising things unnatural, tame, and confined in terms of things natural, wild, and free."[32] John Muir, in a similar spirit of reappraisal, had noted earlier the difference between the wild mountain sheep of the Sierra and the ubiquitous domestic variety. The latter, which Muir described as "hooved locusts," were only, in his estimation, "half alive" in comparison with their natural and autonomous counterparts.[33] One of the more distressing aspects of the animal liberation movement is the failure of almost all its exponents to draw a sharp distinction between the very different plights (and rights) of wild and domestic animals.[34] But this distinction lies at the very center of the land ethic. Domestic animals are creations of man. They are living artifacts, but artifacts nevertheless, and they constitute yet another mode of extension of the works of man into the ecosystem. From the perspective of the land ethic a herd of cattle, sheep, or pigs is as much or more a ruinous blight on the landscape as a fleet of four-wheel drive off-road vehicles. There is thus something profoundly incoherent (and insensitive as well) in the complaint of some animal liberationists that the "natural behavior" of chickens and bobby calves is cruelly frustrated on factory farms. It would make almost as much sense to speak of the natural behavior of tables and chairs.

[31]After so much strident complaint has been registered here about the lack of freshness in self-proclaimed "new" environmental ethics (which turn out to be "old" ethics retreaded) there is surely an irony in comparing the (apparently brand new) Leopoldian land ethic to Plato's ethical philosophy. There is, however, an important difference. The humane moralists have simply revived and elaborated Bentham's historical application of hedonism to questions regarding the treatment of animals with the capacity of sensibility. There is nothing new but the revival and elaboration. Plato, on the other hand, never develops anything faintly resembling an *environmental* ethic. Plato never reached an ecological view of living nature. The wholes of his universe are body, soul, society, and cosmos. Plato is largely, if not exclusively, concerned with moral problems involving individual human beings in a political context and he has the temerity to insist that the good of the whole transcends individual claims. (Even in the *Crito* Plato is sympathetic to the city's claim to put *Socrates* to death however unjust the verdict against him.) Plato thus espouses a holistic ethic which is valuable as a (very different) paradigm to which the Leopoldian *land* ethic, which is also holistic but in relation to a very different whole, may be compared. It is interesting further that some (but not all) of the analogies which Plato finds useful to convey his holistic social values are also useful to Leopold in his effort to set out a land ethic.

[32]Leopold, *Sand County Almanac*, p. ix.

[33]See John Muir, "The Wild Sheep of California," *Overland Monthly* 12 (1874): 359.

[34]Roderick Nash (*Wilderness and the American Mind*, rev. ed. [New Haven and London: Yale University Press, 1973], p. 2) suggests that the English word *wild* is ultimately derived from *will*. A wild being is thus a willed one—"self-willed, willful, or uncontrollable."

Here a serious disanalogy (which no one to my knowledge has yet pointed out) becomes clearly evident between the liberation of blacks from slavery (and more recently, from civil inequality) and the liberation of animals from a similar sort of subordination and servitude. Black slaves remained, as it were, metaphysically autonomous: they were by nature if not by convention free beings quite capable of living on their own. They could not be enslaved for more than a historical interlude, for the strength of the force of their freedom was too great. They could, in other words, be retained only by a continuous counterforce, and only temporarily. This is equally true of caged wild animals. African cheetas in American and European zoos are captive, not indentured, beings. But this is not true of cows, pigs, sheep, and chickens. They have been bred to docility, tractability, stupidity, and dependency. It is literally meaningless to suggest that they be liberated. It is, to speak in hyperbole, a logical impossibility. Certainly it is a practical impossibility. . . .

*   *   *

The land ethic, it should be emphasized, as Leopold has sketched it, provides for the *rights* of nonhuman natural beings to share in the life processes of the biotic community. The conceptual foundation of such rights, however, is less conventional than natural, based upon, as one might say, evolutionary and ecological entitlement. Wild animals and native plants have a particular place in nature, according to the land ethic, which domestic animals (because they are products of human art and represent an extended presence of human beings in the natural world) do not have. The land ethic, in sum, is as much opposed, though on different grounds, to commercial traffic in wildlife, zoos, the slaughter of whales and other marine mammals, etc., as is the human ethic. Concern for animal (and plant) rights and well-being is as fundamental to the land ethic as to the humane ethic, but the difference between naturally evolved and humanly bred species is an essential consideration for the one, though not for the other.

The "shift of values" which results from our "reappraising things unnatural, tame, and confined in terms of things natural, wild, and free" is especially dramatic when we reflect upon the definitions of *good* and *evil* espoused by Bentham and Mill and uncritically accepted by their contemporary followers. Pain and pleasure seem to have nothing at all to do with good and evil if our appraisal is taken from the vantage point of ecological biology. Pain in particular is primarily information. In animals, it informs the central nervous system of stress, irritation, or trauma in outlying regions of the organism. A certain level of pain under optimal organic circumstances is indeed desirable as an indicator of exertion—of the degree of exertion needed to maintain fitness, to stay "in shape," and of a level of exertion beyond which it would be dangerous to go. An arctic wolf in pursuit of a caribou may experience pain in her feet or chest because of the rigors of the chase. There is nothing bad or wrong in that. Or, consider a case of injury. Suppose that a person in the course of a wilderness excursion sprains an ankle. Pain informs him or her of the injury and by its intensity the amount of further stress the ankle may endure in the course of getting to safety. Would it be better if pain were not experienced upon injury or, taking advantage of recent technology, anaesthetized? Pleasure appears to be, for the most part (unfortunately it is not always so) a reward accompanying those activities which contribute to organic maintenance, such as the pleasures associated with eating, drinking, grooming, and so on, or those which contribute to social solidarity like the pleasures of dancing, conversation, teasing, etc., or those which contribute to the continuation of the species, such as the pleasures of sexual activity and of being parents. The doctrine that life is the happier the freer it is from pain and that the happiest life conceivable is one in which there is continuous pleasure uninterrupted by pain is biologically preposterous. A living mammal which experienced no pain would be one which had a lethal dysfunction of the nervous system. The idea that pain is evil and ought to be minimized or eliminated is as primitive a notion as that of a tyrant who puts to death messengers bearing bad news on the supposition that thus his well-being and security is improved.

More seriously still, the value commitments of the humane movement seem at bottom to betray a world-denying or rather a life-loathing philosophy. The natural world as actually constituted is one in which one being lives at the expense of others. Each organism, in Darwin's metaphor, struggles to maintain its own organic integrity. The more complex animals seem to experience (judging from our own case, and reasoning from analogy) appropriate and adaptive psychological accompaniments to organic existence. There is a palpable passion for self-preservation. There are desire, pleasure in the satisfaction of desires, acute agony attending injury, frustration, and chronic dread of death. But these experiences are the psychological substance of living. To live *is* to be anxious about life, to feel pain and pleasure in a fitting mixture, and sooner or later to die. That is the way the system works. If nature as a whole is good, then pain and death are also good. Environmental ethics in general require people to play fair in the natural system. The neo-Benthamites have in a sense taken the uncourageous approach. People have attempted to exempt themselves from the life/death reciprocities of natural processes and from ecological limitations in the name of a prophylactic ethic of maximizing rewards (pleasure) and minimizing unwelcome information (pain). To be fair, the humane moralists seem to suggest that we should attempt to project the same values into the nonhuman animal world and to widen the charmed circle—no matter that it would be biologically unrealistic to do so or biologically ruinous if, per impossible, such an environmental ethic were implemented.

There is another approach. Rather than imposing our alienation from nature and natural processes and cycles of life on other animals, we human beings could reaffirm our participation in nature by accepting life as it is given without a sugar coating. Instead of imposing artificial legalities, rights, and so on on nature, we might take the opposite course and accept and affirm natural biological laws, principles, and limitations in the human personal and social spheres. Such appears to have been the posture toward life of tribal peoples in the past. The chase was relished with its dangers, rigors, and hardships as well as its rewards: animal flesh was respectfully consumed; a tolerance for pain was cultivated; virtue and magnanimity were prized; lithic, floral, and faunal spirits were worshipped; population was routinely optimized by sexual continency, abortion, infanticide, and stylized warfare; and other life forms, although certainly appropriated, were respected as fellow players in a magnificent and awesome, if not altogether idyllic, drama of life. It is impossible today to return to the symbiotic relationship of Stone Age man to the natural environment, but the ethos of this by far the longest era of human existence could be abstracted and integrated with a future human culture seeking a viable and mutually beneficial relationship with nature. Personal, social, and environmental *health* would, accordingly, receive a premium value rather than comfort, self-indulgent pleasure, and anaesthetic insulation from pain. Sickness would be regarded as a worse evil than death. The pursuit of health or wellness at the personal, social, and environmental levels would require self-discipline in the form of simple diet, vigorous exercise, conservation, and social responsibility.

Leopold's prescription for the realization and implementation of the land ethic—the reappraisal of things unnatural, tame, and confined in terms of things natural, wild, and free—does not stop, in other words, with a reappraisal of nonhuman domestic animals in terms of their wild (or willed) counterparts; the human ones should be similarly reappraised. This means, among other things, the reappraisal of the comparatively recent values and concerns of "civilized" *Homo sapiens* in terms of those of our "savage" ancestors.[35] Civilization has insulated and alienated us from the rigors and challenges of the natural environment. The hidden agenda of the humane ethic is the imposition of the anti-natural prophylactic ethos of comfort and soft pleasure on an even wider scale. The land ethic, on the other hand, requires a shrinkage, if at all possible, of the domestic sphere; it rejoices in a recrudescence of wilderness and a renaissance of tribal cultural experience.

The converse of those goods and evils, axiomatic to the humane ethic, may be illustrated and focused by the consideration of a single issue raised by the humane morality: a vegetarian diet. Savage people seem to have had, if the attitudes and values of surviving tribal cultures are representative, something like an intuitive grasp of ecological relationships and certainly a morally charged appreciation of eating. There is nothing more intimate than eating, more symbolic of the connectedness of life, and more mysterious. What we eat and how we eat is by no means an insignificant ethical concern.

From the ecological point of view, for human beings universally to become vegetarians is tantamount to a shift of trophic niche from omnivore with carnivorous preferences to herbivore. The shift is a downward one on the trophic pyramid, which in effect shortens those food chains

---

[35]This matter has been ably and fully explored by Paul Shepard, *The Tender Carnivore and the Sacred Game* (New York: Scribner's, 1973). A more empirical study has been carried out by Marshall Sahlins, *Stone Age Economics* (Chicago: Aldine/Atherton, 1972).

terminating with man. It represents an increase in the efficiency of the conversion of solar energy from plant to human biomass, and thus, by bypassing animal intermediates, increases available food resources for human beings. The human population would probably, as past trends overwhelmingly suggest, expand in accordance with the potential thus afforded. The net result would be fewer nonhuman beings and more human beings, who, of course, have requirements of life far more elaborate than even those of domestic animals, requirements which would tax other "natural resources" (trees for shelter, minerals mined at the expense of topsoil and its vegetation, etc.) more than under present circumstances. A vegetarian human population is therefore *probably* ecologically catastrophic.

Meat eating as implied by the foregoing remarks may be more *ecologically* responsible than a wholly vegetable diet. Meat, however, purchased at the supermarket, externally packaged and internally laced with petrochemicals, fattened in feed lots, slaughtered impersonally, and, in general, mechanically processed from artificial insemination to microwave roaster, is an affront not only to physical metabolism and bodily health but to conscience as well. From the perspective of the land ethic, the immoral aspect of the factory farm has to do far less with the suffering and killing of nonhuman animals than with the monstrous transformation of living things from an organic to a mechanical mode of being. Animals, beginning with the Neolithic Revolution, have been debased through selective breeding, but they have nevertheless remained animals. With the Industrial Revolution an even more profound and terrifying transformation has overwhelmed them. They have become, in Ruth Harrison's most apt description, "animal machines." The very presence of animals, so emblematic of delicate, complex organic tissue, surrounded by machines, connected to machines, penetrated by machines in research laboratories or crowded together in space-age "production facilities" is surely the more real and visceral source of our outrage at vivisection and factory farming than the contemplation of the quantity of pain that these unfortunate beings experience. I wish to denounce as loudly as the neo-Benthamites this ghastly abuse of animal life, but also to stress that the pain and suffering of research and agribusiness animals is not greater than that endured by free-living wildlife as a consequence of predation, disease, starvation, and cold—indicating that there is something immoral about vivisection and factory farming which is not an ingredient in the natural lives and deaths of wild beings. That immoral something is the transmogrification of organic to mechanical processes.

Ethical vegetarianism to all appearances insists upon the human consumption of plants (in a paradoxical moral gesture toward those animals whose very existence is dependent upon human carnivorousness), even when the tomatoes are grown hydroponically, the lettuce generously coated with chlorinated hydrocarbons, the potatoes pumped up with chemical fertilizers, and the cereals stored with the help of chemical preservatives. The land ethic takes as much exception to the transmogrification of plants by mechanicochemical means as to that of animals. The important thing, I would think, is not to eat vegetables as opposed to animal flesh, but to resist factory farming in all its manifestations, including especially its liberal application of pesticides, herbicides, and chemical fertilizers to maximize the production of *vegetable* crops.

The land ethic, with its ecological perspective, helps us to recognize and affirm the organic integrity of self and the untenability of a firm distinction between self and environment. On the ethical question of what to eat, it answers, not vegetables instead of animals, but organically as opposed to mechanicochemically produced food. Purists like Leopold prefer, in his expression, to get their "meat from God," i.e., to hunt and consume wildlife and to gather wild plant foods, and thus to live within the parameters of the aboriginal human ecological niche.[36] Second best is eating from one's own orchard, garden, henhouse, pigpen, and barnyard. Third best is buying or bartering organic foods from one's neighbors and friends.

CONCLUSION

*   *   *

. . . The debate over animal liberation, in short, should be conceived as triangular, not polar, with land ethics or environmental ethics, the third and, in my judgment, the most creative, interesting, and practicable alternative. Indeed, from this third point of view moral humanism and humane moralism appear to have much more in common with one another than either have with environmental or land ethics. On reflection one might even be led to suspect that the noisy debate between these parties has served to drown out the much deeper challenge to "business-as-usual" ethical philosophy represented by Leopold and his exponents, and to keep ethical philosophy firmly anchored to familiar modern paradigms.

*   *   *

---

[36]The expression "our meat from God" is found in Leopold, *Sand County Almanac*, p. viii. Leopold mentions "organic farming" as something intimately connected with the land ethic; in the same context he also speaks of "biotic farming" (p. 222).

Anthropocentrism, Atomism, and Environmental Ethics

Donald Scherer

I conceive this paper as part of an ongoing discussion about the shape of an environmental ethic. Since Ralston's crystallizing article,[1] an environmental ethic has been conceived as one whose fundamental principles are responsive to environmental considerations. Ralston follows Leopold in thinking of an ethic as environmental which places fundamental value in the functioning of the ecosystem. Similarly, Callicott[2] insists that an environmental ethic is one in which the most fundamental value is that which conduces to the maintenance and vitality of the ecosystem. Let this be assumed. How holistic, then, must an ecosystematic ethic be?

Callicott's ethic implies that a species has value because it occupies an important (functional, stabilizing) niche in an ecosystem, and a population of that species has value (I infer) because it has the appropriate demographic characteristics required for the population to perform the ecosystematic functions of the species. Callicott is clear that in this light, abortion and infanticide, among various other practices, will be acceptable for keeping the level of any population (including a human population) appropriate to the maintenance of the ecosystem.[3] Human beings, thus, have no special prerogative in this system of ethics: Callicott has clearly enunciated an ethic which is not specieist. It is ecosystematic, rather than anthropocentric.

At the same time Callicott has enunciated an ethic which is holistic, rather than atomistic. From within the Western liberal democratic tradition one might be genuinely concerned about the status of individual rights within Callicott's ethic. Clearly, in Callicott's view, abortion, infanticide, nonvoluntary euthanasia, war and other means for the elimination of the less fit may be unobjectionable because they are ecosystematically unobjectionable. Such holism not only includes non-individualistic values; it excludes individualistic values.

By defining holism and atomism as contraries, I set the conceptual stage to ask how atomistic or holistic an ethic which recognizes the varieties of environmental value can be. More specifically, what varieties of environmental value exist?

Is the price of a non-anthropocentric ethic an ethic which removes the individual as a locus of value? Should the development of individual rights,

[1]Holmes Rolston III, "Is There an Ecological Ethic?" *Ethics*, 1975, pp. 93–109.

[2]J. Baird Callicott, "Animal Liberation: A Triangular Affair," *Environmental Ethics*, 1980, pp. 311–38.

[3]Ibid., pp. 326–34.

Source: Reprinted by permission of the author and *Environmental Ethics*, 4, no. 2 (Summer 1982), 115–23.

along with the sensitivities which support it, be recognized as simply an outgrowth of the cancer of anthropocentrism?

I am not sure I know the answers to the questions I raise, but I should like to go some distance toward providing an answer. My goal is to provide a sketch of an ethic which is at once non-anthropocentric and yet less holistic than Callicott's. If this conception can be presented, then the discussion about the acceptability of this conception as a conception of environmental ethics and the advantages and disadvantages of this conception compared to Callicott's holistic conception can be discussed at another time.

I do not choose to quarrel with Callicott's view that there can be an ethic only if there are evaluators, beings who attribute value.[4] But the attribution of value is clearly quite independent of judgments both of one's interest and of the interest of any of those regarded as one's kind. In order to keep this clear, let us confine our discussion to successive specifications of an imaginary planet of which earthlings are totally ignorant and with which earthlings shall never, by hypothesis, have any contact, direct or indirect. Without any contact, no advantage shall accrue to any earthling from anything which might happen on the imagined planet. No earthling has any interest, then, in what happens on the planet and, *a fortiori,* no evaluation a human being might make about anything concerning the planet would reflect any human being's interest in what happened on the planet.

In the first of successive imaginings of this planet, let us imagine it as Lifeless. What happens on the planet, therefore, can be exhaustively described in geological, meteorological and solar terms. Many earthquakes occur in a certain region of the planet. There are only small variations in the temperature ranges between the poles and the equator. The sun provides the limited heat of a white dwarf, for examples. If we confine our assertions to such as have no implications that life might exist on the planet, I submit we shall have no basis upon which to justify an assertion that anything happening on the planet is of any value whatever.

Indeed, so long as the planet remains lifeless, it might seem that no sense will accrue to evaluative judgments. After all, would there be any sense to saying that the sun is not very good for heating up the rock? Or that the wind is very good at eroding the mountain side? It seems that if such assertions about lifeless mean anything, they mean something entirely reducible to efficiency or effectiveness. The sun takes thus and so long to heat the rock 10°C. The slope of the mountainside becomes 7° shallower over 70 years. The assertions seem to carry no additional meaning because there is no organism[5] for whom the heating of the rocks or the eroding of the mountainside is of (positive or negative) value.

I am tempted to conclude that statements of value can have only a

---

[4]But see Holmes Rolston's "Are Values in Nature Objective or Subjective," on this point.

[5]An organism is, by definition, a special kind of disentropic entity, namely a programmatic, patterned entity whose interdependent parts have specialized functions. As I proceed hereafter to discuss only planets inhabited by organisms, it is interesting to speculate on the value, e.g., of coral, which are programmatic, patterened, disentropic entities which lack interdependent parts with specialized functions.

meaning capable of reductivist translation on Lifeless, a conclusion which I believe is supported by the foregoing considerations. This conclusion, however, seems to me a bit sweeping. Without any life, the planet may still be one on which the evolution of life is not impossible. For example, conditions on the planet may be conducive to the development of life. If so, it would not be too much to assert, from a disinterested point of view, that the conditions on the planet are *good for* the development of life.

Clearly, some may be inclined to reduce this assertion to the ground provided for it. That is, to say that conditions on the planet are good for the development of life may seem to mean no more than that the conditions conduce to or make probable the development of life on the planet. While I am inclined to agree that the evaluative statement implies the descriptive statement, yet I think the suggestion of the equivalence of these statements is misguided. I should want to deny the equivalence because the evaluation can be read as a statement from the point of view of the life which might come to exist on the planet. From that perspective there is the good of the potential life. To be sure, "the good of the potential life" is an expression of vastly indefinite meaning, indefinite because of the indefiniteness of the kind of life to which the expression refers. The good of a tulip, the good of an octopus and the good of an amoeba are at least referentially very different. But however different these goods may be and however indefinite the expression "the good of the potential life" may be, the fact remains that in introducing the perspective of a living thing, even a potential living thing, we introduce a perspective from which geological, meteorological and solar conditions have value. Beyond its descriptive implications, "These conditions are good for the development of life" shows an awareness and an acceptance of the (potential) existence of a locus of value.[6] I conclude then that even in referring to a lifeless planet, it does make a non-reductivist sense to speak of the conditions as of value relative to the life which may develop on the planet.

Let us now rename our imaginary planet Flora, in accordance with the new assumption that a certain sort of life form does exist on it. Suppose that on Flora are entities which ingest substances, excrete other substances, grow, reproduce and then after some time perish; that is, permanently cease all of the above functions. (One might analogize these entities to plants, though I do not postulate tropisms for these entities.) The entities found on Flora but not on Modified Lifeless create new possibilities for disinterested evaluations. Geological, meteorological and solar conditions are now either conducive or nonconducive to the continued functioning of individual flora, of populations of species of flora, of individual species of flora and of life in general on Flora. Similarly, the functioning of individual flora, of populations, and of species of flora is conducive or nonconducive to the continued functioning of other individual flora, populations or kinds of flora and of flora in general. *De facto* conflicts and coordinations of living things for the first time occur, carrying implications of value for individuals, populations, species and the planetary ecosystem.

As with reference to Modified Lifeless, so with reference to Flora, it

[6]I do not claim to say whether an "ought" can be derived from an "is."

will be difficult to understand these statements about what conduces to what simply as causal claims—that is, reductively—inasmuch as individuals, populations, and kinds of flora, along with the entire ecosystem, are reasonably understood as loci of value.

Yet it may be thought that something queerly anthropocentric is imported with the notion of a locus of value. What is a "locus of value" but a fancy way of speaking which assumes a conscious agent, striving for its own good? Rather than an agent, flora are *organisms* in the sense that a certain interdependent organization of functions is necessary for the continued functioning of each floral organism. Independent of consciousness, much less agency, an individual floral organism occupies a space (locus) at which an interdependent functioning occurs. As soon as an individual or a population is sufficiently complex that a coordination of its functions is required for the continued functioning of the unit, a locus of value exists in that coordinated, interdependent functioning.

Let us now rename our imaginary planet Fauna, in accordance with another new assumption about the kind of life forms it supports. Whereas the individuals on Flora were defined without any capacities to move in place, to move from place to place, to sense conditions beyond the spatial limits of their organisms or to respond differentially to those sensed conditions, let us imagine that Fauna has on it individuals with those four capacities as well as each of the capacities previously ascribed to creatures on Flora. (The creatures of Fauna are in may ways comparable to animals on earth, although it should be noted that I have not defined these creatures as necessarily heterotropic. If any fauna are heterotropic upon other organisms, their existence entails essential conflict among organisms.) The two capacities for motion and the capacities for awareness and response create powers which expand the capacity of the fauna to perform the functions they share with Flora's inhabitants. The creatures of Fauna have increased control over how they shall live and how they shall perform their specific functions. For instance, the new powers create the potential for an individual to move and respond so as to magnify or diminish the conflicts and coordinations we noted might exist on Flora.

Interestingly, these powers seem to shift the locus of value toward individuals. Consider that on Flora no "behaving" existed. Thus all talk about value was talking about interdependent functioning. This might be the functioning of parts of the organism, the functioning of organisms within a population, the functioning of organisms or populations within a species, or the functioning of individuals, populations or species within the maintenance of an ecosystem viable for flora. Whatever, all talk about value was talk about interdependent functioning. The capacities for motion and for information processing (modified responses in the light of received sensory stimuli) give new sense to the concept of a locus of value as applied to individuals. (But since it is only individuals who have these new capacities, it is only they to whom this expanded concept of a locus of value applies.)[7]

---

[7]Plants on earth have tropisms. I should find it arbitrary to deny tropisms as behavior. Thus tropic individuals, including plants, are loci of value as non-tropic organizations are not.

To overemphasize this point, let us understand by an agent simply an individual which is capable of differential responses to its environment *and* such that it normally responds so as to conduce to its functioning and its continued functioning. Agency is thus defined in terms of self-interest. And the conception of a locus of value is expanded by adding the concept of self-interest to the previous floral concept. To correct the overemphasis, let us note that the addition of faunal powers is not univocally tied, at least conceptually, to self-interest, the above notwithstanding. For nothing in the foregoing ties the powers of selective response to sensation and motion to a motivation for *self*-aggradizement or even *self*-preservation. It is quite possible, the above definition of agency to the contrary, that fauna will be motivated by some goal for family, for the population, for the species or for fauna in general. Still, what remains of the claim that the addition of the faunal powers seems to shift the locus of value toward individuals is this: that consistency in the behavior of individual fauna, whether that behavior be self-interestedly or altruistically motivated, provides sense and grounding for the claim that the individuals are valuers; that is, that their behavior manifests the placement of value. Whatever may be the final word about what is good, the existence of value placers, that is, individuals with coherent behavior patterns, defines an enlarged (individualistic!) perspective from which disinterested earthlings observers of Fauna can attribute value.

As we earlier modified our assumption about Lifeless, so let us now consider Modified Fauna. Having previously assumed the existence of the faunal powers, let us now assume both that faunal powers require periods of development and that there is no clear fixed upper limit of the development of the faunal powers. With these new assumptions come new possibilities of evaluative judgments. Certain environments *conduce* to the sharpening of these powers. Certain environments are *safe* for fauna while these powers are developing. The development of certain combinations of powers is *self-reinforcing*, while the development of other combinations is *self-defeating*. Individual specialization in the development of various combinations of powers may *fortify* the population or the species. In a word, a host of goods instrumental to the functioning of individuals, populations and species occur because development is a reality.

These goods, however, are not properly conceived as entirely instrumental. Once it is postulated that there is no clear upper limit on the development and combination of these powers, the distinction between a difference of degree and a difference of kind is blurred. Evolutionary processes will intensify this blurring. The result may be that the development of powers to a hitherto unknown degree may change what has constituted the interdependent functioning of the individual, the population or the species. In such cases what began as an instrumental good becomes a power for transforming the character of the good of the individual, the population or the species.

Before proceeding, let us attempt to summarize. Environmental conditions, and organisms' functionings, behaviors and developments may conduce to the flourishing or the perishing of individuals, populations, species or life in general. Each of these is a basis for an attribution of value, even by a disinterested observer.

Proceeding now, let us rename our imaginary planet once more. So far we have said nothing to indicate the existence of any species which is both adaptable to many environments and adapts to those environments in large part by adapting the environments, over time far exceeding the uses of the environments, to the preferred living conditions of the species. Imagining such a species, let us rename our planet Manipulation. Naturally the manipulation of environments is going to involve making some environments less suitable as habitats for some non-manipulators. Thus, these manipulations may be both good for the manipulators and bad for certain non-manipulators. The existence of manipulators significantly intensifies the probability of interspecies conflicts.

Thus, the lot of manipulators is from the outset a precarious one. (1) If some non-manipulators are threatened by the manipulators or the impact of the manipulators on the non-manipulators' environment(s), the non-manipulators may use whatever power they have at their disposal to subdue the manipulators or to cause them to abandon their manipulation of those environments. On the other hand, if the manipulators are able to enforce their manipulations, they *ipso facto* become the dominant species in the environment. (2) Moreover, when the manipulators change an environment, making it in some way more favorable to them, they may be making it, in other ways or at later times, less favorable to them. Consequently another complexity of evaluation is introduced and a problem of ignorance emerges to cloud the truth of certain evaluations.

A further evaluative complexity introduced by manipulative species is that the same situation, circumstances, etc., may be threatening to the species or to individuals of the species, while, if the environment were suitably transformed, the otherwise same situation might become not only neutral but conducive to the species' development. Thus, relative to one future, perhaps involving certain manipulations, a given situation may be bad, while relative to another future, involving certain other manipulations, that same situation may be very good. Accordingly, manipulative capacities relativize a situation's value to alternative futures and, as well, to the alternative values that those futures emphasize.

A tool-making manipulator intensifies the relativization of values to the extent that a tool makes new manipulations possible. Tool making also extends the argument that if there is no upper limit on the development of capacities, then the distinction between what the species is, what its functioning is, and what it might become is blurred. A particular environment or a particular substance might be "useless" without a particular manipulative capacity while being a "valuable resource" once the capacity was developed, a fact not lost on earthly economists.

Let us now consider Modified Fauna-Manipulation. The modification I have in mind is to postulate that some fauna or some manipulators are self-aware creatures. (A logical point is involved in this conception: the relationship between self-awareness and manipulation is contingent.) In calling the creatures self-aware I mean that each is aware of self and other members of the species as "developing to flourish," without, or through, manipulation. The individuals are aware of themselves as capable of flourishing and vulnerable to perishing. Each enjoys flourishing and developing to flourish. Moreover, each realizes how conflicts can not only prevent or diminish the development or flourishing of others but also mar the enjoyment of that development or flourishing.

Let us imagine that such a species develops and enforces a code of behaviors for ensuring both that the development or flourishing of one individual of any species shall only minimally conflict with the development or flourishing of other individuals, populations, or species and that no activity shall undermine the vitablity of the ecosystem. The sensitivities that lead to the development of the code and the code itself ground new possibilities of judgments of new kinds of goods, namely (a) self-determination, which is itself the individual's expression of itself as a locus of value, and (b) a social order judged as good or bad insofar as it conduces to the expression of (self-respecting and other-respecting) valuing in the behavior and self-awareness of individuals. (Such a code would, I suppose, determine an environmental ethic.)

If such a social order is good, it will include an understanding of permissions and of prohibitions of various kinds of behaviors of individuals. If each individual is at liberty to act in certain ways, others are prohibited from prohibiting exercise of this liberty. In a word, then, the new kind of good involved in a good social order among such creatures is a social order which establishes and maintains a system of *prima facie* individual rights.

Here I conclude my thought experiment and turn to assessing its significance. The thought experiment has manifested non-self-interested forms of human valuing. We had discovered interdependent functioning, behaving, development, manipulative capacities, self-awareness of potentials and vulnerabilities, self-determination, conflicts and coordinations of any and all of the above, and codes of behavior designed to promote flourishing as sources of value. It remains now to say what this has to do with ethics and with environmental ethics.

By an ethic I understand a statement of the most general principles to which conduct should adhere. The ethic I envision is teleological. I have characterized the sources of value, independent of interest because the principles of the ethic will be very abstract hypotheses for minimizing and resolving conflicts, maximizing coordinations and prioritizing values to enhance the existence of sources of positive value. Because of their hypothetical character, the principles will, in theory, be subject to revision. Because of their abstractness, most of the revision will be absorbed by more concrete prescriptions derived from those principles.

But, it will be asked, how can what is proposed amount to an ethic if it provides only the easy advice that avoidable conflicts should be avoided? Surely one important function of an ethic must be to say how the hard cases are to be handled. My first answer to this question, one which philosophers with a love of completeness will disdain, seems to me extensionally the more important. The way to deal with conflicts of positive values is threefold: avoid them, dissolve them or minimize them. The same ecosystematic richness which implies that one can never do just one thing equally implies that one can, at least almost always, achieve a given goal in a large variety of ways. While some of those ways will be more self-interestedly advantageous, other ways will often be respectful of the previously explicated range of disinterested values. No ethic can be conceived independent of a motivational system widely internalized within individuals' primary socialization. To imagine an environmental ethic in practice is to imagine a society in which agents have internalized the range of disinterested values explicated above. Such agents have bound their integrity to the harmonization of values, rather than to maximization of any particular (self-interested!) value. Such agents would find few conflicts unavoidable. W. H. Murty suggests that the evolution of a cultural species implies the exhaustion/replacement of resources we witness,[8] whereas I notice that in the United States, where the social licensure of the pursuit of self-interest far outstrips that of Europe and Japan, the exhaustion/replacement of resources is also intensified. Indeed conflicts would seem to be inevitable only concerning two matters of energy: (1) some organisms gain energy by eating other organisms, and (2) some population's energy (or other resource) use may exceed the carrying capacity of the land. (I assume a definition of carrying capacity relative to available technology.)

But if some conflicts are unavoidable and others will arise, then surely an ethic should outline how these conflicts are to be resolved. Fair enough: the conflicts arise in an environment within which only some species are capable of formulating general predictions about the conflicts. They alone, therefore, can undertake action for the sake of avoiding, dissolving or minimizing the conflict. Hence, as Callicott has argued,[9] the obligations for responding to those conflicts must fall upon those agents. Although they have a right to self-development, this right implies no right to self-interest since the right of any individual to self-development is simply an instance of a right which belongs universally to creatures capable of development. Their own worth can exist only within a functioning ecosystem, whose harmony thus takes precedence over self-interested preferences, but not over *universalizable* individual rights.

I read Callicott as arguing that if the life styles of human beings are taken as given, then the human population on earth is excessive. He concludes that some human individuals, detrimental to a thriving ecosystem, are expendable. Appreciating Potter's point about alternative starting points,[10] I argue that in order for individuals to have universalizable rights within a thriving ecosystem, life styles of self-interest must be curtailed.

But is this ethic in any special way environmental? I think so for several reasons. First, the interdependent functioning of not only individuals, but also populations and species, a value discovered on Flora, is in no way mitigated or denied by the other values subsequently discovered.

[8]W. H. Murty, "Anthropocentrism: A Modern Version," *Science* 187 (1975): 1168–72.

[9]J. Baird Callicott, "Elements of an Environmental Ethic," *Environmental Ethics*, 1979, pp. 71–82, esp. pp. 72–77.

[10]Ralph Potter, "The Simple Structure of the Population Debate," in *Population Policy and Ethics* (ed. Veatch), 1975.

Indeed, the entire set of subsequent values is derivative from, because they are physically dependent upon, a viable ecosystem. The maintenance of the ecosystem will thus be a prioritized norm of an ethic recognizing the foundational character of ecosystematic value. Second, the developments on Fauna and on Manipulation create possibilities of fits between living things and their environments which do not exist on Flora. In part the values discovered on Fauna and Manipulation have their source in these creature-environment fits. Third, the non-anthropomorphic, disinterested character of the discovery of the values on which the ethic rests reminds us that the ethic is a set of principles designed to enhance the harmony of the environment and the possibilities of creatures' flourishing within it. Fourth, the ethic is an ethic which is realisitc about the kinds of species included in this world's environment. Failure to correctly characterize the kinds of species in an environment can only lead to an ethic which fantasizes coordinations which could never be. For is not the real problem of environmental ethics that humankind is a manipulative species? Fifth, the ethic aims at the harmonization of value. Consider the ethic I imagine on Modified Fauna–Manipulation. Add to it the prioritized principle that no acceptable action may damage the vitality or imperil the existence of the ecosystem. Surely such an ethic is environmental, but much more atomistic than Callicott's. For expressions of individualistic valuing may vastly modify the ecosystem while its vitality is maintained. When manipulative species are involved, the crucial questions concern the real ecological limits of that vastness.

What does all of this suggest? I do not mean to attempt to be definitive about the shape of an adequate environmental ethic. What I have attempted to do is (1) to divorce attributions of value from judgments of the interest of the attributor, (2) to develop the concept of a locus of value, (3) to explore the interconnections between the goods of individuals and the goods of populations, species and of life, (4) to outline how a non-anthropocentric conception of value is possible without being holistic, and (5) to suggest the reasonableness on naturalistic grounds of the attribution of some sorts of rights to individuals who have certain kinds of awareness. I trust that the extent to which I have faithfully tried to include (3) in my agenda shows how open I remain to exploring the intricate connections between the individual and the holistic good.

Four Forms of Ecological Consciousness Reconsidered

John Rodman

The primary purpose of this paper is to describe and evaluate as succinctly as possible four currents of thought discernible in the history of the contemporary environmental movement. The secondary purpose is to recommend the still-emergent fourth form (Ecological Sensibility) as the starting point for a general environmental ethic. Along the way, I hope to suggest something of the complexity and ambiguity of the various forms—qualities sometimes lost in the rush to condemn the "shallow" and extoll the "deep."

1. RESOURCE CONSERVATION

The basic thrust of the Resource Conservation standpoint, taken in its turn-of-the-century context and seen as its advocates saw it, was to restrain the reckless exploitation of forests, wildlife, soils, etc., characteristic of the pioneer stage of modern social development by imposing ethical and legal requirements that "natural resources" be used "wisely," meaning (in Gifford Pinchot's words) that they should be used "for the greatest good of the greatest number" (of humans), as distinct from being used to profit a few, and that the good should be considered over "the long run," that is, in terms of a sustainable society. Now that the novelty of this standpoint has worn off and more radical views have arisen, it is clear that the ethic of "wise use" remained within the worldview of anthropocentric utilitarianism, since it assumed (without arguing the point) that nonhuman natural entities and systems had only instrumental value as (actual or potential) "resources" for human use, so that the only reasons for humans to restrain their treatment of nonhuman nature were prudential ones flowing from considerations of enlightened self-interest.

What is a self and what is an interest, however, are not exactly given once and for all. To Pinchot's identification of human interests with economic prosperity and national power others have subsequently added such things as esthetic enjoyment, scientific knowledge, and (more recently) biological survival. To Pinchot's and Theodore Roosevelt's extension of the

Source: An earlier version of the "four forms" analysis was developed in a series of papers written in 1976–77. These included "The Liberation of Nature?" (*Inquiry*, 20, spring 1977), "Four Forms of Ecological Consciousness, Part One: Resource Conservation" (a paper presented at the annual meeting of the American Political Science Association, 1976), and the papers listed below in notes 2 and 3. The present essay is based on a paper read to the Department of Philosophy, Research School of Social Sciences, The Australian National University, where I was a Visiting Fellow in the summer of 1981. It attempts to restate the "four forms" analysis so as to clear up misunderstandings, deal with criticisms, and incorporate suggestions. It omits much of the historical material and many peripheral arguments in an effort to focus on the central issues.

self in space and time to comprise a national society and to include the interests of overlapping generations (ourselves, "our children, and our children's children"), others have superadded the notion of the human species as a kind of planetary society and the notion of obligations to a remoter posterity to which we are linked by the half-life of radioactive nuclear waste. Clearly, it is possible to engage in a good deal of persuasion by using and extending key terms and commitments within the Resource Conservation standpoint, as, for example, when Aldo Leopold redefined wealth and poverty in esthetic terms so that an economically poor landscape might be seen as rich in beauty and therefore worth preserving. In the case of esthetic contemplation and certain kinds of disinterested scientific knowledge (e.g., that of the field naturalist), we approach the boundary of the Resource Conservation position in the sense that these are undeniable human interests that are so distant from the original and core (economic) sense of "use" (which involved the damming, logging, bulldozing, and transformation of nature into manufactured products) that the non- (or at least significantly less-) exploitative, more respectful senses of "use" can provide bridges for crossing over into the notion that there is intrinsic value in (some) natural entities and systems, which, after all, are beautiful or interesting to us partly in virtue of qualities that inhere *in them*.

Insofar as the Resource Conservation standpoint is retained in its core assumptions, however, it is vulnerable on several related grounds. First, the reduction of intrinsic value to human beings and the satisfaction of their interests is arbitrary, since it is neither necessary (for there are other human cultures that have not so reduced value), nor justified (for nobody has yet successfully identified an observable, morally relevant quality that both includes all humans and excludes all nonhumans). Second, the commitment to maximizing value through maximizing human use leads logically and in practice to an unconstrained total-use approach, whose upshot is to leave nothing in its natural condition (for that would be a kind of "waste," and waste should be eliminated); all rivers should be dammed for irrigation and hydropower, and all native forests replaced with monocultural tree plantations managed for "harvest." Given the arbitrariness of the first principle, the second amounts to an unjustifiable species imperialism.

Granted all this, it would be unfortunate if the contemporary environmental movement turned out to be simply what Stewart Udall once called it, "the third wave of conservation." Yet it is also important to recognize the (limited) validity of the Resource Conservation standpoint in terms of its historical thrust. It emerged, in large part, as an attempt to constrain the destructive environmental impact of individuals and corporations who exploited nature for profit without sufficient regard for the larger social good or for the welfare of future generations. That issue has not died or become unimportant because broader ones have arisen. Some acts are wrong on several grounds: this is what makes possible the formation of honest coalitions, which are indispensable to political efficacy. Put in the most general way, the original thrust of the Resource Conservation movement was to enlarge in space and time the class of beings whose good ought to be taken into account by decision-makers, and to draw from that some conclusions about appropriate limits on human conduct. That Pinchot and his followers were inhibited by an unquestioning, almost unconscious, fidelity to an anthropocentric reduction of intrinsic value is cause for regret and for criticism, but the direction of thrust warrants respect from even the most radical environmentalists. In retrospect, the Resource Conservation standpoint appears to have been an early ideological adaptation on the part of a society that was still in the pioneering or colonizing stage of succession but had begun to get glimpses of natural limits that would require different norms of conduct for the society to become sustainable at a steady-state level. How different those norms might have to be was not yet clear.

2. WILDERNESS PRESERVATION

At approximately the same time (1890–1914) that the Conservation movement was defining itself against the forces of unbridled resource exploitation, the Wilderness Preservation tradition, represented in part by John Muir and the Sierra Club, was also emerging as a social force.[1] At first allied with Pinchot against the common enemy and under the common banner of "conservation," Muir parted ways with him over issues such as the leasing of lands in the federal forest reserves to commercial grazing corporations and over the proposal to dam Hetch Hetchy Valley to make a reservoir for the growing population of San Francisco. What seemed a wise use to Pinchot, weighing the number of city dwellers, seemed a "desecration" to Muir. In contrast to the essentially economic language of Resource Conservation, Preservationists tended to articulate their vision in predominantly religious and esthetic terms. Beneath Muir's somewhat parochial tendency to depict particular landscapes as "temples" and "cathedrals" lay both a rather pantheistic view of nature as animated by a divine power ("God" being sometimes equated with "Beauty") and also a very ancient and widespread notion that certain natural areas were sacred places where human beings could encounter the holy. This has been a potent and enduring strand in American environmentalism, going back to Emerson and Thoreau. Sociologist Arthur St. George concluded his study of Sierra Club members in the 1970s with the finding that their basic values were (still) "religious and esthetic." Surely Muir would have applauded, had he been alive in 1966, when the Sierra Club took out full-page newspaper ads satirizing the Bureau of Reclamation's claim that damming the Grand Canyon for irrigation, etc., would enhance its recreational value: "Should we also flood the Sistine Chapel so tourists can get nearer the ceiling?" The implied analogy between Grand Canyon and a chapel full of priceless works of art was not only clever but faithful to a long-standing tradition.
When the religious element in the Preservationist tradition becomes

---

[1] The hedge ("in part") is meant to acknowledge that, although Muir did articulate the standpoint that I describe, there were other elements in his writings as well. I am analyzing a particular point of view, not presenting an exhaustive analysis of John Muir.

explicit, some philosophers are embarrassed and inclined to dismiss it in a sentence or two as "mysticism," "superstition," "irrationalism," or at least as an unnecessary and misleading backdrop that disguises the real thing at stake and will surely lead other people to discount the case for preserving wilderness. Perhaps this reaction stems, at least in part, from assuming that the important issues are metaphysical ones (Does God exist? Is (S)he present in nature?) instead of experiential ones (What do people tend to feel in certain natural settings, and, given their cultural background, how do they tend to articulate those feelings?). I have given elsewhere[2] a rather psychological interpretation of the wilderness experience, which may help salvage it as an intelligible phenomenon for secular minds at the cost of prompting the question whether the value of Nature for the Preservationist lies solely in its therapeutic utility for what Muir described as "thousands of tired, nerve-shaken, over-civilized people." If the answer is yes, then Wilderness Preservation should be seen as a genteel variant on Resource Conservation. There is no doubt that the passage of time affects our perspective on this kind of thing. The more distant we are from Pinchot's struggle against "reckless" resource exploitation, the easier it is to see Resource Conservation as simply a more prudent form of resource exploitation. The more distant we are from the split between Muir and Pinchot, and the more aware we have become of alternative positions that assert the intrinsic value of nature with less ambiguity, the more inclined we are to see this once world-historical schism as a family quarrel between advocates of two different forms of human use—economic and religio-esthetic. On the other hand, if Muir had been asked outright whether Yosemite had value in itself, or for its own sake, independent of there being any actual or potential people to experience it, he would have surely said that it did. Whether this would be value independent of a divine, creative force lurking in the universe, however, is doubtful. The Preservationist notion of nature's value is thus in continual danger of being reduced by critics one way or another—either to subjective human experience or to an (allegedly) objective deity that is manifested in nature. For the person unsatisfied by the former but unable to believe in the latter, the Preservationist view poses serious difficulties.

Since this issue can be argued back and forth without any clear conclusion being reached, I should like to approach it from a slightly different tack, focusing on the esthetic that mediates the experience of the holy. In general, esthetic considerations are very subjective and therefore shaky foundations on which to base any kind of ethic. The specific problem with the Preservationist tradition emerges when we consider that until the eighteenth century most Europeans, including early American settlers, viewed "wilderness" and especially mountains with horror and dread, and that the emergence of wilderness-appreciation and mountain-climbing as cults accompanied the emergence of the Romantic esthetic of "the sublime and the

[2]"Theory and Practice in the Environmental Movement," in *The Search for Absolute Values in a Changing World*, vol. 1 (New York: The International Cultural Foundation, 1978), p. 49.

beautiful," especially the sublime, meaning essentially the feeling of awe experienced in the presence of overwhelming power, magnitude, or antiquity. For two centuries the esthetic of the sublime has, in effect, defined outdoor sacred space for people of European background, who, consequently, have often had difficulty relating to the claims of aboriginal peoples whose sacred places do not always conform to our ideas of what a sacred place is like. Preservationist efforts have tended to focus on protecting more-or-less pristine wilderness at the expense of disturbed areas, and on saving the Sierras, the Grand Canyons, and the giant sequoias of life as the natural environments of peak experiences, while the marshes and the brushlands have gradually disappeared under the impact of less exalted forms of human "growth." Of course, it is not *a priori* false that some natural areas are more valuable than others; and, given environmentalists' limits of numbers, time, and energy, priorities may be a practical necessity. Still, the particular pattern of discrimination exhibited by the history of the Preservation movement stems all too clearly from historically transient esthetic tastes and bears too little relation to sustaining healthy ecological systems.

An esthetic of nature can evolve (e.g., to incorporate an appreciation of small organisms and of complex and intricate interrelatedness), and an organized movement can evolve away from esthetics. As Sierra Club members become also Friends of the Earth, they lose a certain ferocity of commitment that is probably possible only to places that are special, while they gain a more generalized commitment to defending ecological values. In special cases, when grand, ancient, or otherwise awe-inspiring wild areas are threatened, the Preservationist tradition still provides a wellspring of powerful feeling and rhetoric that can be tapped. But, even within a more-or-less pantheistic framework, sacred places exist in contrast to profane ones, and the Preservationist tradition cannot—without serious attenuation of its core values or indulgence in gross eclecticism—do the work of a general environmental ethic.

3. MORAL EXTENSIONISM

Moral Extensionism (which I called "Nature Moralism" in earlier papers) is an appropriately awkward term invented to designate a wide range of positions whose common characteristic is that they contend that humans have duties not only concerning but also directly to (some) nonhuman natural entities, that these duties derive from rights possessed by the natural entities, and that these rights are grounded in the possession by the natural entities of an intrinsically valuable quality such as intelligence, sentience, or consciousness. Quite different versions of this position can be found in the writings of such people as John Lilly, Peter Singer, Christopher Stone, and certain philosophers in the tradition of Whitehead (notably, Charles Hartshorne and John Cobb). All these writers *appear* to break with the anthropocentric bias of Resource Conservation and to resolve the ambiguity of Preservationism by clearly attributing intrinsic value to (at least some) natural items in their own right. The ground for human self-restraint towards nonhuman nature thus becomes moral in a strict sense (respect for rights) rather than prudential or reverential. Yet more radical environmentalists (e.g., the Routleys, Rodman, Callicott, Sessions, Devall, et al.) object that the break with anthropocentrism and the resolution of the ambiguity are incomplete, and that all the variants of this position are open to the criticism that they merely "extend" (rather than seriously question or radically change) conventional anthropocentric ethics, so that they are vulnerable to revised versions of the central objection to the Resource Conservation standpoint, namely, that they are chauvinistic, imperialistic, etc.

Consider, for a starter, John Lilly's view that we ought to protect dolphins because they are very intelligent. Or consider, further along the spectrum of variants on this position, Peter Singer's argument that all sentient beings (animals down through shrimps) have an equal right to have their interests taken into consideration by humans who are making decisions that might cause them pain (pain being bad, and acts that cause unnecessary pain being wrong). Then consider, at the far end of the spectrum, the claim of various writers that all natural entities, including plants and rocks, have certain rights (e.g., a right to live and flourish) because they all possess some trait such as consciousness (though some possess it more fully than others). In the first two cases the scope of moral concern is extended to include, besides humans, certain classes of nonhumans that are like humans (with regard to the specified quality), while the vast bulk of nature is left in a condition of unredeemed thinghood. In Singer's version, anthropocentrism has widened out to a kind of zoocentric sentientism, and we are asked to assume that the sole value of rainforest plant communities consists in being a natural resource for birds, possums, veneer manufacturers, and other sentient beings. In the third case, we are asked to adopt the implausible assumption that rocks (for example) are conscious. In all three cases we end up with an only slightly modified version of the conventional hierarchy of moral worth that locates humans at the top of the scale (of intelligence, consciousness, sentience), followed by "higher" animals, "lower" animals, plants, rocks and so forth. "Subhumans" may now be accorded rights, but we should not be surprised if their interests are normally overridden by the weightier interests of humans, for the choice of the quality to define the extended base class of those entitled to moral consideration has weighted the scales in that way.

Moreover, extensionist positions tend (when consistent, at least) to perpetuate the atomistic metaphysics that is so deeply imbedded in modern culture, locating intrinsic value only or primarily in individual persons, animals, plants, etc., rather than in communities or ecosystems, since individuals are our paradigmatic entities for thinking, being conscious, and feeling pain. Yet it seems bizarre to try to account wholly for the value of a forest or a swamp by itemizing and adding up the values of all the individual members. And it is not clear that rights and duties (of which our ideas are fundamentally individualistic) can be applied to ecosystem relationships without falling into absurdity. Pretty clearly what has happened is that, after both the prudential and the reverential stages of ideological adaptation represented by Resource Conservation and Wilderness Preservation came to seem inadequate, a more radical claim that nature had value "in its own right" seemed in order. Many of the attempts to make that claim plausible have, however, tried to extend the sphere of intrinsic value and therefore of obligatory moral concern by assimilating (parts of) nature to inappropriate models, without rethinking very thoroughly either the assumptions of conventional ethics or the ways in which we perceive and interpret the natural world. It is probably a safe maxim that there will be no revolution in ethics without a revolution in perception.

4. ECOLOGICAL SENSIBILITY

The last form that I shall discuss is still emergent, so that description is not easily separated from prescription. The term "sensibility" is chosen to suggest a complex pattern of perceptions, attitudes, and judgments which, if fully developed, would constitute a disposition to appropriate conduct that would make talk of rights and duties unnecessary under normal conditions. At this stage of development, however, we can analytically distinguish three major components of an Ecological Sensibility: a theory of value that recognizes intrinsic value in nature without (hopefully) engaging in mere extensionism (in the sense discussed in section 3); a metaphysics that takes account of the reality and importance of relationships and systems as well as of individuals; and an ethics that includes such duties as noninterference with natural processes, resistance to human acts and policies that violate the noninterference principle, limited intervention to repair environmental damage in extreme circumstances, and a style of coinhabitation that involves the knowledgeable, respectful, and restrained use of nature. Since there is not space to discuss all these components here, and since I have sketched some of them elsewhere,[3] I shall focus here on two basic dimensions of the theory of value, drawing primarily upon the writings of Leopold,[4] the Routleys,[5] and Rodman.

The first dimension is simple but sweeping in its implications. It is based upon the obligation principle that one ought not to treat with disrespect or use as a mere means anything that has a *telos* or end of its own— anything that is autonomous in the basic sense of having a capacity for internal self-direction and self-regulation. This principle is widely accepted but has been mistakenly thought (e.g., by Kant and others) to apply only to persons. Unless one engages in a high redefinition of terms, however, it more properly applies to (at least) all living natural entities and natural systems. (I leave aside in this essay the difficult and important issue of

[3]"Ecological Resistance: John Stuart Mill and the Case of the Kentish Orchid," paper presented at the annual meeting of the American Political Science Association, 1977.

[4]Aldo Leopold, *A Sand County Almanac* (New York: Oxford University Press, 1949).

[5]Richard and Val Routley, "Human Chauvinism and Environmental Ethics," in *Environmental Philosophy*, eds. Don Mannison, Michael McRobbie, and Richard Routley (Department of Philosophy, Research School of Social Sciences, The Australian National University, 1980); Val and Richard Routley, "Social Theories, Self Management, and Environmental Problems," in ibid.

physical systems.) The vision of a world composed of many things and many kinds of things, all having their own *telē*, goes back (except for the recognition of ecosystems) to Aristotle's metaphysics and philosophy of nature and does therefore not involve us in the kinds of problems that arise from extending the categories of modern Liberal ethics to a natural world made up of the dead "objects" of modern thought. (To mention Aristotle is not, of course, to embrace all of his opinions, especially the very anthropocentric *obiter dicta*—e.g., that plants exist for the sake of animals, animals for humans, etc.—that can be found in his *Ethics* and *Politics*.) This notion of natural entities and natural systems as having intrinsic value in the specific and basic form, of having *telē* of their own, having their own characteristic patterns of behavior, their own stages of development, their own business (so to speak), is the basic ground in which is rooted the attitude of respect, the obligation of noninterference, etc. In it is rooted also the indictment of the Resource Conservation standpoint as being, at bottom, an ideology of human chauvinism and human imperialism.

It may be objected that our paradigmatic notion of a being having a *telos* is an individual human being or a person, so that viewing nature in terms of *telē* involves merely another extension of an all-too-human quality to (part of) nature, retaining the conventional atomistic metaphysics and reinstating the conventional moral pecking order. I do not think that this is the case. It seems to me an observable fact that thistles, oak trees, and wombats, as well as rainforests and chaparral communities, have their own characteristic structures and potentialities to unfold, and that it is as easy to see this in them as it is in humans, if we will but look.

For those unaccustomed to looking, Aldo Leopold's *Sand County Almanac* provides, in effect, a guidebook. Before the reader is introduced to the "land ethic" chapter (which is too often read out of the context of the book as a whole), (s)he is invited to accompany Leopold as he follows the tracks of the skunk in the January snow, wondering where the skunk is heading and why; speculating on the different meanings of a winter thaw for the mouse whose snow burrow has collapsed and for the owl who has just made dinner of the mouse; trying to understand the honking of the geese as they circle the pond; and wondering what the world must look like to a muskrat eye-deep in the swamp. By the time one reaches Leopold's discussion of the land ethic, one has grown accustomed to thinking of different animals— and (arguably), by extension, different natural entities in general—as subjects rather than objects, as beings that have their own purposes, their own perspectives on the world, and their own goods that are differentially affected by events. While we can never get inside a muskrat's head and know exactly what the world looks like from that angle, we can be pretty certain that the view is different from ours. What melts away as we become intrigued with this plurality of perspectives is the assumption that any one of them (for example, ours) is privileged. So we are receptive when the "land ethic" chapter suggests that other natural beings deserve respect and should be treated as if they had a "right" in the most basic sense of being entitled to continue existing in a natural state. To want from Leopold a full-scale theory of the rights of nature, however, would be to miss the point, since the idea of rights has only a limited application. Moreover,

Leopold does not present logical arguments for the land ethic in general, because such arguments could not persuade anyone who still looked at nature as if it were comprised of objects or mere resources, and such arguments are unnecessary for those who have come to perceive nature as composed of subjects. When perception is sufficiently changed, respectful types of conduct seem "natural," and one does not have to belabor them in the language of rights and duties. Here, finally, we reach the point of "paradigm change."[6] What brings it about is not exhortation, threat, or logic, but a rebirth of the sense of wonder that in ancient times gave rise to philosphers but is now more often found among field naturalists.

In further response to the objection that viewing nature in terms of *telē* is simply another version of anthropocentric Moral Extensionism, consider that a forest may be in some ways more nearly paradigmatic than an individual human for illustrating what it means to have a *telos*. A tropical rainforest may take 500 years to develop to maturity and may then maintain a dynamic, steady-state indefinitely (for millions of years, judging from fossils) if not seriously interfered with. It exhibits a power of self-regulation that may have been shared to some extent by millennia of hunter-gatherer societies but is not an outstanding characteristic of modern humans, taken either as individuals or as societies. While there may therefore be some differences in the degree to which certain aspects of what it means to have a *telos* are present in one organism or one system compared with another, the basic principle is that all items having a *telos* are entitled to respectful treatment. Comparisons are more fruitfully made in terms of the second dimension of the theory of value.

The second dimension incorporates a cluster of value-giving characteristics that apply both to natural entities and (even more) to natural systems: diversity, complexity, integrity, harmony, stability, scarcity, etc. While the *telos* principle serves primarily to provide a common basic reason for respectful treatment of natural entities and natural systems (ruling out certain types of exploitative acts on deontological grounds), and to provide a criterion for drawing morally relevant distinctions between natural trees and plastic trees, natural forests and timber plantations, etc., this cluster of value-giving qualities provides criteria for evaluating alternative courses of permissible action in terms of optimizing the production of good effects, the better action being the one that optimizes the qualities taken as an interdependent, mutually constraining cluster. Aldo Leopold seems to have had something like this model in mind when he stated the land ethic in these terms:

> A thing is right when it tends to preserve the integrity, stability, and beauty of the biotic community. It is wrong when it tends otherwise.

(We may wish to modify Leopold's statement, omitting reference to beaut and adding additional criteria, especially diversity [which stands as a princi-

---

[6]Obviously, I believe that those who see Leopold's land ethic as a mere extension of conventional ethics are radically mistaken.

ple in its own right, not merely as a means to stability]; moreover, an action can be right or wrong in reference to individuals as well as communities— but Leopold was redressing an imbalance, calling our attention to the su- pra-individual level, and can be forgiven for overstating his case.) More controversially, the cluster of ecological values can also be used to appraise the relative value of different ecosystems when priorities must be set (given limits on time, energy, and political influence) by environmentalists work- ing to protect nature against the bulldozer and the chain saw. The criteria of diversity, complexity, etc., will sometimes suggest different priorities than would result from following the esthetic of the sublime or a criterion such as sentience, while a fully pantheistic philosophy of preservation pro- vides no criteria at all for discriminating cases.

What can be said in justification of this cluster of ecological values? It is possible for human beings to hold such values. Those who do not, and those who are not sure whether they do or not, may wish to imagine alternative worlds, asking whether they prefer the diverse world to the monocultural world, and so forth. But it would be naive to assume that such thought experiments are conducted without any significant context. For example, I am aware that my preference for diverse, complex, and stable systems occurs in a time that I perceive as marked by an unpreceden- tedly high rate of species extinction and ecosystem simplification. In this situation, diversity has scarcity value in addition to its intrinsic value, in addition to its instrumental value as conducive to stability. This illustrates a general characteristic of the cluster of ecological values: the balance is not static but fluctuates in response to changes in the environment, so that different principles are more or less prominent at different times.

Since the cluster of value-giving principles applies generally through- out the world to living natural entities and systems, it applies to human beings and human societies as well as to the realm of nonhuman nature. To the extent that diversity on an individual human level is threatened by the pressures of conformity in mass society, and diversity of social ways of life is threatened by the pressures of global resource exploitation and an ideology of world-wide "development" in whose name indigenous peoples are being exterminated along with native forests, it would be short-sighted to think of "ecological issues" as unrelated to "social issues." From an ecological point of view, one of the most striking socio-political phenomena of the twentieth century—the rise of totalitarian dictatorships that forcibly try to eliminate the natural condition of human diversity in the name of some mono- cultural ideal (e.g., an Aryan Europe or a classless society)— is not so much a freakish aberration from modern history as it is an intensification of the general spirit of the age. Ecological Sensibility, then is "holistic" in a sense beyond that usually thought of: it grasps the underlying principles that manifest themselves in what are ordinarily perceived as separate "social" and "environmental" issues.[7] More than any alternative environmental ethic, it attains a degree of comprehension that frees environmentalists

[7]See also Rodman, "Paradigm Change in Political Science," *American Behavioral Scientist* 24, 1 (September–October 1980): 67–69.

from the charge of ignoring "people problems" in their preoccupation with saving nature. Insofar as Ecological Sensibility transcends "ecology" in the strict sense, its very name is metaphorical, drawing on a part to suggest the whole. Starting with issues concerning human treatment of the natural environment, we arrive at principles that shed light on the total human condition.

PART TWO
SPECIFIC
ENVIRONMENTAL
PROBLEMS

INTRODUCTION

Environmental ethics has also been conceived as focused on this question: "When we confront the social problems of our time, how should we act so as to stop shortchanging the environmental dimension of our problems?" Many philosophers have been less concerned with developing a whole new way of thinking and more concerned with helping us recognize that environmental problems reflect conflicts among basic social values. If individuals are to have the freedom to act as they choose, how can society assure that sufficient resources will be available for such public goods as a common defense, education, transportation, recreation, and a clean environment? If public decisions are going to be made in an objective, verifiable manner, what values will those decisions reflect and what values will be ignored? Do we want preferences or collective values to inform the choices that shape our natural and social environment?

In selecting articles reflecting current thinking about the environmental aspects of contemporary problems, the editors have sought to focus on major problems with a significant environmental dimension, but not to duplicate material available elsewhere. The issue of animal liberation, for example, is thoroughly explored in *Animal Rights and Human Obligations,* eds. Regan and Singer. The issue of world hunger and justice is considered in *World Hunger and Moral Obligation,* eds. Aiken and LaFollette. The issue of the rights of future generations is considered in *Obligations to Future Generations,* eds. Sikora and Barry, and in *Responsibilities to Future Generations,* ed. Ernest Partridge. Here, the focus is on three broad issues: (1) What values should be reflected in human land use? (2) What are the strengths and weaknesses of using cost-benefit analyses for determining environmental policies? (3) What values, individual or collective, should inform public choices concerning environmental policy?

LAND USE

In the English-speaking world in modern times, land has been conceived as the property of people and has been defined in terms of its usefulness to people as a resource. The very concept of land as property implies, as Leopold notes, that land is not conceived as having rights. Rather, to say that a human being owns a piece of land has traditionally meant that the person has a collection of rights over the land, rights to control the use of the land, to develop the land, to rent or sell it, or to exclude others from using it, even the right to destroy the land or to impair its usefulness in various ways. In the first article in this section, Eugene Hargrove outlines how the development of the concept of property ownership has tended to downplay any duties of property owners that might correlate with their rights.

But the environmental fact is that the nearness of one property to another and the operation of wind and water upon properties imply that what one person does with a property has implications for what another can do. What, then, is an environmentally informed understanding of the maxim of equal freedom for all? This question is very much a live issue in the United States. The tradition of freedom is represented in the affirmation that the government shall not take an individual's property without just compensation. But concern for harm to others underlies the affirmation that the police power of the state is rightly employed against an individual when that individual's property use causes a public nuisance. How are these two affirmations to be reconciled? If the state restricts property use, when is it a "taking" for the public good and when is it a restraint of a public nuisance? Much of the complexity of this question is environmental. How should we understand causation within ecosystems? In the light of ecological interdependencies, how widely should individual duties be defined? Philip Soper's "critical features" doctrine and Chief Justice Hallow's reasoning are initial attempts to answer these broad questions.

Anglo-American Land Use Attitudes

Eugene C. Hargrove

* * *

LANDHOLDING AMONG EARLY GERMAN AND SAXON FREEMEN

About two thousand years ago most of Europe was occupied by tribes of peoples known collectively today as the Celts. At about that time, these peoples came under considerable pressure from the Romans moving up from the south and from Germanic tribes entering central Europe from the east. Five hundred years later, the Celts had either been subjugated by the German and Roman invaders or pushed back into Ireland and fringe areas of England. The Roman Empire, too, after asserting its presence as far north as England, was in decay. Roman influence would continue in the south, but in northern and central Europe as well as in most of England German influence would prevail.

The Germanic tribes which displaced the Celts and defeated the Romans were composed of four classes: a few nobles or earls, a very large class of freemen, a smaller class of slaves, and a very small class of semifree men or serfs. Freemen were the most common people in early German society. They recognized no religious or political authority over their own activities, except to a very limited degree. As *free* men, they could, if they desired, settle their accounts with their neighbors and move to another geographical location. Each freeman occupied a large amount of land, his freehold farmstead, on which he grazed animals and, with the help of his slaves, grew crops. When necessary, he joined together with other freemen for defense or, more often, for the conquest of new territories.[1]

Freemen were the key to German expansion. When overcrowding occurred in clan villages and little unoccupied land remained, freemen moved to the border and with other freemen defeated and drove away the neighboring people. Here they established for themselves their own freehold farmsteads. Their decendants then multiplied and occupied the vacant land between the original freehold estates. When land was no longer available, clan villages began to form again and many freemen moved on once more to the new borders to start new freehold farmsteads. In this way,

---

[1]The account given in this section is based most directly on Denman W. Ross, *The Early History of Land-Holding Among the Germans* (Boston: Soule and Bugbee, 1883), and Walter Phelps Hall, Robert Greenhalgh Albion, and Jennie Barnes Pope, *A History of England and the Empire—Commonwealth*, 4th ed. (Boston: Ginn, 1961).

Source: Reprinted by permission of the author and *Environmental Ethics*, 2, no. 2 (Summer 1980), 121–48.

the Germans slowly but surely moved onward across nothern and central Europe with freemen leading the way until no more land was available.

Strictly speaking, a freeman did not own his land. The idea of land-ownership in the modern sense was still many centuries away. In England, for example, landowning did not become a political and legal reality until 1660 when feudal dues were finally abolished once and for all. Freemen, however, lived in prefeudal times. They usually made a yearly offering to the local noble or earl, but technically this offering was a gift rather than a feudal payment and had nothing to do with their right to their land. As the term *freehold* suggests, a freeman held his land freely without any forced obligations to an overlord or to his neighbors.

In early times, when land was readily available, each freeman occupied as much land as he needed. There was no set amount that a free-man ought to have and no limit on his holdings, except that he could not hold more land than he could use. Thus, in effect, his personal dominion was restricted only by the number of animals that he had available for grazing and the number of slaves he had for agricultural labor. Sometimes, when the land began to lose its fertility, he would abandon his holdings and move to some other unoccupied location nearby. The exact location of each holding was only vaguely determined, and when disputes arose about boundaries, they were settled with the help of the testimony of neighbors or, when that failed, by armed combat between the parties involved.

Much of the unoccupied land was held in common with other free-men in accordance with various local arrangements. Sometimes the use was regulated by establishing the number of cattle that each freeman could place on the land. In other cases, plots were used by different freeman every year on a rotational basis.

When unoccupied border lands were no longer available for new freemen to settle, the way of life of the freemen began to change. The primary problem was one of inheritance. In the beginning, land had never been divided; rather, it has always been "multiplied" as sons moved to adjacent areas and established new freehold farmsteads. Eventually, how-ever, it became necessary for the sons to divide the land which had been held by their father. A serious problem then developed, for, if division took place too many times, then the holdings became so small that they had little economic value, and the family as a whole slipped into poverty.

The solution was *entail*, i.e., inheritance along selected family lines. The most common form of entail was *primogeniture*, according to which the eldest son inherited everything and the others little or nothing. In this way, the family head remained powerful by keeping his landholdings intact, but most of his brothers were condemned to the semifree and poverty-stricken life of serfdom. As a result of these new inheritance practices, the number of freemen became an increasingly smaller portion of the society as a whole as most of the rest of the population, relatives included, rapidly sank to the level of serfs.

Another problem affecting freemen was taxation. The custom of giv-ing an offering to the local noble was gradually replaced by a tax, and once established, taxes often became large burdens on many of the poorer freemen who in many instances paid taxes while other richer landholders were exempted. In such circumstances, freemen often gave up their status and their lands to persons exempted from the taxes and paid a smaller sum in rent as tenants.

* * *

These feudal conditions did not appear in England until long after they were firmly established in Europe. At the time of the conquest of England by William the Conqueror most Englishmen were freemen. Thus, in England, unlike in Germanic Europe, prefeudal conditions did not slip away gradually but were abruptly replaced by a feudal system imposed on much of the native population by the victorious Normans. Under such circumstances, freemen declined in numbers, but struggled as best they could to maintain their freeman status in opposition to Norman rule and as a part of their Saxon heritage. As a result, freemen managed to maintain a presence in England no longer conceivable in Europe. Through them, memories of the heyday of the flamboyant Saxon freemen remained to shade political thought and to shape land use attitudes for centuries after the conquest. Ironically, the conquest drew attention to a class status which might otherwise have quietly passed away.

There were four major political divisions in Saxon England: the kingdom, the shire (called the *county* after the arrival of the Normans), the hundred, and the township, the last two being subdivisions of the shire or county. Throughout English history the exact nature of the government of the kingdom fluctuated, sometimes very radically. Changes occurred in the hundreds and the townships as the courts at these levels were gradually replaced by those of the local nobility, probably with the support of the government of the kingdom. The shire or county and its court or moot, however, persisted unchanged and continued to be one of the most important political units from the earliest Saxon times in England to the present day in both England and the United States.

The county court met to deal with cases not already handled by the hundred moots and with other business of common importance to the community. The meetings were conducted by three men: the alderman, representing the shire; the sheriff, representing the king; and the bishop, representing the church. All freemen in the county had the right to attend the court and participate in the decision process. Most of them, of course, were usually too busy to come except when personal interests were at stake.

There are only small differences between the county courts of Saxon and Norman times and those of modern rural America. The three judges, alderman, sheriff, and bishop, have been replaced by elected judges. Court procedure in most of these courts, however, remains as informal today as it was in pre-Norman England. In many, no record is kept by the court of its decisions and, in such cases, except for word of mouth and intermittent coverage by the news media, little is known of what goes on there. Court judges are primarily concerned with keeping the local landowners contented by resolving local differences and by providing the few community services under the administrative jurisdiction of the court, e.g., maintaining dirt or gravel roads. This casual form of government is replaced only when the county becomes urbanized, thereby enabling residents to incorporate it and enjoy extensive new administrative and legal powers and, of course, responsibilities.

The special considerations given to the local landowner by the modern rural county court reflects the relationship of Saxon freemen to the court at the time when such courts first came into existence. The court evolved out of the freemen's custom of consulting with his neighbors during local disputes as an alternative to physical combat between the parties involved. Thus, rather than being something imposed on the freemen from above, the court was created by them for their own convenience. Since the freemen gave up little or none of their personal power, the power of the court to enforce its decisions was really nothing more than the collective power of the freemen ultimately comprising the membership of the court. From the earliest times, freemen had had absolute control over all matters pertaining to their own landholdings. When county courts were formed, freemen retained this authority over what they considered to be their own personal affairs. This limitation on the power of the court was maintained for more than a thousand years as part of the traditional conception of what a county court is, and how it is supposed to function. Today, when a landowner demands to know what right the court or anyone else has to tell him what to do with his own land he is referring to the original limitations set on the authority of the county court, and is appealing to the rights which he has informally inherited from his political ancestors, Saxon or German freemen—specifically, the right to do as he pleases without considering any interests except his own.

A modern landowner's argument that he has the right to do as he wishes is normally composed of a set series of claims given in a specific order. First, he points out that he or his father or grandfather worked the land in question. Second, he asserts that his ownership of the land is based on the work or labor put into it. Finally, he proclaims the right of uncontrolled use as a result of his ownership claim. Not all of this argument is derived directly from the freemen's world view. As mentioned above, the modern concept of ownership was unknown to freemen who were engaged in landholding rather than landowning. In other respects, however, there are strong similarities between the views of modern landowners and those of the freemen.

Landholding among German freemen was based on work. A freeman, like the nineteenth-century American homesteader, took possession of a tract of land by clearing it, building a house and barns, and dividing the land into fields for the grazing of animals and for the growing of crops. In this way, his initial work established his claim to continued use.

This emphasis on work as the basis for landholding is especially clear in connection with inheritance. When plenty of vacant land was available, landholdings were never divided among the sons, but, as described above, the sons moved to unoccupied land nearby and started their own freehold farmsteads. Thus, inheritance in those early times was not the acquisition of land itself but rather the transferral of the right to acquire land through work. This distinction is reflected in the early German word for inheritance, *Arbi* in Gothic and *Erbi* in Old High German, both of which have the same root as the modern High German word, *Arbeit,* meaning work.[2]

Thus freemen were interested in land use rather than landownership. The right to land was determined by their social status as freemen and not by the fact that they or their fathers had occupied or possessed a particular piece of ground. The specific landholdings, thus, were not of major importance to the early freemen. Conceivably, they might move several times to new landholdings, abandoning the old, without the size of their landholdings being affected in any way. As mentioned above, it was their ability to use their holdings, the number of grazing animals, and slave workers they owned, not some form of ownership, which determined the size of their landholdings at any particular time in their lives.

Of course, once unoccupied land ceased to be readily available, freemen started paying much more attention to their land as property, encouraging the development of the idea of landownership in the modern sense. When the inheritance of sons became only the right to work a portion of their father's holdings, the transition from landholding to landowning was well on its way.

Until the time when there were no more unoccupied lands to move to, there was really no reason for freemen to be concerned with proper use or management of their land or for them to worry about possible long-term problems for themselves or their neighbors resulting from misuse and abuse of particular pieces of land. When a freeman lost his mobility, however, he did start trying to take somewhat better care of his land, occasionally practicing crop rotation and planting trees to replace those he cut down, but apparently these new necessities had little influence on his general conviction that as a freeman he had the right to use and even abuse his land as he saw fit.

Today's rural landowner finds himself in a situation not unlike that of freemen in the days when inheritance became the division of land rather than the multiplication of it. In the late eighteenth century and during most of the nineteenth, American rural landowners led a way of life much like that of prefeudal German freemen; now modern landowners face the same limitations their freeman ancestors did as feudal conditions began to develop. Although willing to take some steps toward good land management, especially those which provide obvious short-term benefit, when faced with broader issues involving the welfare of their neighbors and the local community and the protection and the preservation of the environment as a whole, they claim ancient rights which have come down to them from German freemen, and take advantage of their special influence with the local county court, a political institution as eager to please them today as it was more than a thousand years ago.

[2]Ross, *Land-Holding,* p. 24.

THOMAS JEFFERSON AND THE ALLODIAL RIGHTS
OF AMERICAN FARMERS

When British colonists arrived in North America, they brought with them the land laws and land practices that were current in England at that time. These included entail, primogeniture, and most other aspects of the feudal tenure system which had taken hold in England after the Norman Conquest. The American Revolution called into question the right of the king of England to lands in North America which in turn led to attempts to bring about major land reform—specifically, efforts to remove all elements of the feudal system from American law and practice and replace them with the older Saxon freehold tenure system. At the forefront of this movement was a young Virginian lawyer named Thomas Jefferson. According to Jefferson's biographer, Merrill D. Peterson, while social and economic forces may have already made the success of the land reform movement inevitable, Jefferson's efforts, nevertheless, "capped the development and exalted the principle of freehold tenure."[3] In any event, whether or not Jefferson caused the land reform, he did manage to identify himself with the effort to such a degree that his statements on the subject could later be used with great authority to justify additional reform, leading eventually to the Homestead Act of 1862. So great was Jefferson's influence on these later reforms that they are usually erroneously viewed as the fulfillment of a Jeffersonian dream arising out of new democratic principles rather than as the achievement of the much older dream of economically disadvantaged Saxon freemen dating back to the Norman Conquest.

From the first moment that Jefferson began airing his land tenure opinions, however, he made it completely clear that they were based entirely on Saxon, and not on Norman, common law. Thus, he consistently spoke of allodial rights—*allodial* being the adjectival form of the Old English word *allodium* which refers to an estate held in absolute dominion without obligation to a superior—i.e., the early German and Saxon freehold farmstead.

Jefferson's attitudes towards the disposition of land developed naturally out of his early studies of the origins of the British legal system, as he himself notes in a letter written some years later:

> The opinion that our lands were allodial possessions is one which I have very long held, and had in my eye during a pretty considerable part of my law reading which I found alwais strengthened it.

* * *

Jefferson's first public expression of his position came in a political pamphlet titled "A Summary View of the Rights of British America," published in Williamsburg, Philadelphia, and London in 1774 . . . Jefferson

---

[3]Merrill D. Peterson, *Thomas Jefferson and the New Nation: A Biography* (New York, London, and Oxford: Oxford University Press, 1970), p. 113.

claims that all British citizens came to America with the rights of Saxon freemen.

* * *

Noting the right of a Saxon freeman to settle his accounts and move to another realm at his own pleasure without obligation to the lord of his previous domain, Jefferson argues that this is also the case with the British citizens who moved to North America. According to this analogy, England has no more claim over residents of America than Germany has over residents of England. In accordance with Saxon tradition, the lands of North America belong to the people living there and not to the king of England.[4]

Later in the pamphlet, Jefferson expands on this point, arguing that the belief that the king owns North America is based on the erroneous claim that feudal law rather than Saxon law applies in British America:

> The introduction of the Feudal tenures into the kingdom of England, though antient, is well enough understood to set this matter in a proper light. In the earlier ages of the Saxon settlement feudal holdings were certainly altogether unknown, and very few, if any, had been introduced at the time of the Norman conquest. Our Saxon ancestors held their lands, as they did their personal property, in absolute dominion, disencumbered with any superior, answering nearly to the nature of those possessions which the Feudalists term Allodial: William the Norman first introduced that system generally.

According to Jefferson, William the Conqueror confiscated the lands of those who fell at the Battle of Hastings and these lands legally became subject to feudal duties, "but still much was left in the hands of his Saxon subjects, held of no superior, and not subject to feudal conditions." Later, Norman lawyers found ways to impose feudal burdens on the holders of these lands, "but still they had not been surrendered to the king, they were not derived from his grant, and therefore they were not holden of him." . . .

* * *

It is not the king, Jefferson declares, but the individual members of a society collectively or their legislature that determine the legal status of land, and, if they fail to act, then, in accordance with the traditions of Saxon freemen," each individual of the society may appropriate to himself such lands as he finds vacant, and occupancy will give him title."[5] Jefferson was addressing issues of great importance in the history of British legal and political philosophy. William the Conqueror had claimed title to all Anglo-Saxon estates, but the claim had never been fully accepted by the defeated Saxons who had continued to view themselves as freemen without any

---

[4]Thomas Jefferson, "A Summary View of the Rights of British America," In *The Portable Thomas Jefferson*, ed. Merrill D. Peterson (New York: Viking Press, 1975), pp. 4–5.

[5]Ibid., pp. 17–19.

legitimate legal obligation to their Norman rulers beyond what their German heritage had always required. The controversy was still adequately alive in the mid-seventeenth century for Thomas Hobbes, a major British political philosopher, to take up the issue on behalf of the crown. Hobbes writes in the *Leviathan:*

> . . . the First Law, is for Division of the Land it selfe: wherein the Soveraign assigneth to every man a portion, according as he, and not according as any Subject, or any number of them, shall judge agreeable to Equity, and the Common Good.

After a long discussion of the ancient Jewish conquest of Israel, Hobbes continues with the specific claim that Jefferson is disputing:

> . . . though a People coming into possession of a Land by warre, do not alwais exterminate the antient inhabitants . . . , but leave to many, or most, or all of them their Estates; yet it is manifest they hold them afterwards, as of the Victors distribution; as the people of *England* held all theirs of *William the Conquerour.*[6]

Jefferson, of course, did not succeed in refuting the claim of the king of England to all land in British America, but by arguing in terms of this old dispute, he gives his position a legal basis which would have strong appeal among Englishmen with Saxon backgrounds, assuring some political support of the American cause in England.

In 1776, Jefferson got the opportunity to try to turn his theory into practice. Although Jefferson is most famous for writing the *Declaration of Independence,* most of his time that year was spent working on his draft of the Virginia constitution and on the reform of various Virginia laws including the land reform laws. In his draft constitution, Jefferson included a provision which gave every person of full age the right to fifty acres of land "in full and absolute dominion." In addition, lands previously "holden of the crown in feesimple" and all other lands appropriated in the future were to be "holden in full and absolute dominion, of no superior whatever."[7] Although these provisions were deleted, and similar bills submitted to the legislature failed to pass, Jefferson, nevertheless, did succeed in getting the legislature to abolish the feudal inheritance laws, entail and primogeniture.

In a series of letters exchanged with Edmund Pendleton, the speaker of the House of Delegate, during the summer of 1776, Jefferson expresses his desire to reestablish ancient Saxon law in Virginia. In one letter, after insisting that unoccupied land should neither be rented nor given away in return for military service, Jefferson continues:

> Has it not been the practice of all other nations to hold their lands as their personal estate in absolute dominion? Are we not the better for what we have

---

[6]Thomas Hobbes, *Leviathan,* ed. C. B. MacPherson (Middlesex, England: Penguin Books, 1968), pt. 1, Chap. 24.

[7]Thomas Jefferson, "Draft Constitution for Virginia," in *Portable Jefferson,* p. 248.

hitherto abolished of the feudal system? Has not every restitution of the antient Saxon laws had happy effects? Is it not now better that we return at once to that happy system of our ancestors, the wisest and most perfect ever yet devised by the wit of man, as it stood before the 8th century?

As for the government selling the land, Jefferson was completely opposed. "I am against selling the land at all," he writes to Pendleton, "By selling the lands to them, you will disgust them, and cause an avulsion of them from the common union. They will settle the lands in spite of every body." This prediction proved to be remarkably correct as evidenced by the fact that the next eighty years of American history was cluttered with squatters illegally occupying government land and then demanding compensation for their "improvements" through special preemption laws.[8]

In 1784, when he was appointed to head the land committee in the Congress of the Confederacy, Jefferson had a second opportunity to re-establish the Saxon landholding system. Whether Jefferson tried to take advantage of this opportunity is not known because the report of the committee, called the Ordinance of 1784, contains nothing about allodial rights to land. In addition, it even contains recommendations for the selling of western lands as a source of revenue for the government. It should be noted, however, that in one respect at least the document still has a very definite Saxon ring to it. Jefferson managed to include in his report a recommendation that settlers be permitted to organize themselves into new states on an equal footing with the original colonies. This recommendation, which was retained in the Ordinance of 1787, a revised version of the earlier ordinance, not only created the political structure necessary to turn the thirteen colonies into a much larger union of states, but also provided future generations of Americans with an independence and mobility similar to that enjoyed by the early Saxon and German freemen. In his *Summary View* of 1774, as mentioned above, Jefferson had argued that just as the Saxons invading England had had the right to set up an independent government, so British Americans had the right to an independent government in North America. The Ordinances of 1784 and 1787 extended this right to movement and self-determination of American settlers leaving the jurisdiction of established states and moving into the interior of the continent. In large measure, it is thanks to this provision that Americans today are able to move from state to state without any governmental control in the form of visas, passports, immigration quotas, or the like, as unhassled by such details as were early German freemen.

The absence of any provisions specifically granting landowners full and absolute dominion over their land, however, does not mean that Jefferson abandoned this conception of landholding or ownership. Privately and in his published writings he continued to champion the right of Americans to small freehold farmsteads. The only major change seems to be that Jefferson stopped trying to justify his position in terms of historical precedents and instead began speaking in moral terms, claiming that small

[8]Jefferson to Edmund Pendleton, 13 August 1776, in *Papers of Thomas Jefferson*, 1: 492.

independent landholders were the most virtuous citizens any state could ever hope to have. In a letter to John Jay in 1785, Jefferson writes:

> Cultivators of the earth are the most valuable citizens. They are the most vigorous, the most independent, the most virtuous, and they are tied to their country and wedded to it's liberty and interests by the most lasting bands.[9]

In a letter to James Madison in the same year, he adds:

> Whenever there is in any country, uncultivated lands and unemployed poor, it is clear that the laws of property have been so far extended as to violate natural right. The earth is given as a common stock for man to labour and live on. If, for the encouragement of industry we allow it to be appropriated, we must take care that other employment be furnished to those excluded from that appropriation. If we do not the fundamental right to labour the earth returns to the unemployed. It is too soon yet in our country to say that every man who cannot find employment but who can find uncultivated land, shall be at liberty to cultivate it, paying a moderate rent. But it is not too soon to provide by every possible means that as few as possible shall be without a little portion of land. The small landholders are the most precious part of the state.[10]

*   *   *

Had Jefferson been alive in the late nineteenth century when his views were being cited in opposition to the preservation of Yellowstone or were he alive today to see his Saxon freemen busily sabotaging county planning and zoning, he might have become disillusioned with his faith in the virtues of independent rural landowners. Jefferson, after all, as a result of his purchase of the Natural Bridge, perhaps the first major act of nature preservation in North America, ranks as a very important figure in the history of the nature preservation movement. Unfortunately, however, Jefferson's homesteaders and their modern day descendants did not always retain his aesthetic interest in nature or his respect for sound agricultural management which he interwove with his Saxon land use attitudes to form a balanced land use philosophy.

In part, the callousness and indifference of most rural landowners to environmental matters reflects the insensitivity of ancient Saxon freemen who viewed land as something to be used for personal benefit and who, being semi-nomadic, were unconcerned about whether that use would result in irreparable damage to the particular piece of land that they held at any given point in their lives. In addition, however, it can also be traced back to the political philosophy and theory of property of John Locke, a seventeenth-century British philosopher, who had a major impact on the political views of Jefferson and most other American statesmen during the American Revolution and afterwards. This influence is the subject of the next section.

[9]Jefferson to John Jay, 23 August 1785, in *Portable Jefferson*, p. 384.
[10]Jefferson to James Madison, 28 October 1785, in *Portable Jefferson*, p. 397.

JOHN LOCKE'S THEORY OF PROPERTY

As noted above, German and Saxon freemen did not have a concept of landownership, but only of landholding. As long as there was plenty of land for everyone's use, they did not concern themselves with exact boundaries. Disputes arose only when two freemen wanted to use the same land at the same time. By the end of the Middle Ages, however, with land in short supply, landholders began enclosing their landholdings to help ensure exclusive use. Enclosure kept the grazing animals of others away and also provided a sign of the landholder's presence and authority. Although enclosure was only a small step towards the concept of landownership, it nonetheless proved useful as a pseudo-property concept in early seventeenth-century New England, where Puritans were able to justify their occupation of Indian lands on the grounds that the lack of enclosures demonstrated that the lands were vacant. Landownership became an official legal distinction in England after 1660 with the abolishment of feudal dues. The concept of landownership was introduced into British social and political philosophy thirty years later as part of John Locke's theory of property. This theory was presented in detail in Locke's *Two Treatises of Government,* a major work in political philosophy first published in 1690.[11]

Jefferson had immense respect and admiration for Locke and his philosophical writings. On one occasion, he wrote to a friend that Locke was one of the three greatest men that had ever lived—Bacon and Newton being the other two. Jefferson's justification of the American Revolution in "The Declaration of Independence" was borrowed directly from the *Second Treatise.* Many of Jefferson's statements in the document are almost identical to remarks made by Locke. For example, when Jefferson speaks of "life, liberty, and the pursuit of happiness," he is closely paraphrasing Locke's own views. His version differs from Locke's in only one minor respect: Jefferson substitutes for Locke's "enjoyment of property" the more general phrase "the pursuit of happiness," a slight change made to recognize other enjoyments in addition to those derived from the ownership of property. Years later, when Jefferson was accused by John Adams and others of having stolen most of his ideas from Locke's writings, he simply acknowledged his debt, pointing out that he had been asked to write a defense of the American Revolution in 1776, not to create an entirely new and original political philosophy. He added that he had not referred to Locke's writings when writing "The Declaration of Independence" or consciously tried to paraphrase Locke's remarks. Locke's influence on him, however, had been so strong that without his being fully aware of it, bits and pieces of Locke's own words had found their way into the document.[12]

Although Locke's political philosophy proved to be tailor-made for

---

[11]John Locke, *Two Treatises of Government,* ed. Thomas I. Cook (New York and London: Hafner Press, 1947).

[12]Jefferson to John Trumbull, 15 February 1789, in *Portable Jefferson,* pp. 434–35; Locke, *Second Treatise,* sec. 6; Carl Becker, *The Declaration of Independence: A Study in the History of Political Ideas* (New York: Knopf, 1960), pp. 24–28.

the American Revolution, it was actually the partisan product of a some-what earlier period of political turmoil in English history. Locke's *Two Treatises* was written and published near the end of a century characterized by major changes in the British political system. The power of the king and the aristocracy was beginning to give way to the kind of party system which still dominates British and American politics today. Locke had been a theological student at Oxford during Cromwell's dictatorship. During the subsequent reigns of Charles II and James II he was in exile in France and Holland, returning to England during the Glorious Revolution of 1688 with the new rulers, William and Mary. Locke wrote his *Two Treatises* for political purposes. He hoped to justify the revolution settlement and also to help create a political climate favorable to the political party of his late friend, Lord Shaftesbury. This party was an alliance of a few liberal aristo-crats with the discontented rich of London and other major towns.

A new theory of property ownership was important to these people. Previously, property rights had been tied to inheritance and to the divine rights of kings. A person owned property because his father and his fa-ther's father had owned it and also because at some point, at least the-oretically, the property had been given to his family by the king. The king's right to bestow property was based on certain agreements made between God and Adam, and later Noah, in which He gave the entire Earth to the children of God. The king, as a descendant of Adam and more importantly as God's designated agent, served more or less as an executor for the estate. Since the doctrine of the divine rights of the king was being rescinded by act of Parliament, a new theory of property was needed to justify private ownership.

The divine rights of kings had been defended by Robert Filmer in a book titled *Patriarcha*, published posthumously in 1280.[13] The *First Treatise* is a direct and all-out attack on Filmer's arguments. The *Second Treatise* develops Locke's own position. It is this position which I am primarily concerned with here.

In the *Second Treatise* Locke bases property rights on the labor of the individual:

> Though the Earth, and all inferior Creatures be common to all Men, yet, every Man has a *Property* in his own *Person*. This no Body has any Right to but himself. The *Labour* of his Body, and the *Work* of his Hands, we may say, are properly his. Whatsoever then he removes out of the State that Nature hath provided, and left in, he hath mixed his *Labour* with, and joyned to it some-thing that is his own, and thereby makes it his *Property*.[14]

This theory of property served Locke's friends well since it made their property rights completely independent of all outside interest. According to Locke, property rights are established without reference to kings, gov-

---

[13]Robert Filmer, *Patriarcha or the Natural Power of Kings*, in Locke, *Two Treatises*, pp. 299–310.

[14]Locke, *Second Treatise*, sec. 27.

ernments, or even the collective rights of other people. If a man mixes his labour with a natural object, then the product is his.

The relevance of Locke's labor theory to the American homestead land use philosophy becomes especially clear when he turns to the subject of land as property:

> But the *chief matter of Property* being now not the Fruits of the Earth, and the Beasts that subsist on it, but the *Earth it self* as that which takes in and carries with it all the rest; I think it is plain, that *Property* in that too is acquired as the former. *As much land* as a Man Tills, Plants, Improves, Cultivates, and can use the Product of, so much is his *Property.* He by his Labour does, as it were, inclose it from the Common. . . . God, when He gave the World in common to all Mankind, commanded Man also to labour, and the penury of his Condition required it of him. God and his Reason commanded him to subdue the Earth, *i.e.* improve it for the benefit of Life, and therein lay out something upon it that was his own, his labour. He that in Obedience to this Command of God, subdued, tilled, sowed any part of it, thereby annexed to it something that was his *Property,* which another had no Title to, nor could without injury take from him.[15]

In this passage, the right of use and ownership is determined by the farmer's labor. When he mixes his labor with the land, the results are *improvements,* the key term in homesteading days and even today in rural America where the presence of such improvements may qualify landowners for exemption from planning and zoning under a grandfather clause. Since property rights are established on an individual basis independent of a social context, Locke's theory of property also provides the foundation for the landowner's claim that society has little or no role in the management of his land, that nobody has the right to tell him what to do with his property.

* * *

Not everyone in the first half of the nineteenth century shared Jefferson's enthusiasm for land reform based on Saxon common law modified by Locke's theory of property, and for a time the idea of landholding independent of landowning continued to be influential in American political and legal thought. Early versions of the homestead bill before the beginning of the Civil War, for example, often contained inalienability and reversion clauses. According to these, a homesteader had the right to use the land, but could not subdivide it, sell it, or pass it on to his children after his death. These limitations, however, were not compatible with the wishes of potential homesteaders who wanted to be landowners, not just landholders, and, as a result, they were not included in the Homestead Act of 1862. It is unlikely that homesteading based entirely on Saxon common law ever had much chance of passing Congress because early nineteenth-century settlers squatting illegally on Western lands and demanding the enact-

---

[15]Ibid., sec. 32.

ment of special preemption laws had always had landownership as their primary objective.[16]

Because it was probably Locke's theory of property as much as Saxon common law which encouraged American citizens and immigrants to move westward, both should be given a share of the credit for the rapid settlement of the American West which ultimately established a national claim to all the lands west of the Appalachians as far as the Pacific. This past benefit to the American people, nevertheless, should not be the only standard for evaluating this doctrine's continuing value. We must still ask just how well the position is suited to conditions in twentieth-century America.

MODERN DIFFICULTIES WITH LOCKE'S POSITION

One obvious problem with Locke's theory today is his claim that there is enough land for everyone.[17] This premise is of fundamental importance to Locke's argument because, if a present or future shortage of land can be established, then any appropriation of land past or present under the procedure Locke recommends, enclosure from the common through labor, is an injustice to those who must remain unpropertied. By Locke's own estimates there was twice as much land at the end of the seventeenth century as all the inhabitants of the Earth could use. To support these calculations Locke pointed to the "in-land, vacant places of America"— places which are now occupied.[18] Since Locke's argument depends on a premise which is now false, Locke would have great difficulty advancing and justifying his position today.

Another problem is Locke's general attitude towards uncultivated land. Locke places almost no value on such land before it is improved and after improvement he says the labor is still the chief factor in any value assessment:

> . . . when any one hath computed, he will then see, how much *labour makes the far greatest part of the value* of things we enjoy in this World: And the ground which produces the materials, is scarce to be reckon'd in, as any, or at most, but a very small part of it; So little, that even amongst us, Land that is left wholly to Nature, that hath no improvement of Pasturage, Tillage, or Planting, is called, as indeed it is, *waste* and we shall find the benefit of it amount to little more than nothing.

According to Locke's calculations, 99 to 99.9 percent of the value of land even after it is improved still results from the labor and not the land. Although these absurdly high figures helped strengthen Locke's claim that labor establishes property rights over land, by making it seem that it is

[16]Paul W. Gates, *History of Public Land Law Development* (Washington, D.C.: Public Land Law Commission, 1968), pp. 390–93.

[17]Locke, *Second Treatise*, sec. 33.

[18]Ibid., sec. 36.

primarily the individual's labor mixed with the land rather than the land itself which is owned, such estimates, if presented today, would be considered scientifically false and contrary to common sense.[19]

Locke's land-value attitudes reflect a general desire prevalent in Locke's time as well as today for maximum agricultural productivity. From Locke's point of view, it was inefficient to permit plants and animals to grow naturally on uncultivated land:

> . . . I aske whether in the wild woods and uncultivated waste of America left to Nature, without any improvement, tillage, or husbandry, a thousand acres will yield the needy and wretched inhabitants as many conveniences of life as ten acres of equally fertile land doe in Devonshire where they are well cultivated?[20]

The problem, however, is not just productivity and efficiency, but also a general contempt for the quality of the natural products of the Earth. Locke writes with great conviction that "*Bread* is more worth than Acorns, *Wine* than Water, and *Cloth* or *Silk* than Leaves, Skins or Moss."[21] Even though we might be inclined to agree with Locke's pronouncements in certain contexts, the last two hundred years of the American experience have provided us with new attitudes incompatible with those of Locke and his contemporaries, and apparently completely unknown to them, which place high value on trees, water, animals, and even land itself in a wholly natural and unimproved condition. Unlike Locke, we do not always consider wilderness land or uncultivated land synonymous with waste.

At the very core of Locke's land-value attitudes is his belief that "the Earth, and all that is therein, is given to Men for the Support and Comfort of their being." In one sense, this view is very old, derived from the biblical and Aristotelian claims that the Earth exists for the benefit and use of human beings. At the same time, it is very modern because of Locke's twin emphasis on labor and consumption. Both of these activities are of central importance in communistic and capitalistic political systems, and they became so important precisely because the founders and ideologists of each system originally took their ideas about labor and consumption from Locke's philosophy. In accordance with these ideas, the Earth is nothing more than raw materials waiting to be transformed by labor into consumable products. The Greeks and Romans would have objected to this view on the grounds that labor and consumption are too low and demeaning to be regarded as primary human activites.[22] From a twentieth-century standpoint, given the current emphasis on consumption, the neglect of the aesthetic and scientific (ecological) value of nature seems to be a more fundamental and serious objection to this exploitative view.

[19]Ibid., sec. 42–43.

[20]Ibid., sec. 37.

[21]Ibid., sec. 42.

[22]Ibid., sec. 26; for a full discussion of labor and consumption see Hannah Arendt, *The Human Condition* (Chicago and London: University of Chicago Press, 1958), chap. 3.

The worst result of Locke's property theory is the amoral or asocial attitude which has evolved out of it. Locke's arguments have encouraged landowners to behave in an antisocial manner and to claim that they have no moral obligation to the land itself, or even to the other people in the community who may be affected by what they do with their land. This amoral attitude, which has been noted with dismay by Aldo Leopold, Garrett Hardin, and others, can be traced directly to Locke's political philosophy, even though Locke himself may not have intended to create this effect. The reasons why this moral apathy developed are complex.

First, the divine rights of kings had just been abolished. In accordance with this doctrine, the king had had *ultimate* and *absolute* property rights over all the land in his dominion. He could do whatever he wanted with this land—give it away, take it back, use it himself, or even destroy it as he saw fit. Locke's new theory of property stripped the king of this power and authority and transferred these *ultimate* and *absolute* rights to each and every ordinary property owner. This transfer has been a moral disaster in large part because the king's rights involved moral elements which did not carry over to the new rights of the private landowner. As God's agent on Earth, the king was morally obligated to adhere to the highest standards of right and wrong. Furthermore, the king, as the ruler of the land, had a moral and political obligation to consider the general welfare of his entire kingdom whenever he acted. Of course, kings did not always behave as they should have, but, nevertheless, there were standards recognized by these kings and their subjects as to what constituted proper and kingly moral behavior. Private landowners, however, did not inherit these sorts of obligations. Because they were not instruments of church or state, the idea that they should have moral obligations limiting their actions with regard to their own property does not seem to have come up. The standard which landowners adopted to guide their actions was a purely selfish and egotistical one. Because it involved nothing more than the economic interest of the individual, it was devoid of moral obligation or moral responsibility.

* * *

This difficulty is revealed momentarily in the *First Treatise* where Locke argues that property owners have the right to destroy their property if they can derive an advantage from doing so. Locke apparently feels compelled to acknowledge the right of property owners to destroy *in general* in order to justify the killing of animals for food but, obviously uneasy about the point he has just made, he adds that the government has the responsibility of making sure that this destruction does not adversely affect the property of others:

> Property, whose Original is the Right a Man has to use any of the Inferior Creatures, for Subsistence and Comfort of his life, is for the benefit and sole Advantage of the Proprietor, so that he may even destroy the thing, that he has Property in by his use of it, where need requires; but Government being

for the Preservation of every Man's Right and Property, by preserving him from the Violence or Injury of others, is for the good of the Governed.[23]

Ironically, the very rights to property which the government is supposed to protect hinder or even prevent the government from carrying out this responsibility.

*   *   *

Government regulation of individual private landowners has been ineffective historically because, from the very beginnings of American government, representation at state and federal levels has nearly always been based on landownership, an approach which has usually assured rural control of the legislature even when most of the citizens in the state lived in urban population centers. Government leaders intent on acting primarily in the interests of landowners could hardly have been expected to play the preventive role which Locke recommends. The unwillingness of legislators to act in this way in the nineteenth century and most of the twentieth, moreover, further contributed to the amoral belief of rural landowners that they can do whatever they want without being concerned about the welfare or rights of others.

When Jefferson attempted to build American society on a Lockeian foundation of small landowners, he did so in large measure because he believed that small landowners would make the most virtuous citizens. He failed to foresee, however, that the independence provided by Locke's presocietal natural rights would discourage rather than encourage social responsibility, and, therefore, would contribute little to the development of moral character in American landowners. Since social responsibility is basic to our conception of morality today, the claim of landowners that their special rights relieve them of any obligation or responsibility to the community can be regarded only as both socially and morally reprehensible. The position of such rural landowners is analogous to that of a tyrannical king. Tyranny is always justified, when it is justified at all, by a claim that the tyrant has the *right* to do as he pleases regardless of the consequences. In practice, however, the impact of rural landowners more closely approaches anarchy than tyranny, but only because landowners, though sharing a common desire to preserve their special rights. do not always have common economic interests. As a result, landowners are usually more willing to promote the theoretical rights of their fellow property owners than their specific land use and development projects, which as members of society, they may find objectionable or even despicable—in spite of their Saxon and Lockeian heritage rather than because of it.

*   *   *

[23]Locke, *First Treatise*, sec. 92; Locke also addresses this point to some degree in the *Second Treatise*, sec. 31, where he writes that "Nothing was made by God for Man to spoil or destroy." Here Locke emphasizes the abundance of the nautral things supplied by God and states that human beings who set limits on themselves with their reason will not claim more than their fair share.

Today, of course, whenever Locke's theory of property and the heritage of the ancient Saxon freeman surface in county courts, at planning and zoning meetings, and at state and federal hearings on conservation and land management, they still remain a formidable obstacle to constructive political action. As they are normally presented, however, they are certainly not an all-purpose answer to our environmental problems or even a marginally adequate reply to environmental criticism. When a landowner voices a Lockeian argument he is consciously or unconsciously trying to evade the land management issues at hand and to shift attention instead to the dogmatic recitation of his special rights as a property owner.

*   *   *

"Taking" Issues[1]

Philip Soper

Of constitutional obstacles likely to confront future environmental legislation none looms potentially larger than the problem of determining when compensation is required in order to sustain regulations restricting the use of private property. The problem, which arises from the Fifth Amendment's provision that "private property" shall not "be taken for public use without just compensation," is likely to become increasingly important for two reasons. First, despite extensive scholarly discussion[2] and literally thousands of state court opinions on the issue, the line between constitutional "takings," which require compensation, and exercises of "the police power," which do not, has never been drawn clearly enough to justify confident prediction of the outcome of the issue in all cases. Second, although the resulting uncertainty would perhaps be less significant if the

[1]The discussion in this section reflects the results of a similar exploration of the "taking issue" prepared by the author as a staff member of the Council on Environmental Quality (CEQ) for use in the Council's fourth Annual Report. *See* CEQ, Fourth Annual Report, chapter 4 (September 1973).

[2]See, e.g., Van Alstyne, *Statutory Modification of Inverse Condemnation: The Scope of Legislative Power,* 19 Stan. L. Rev. 727 (1967); Van Alstyne, *Taking or Damaging by Police Power: The Search for Inverse Condemnation Criteria,* 44 S. Cal. L. Rev. 1 (1970); Michelman, *Property, Utility, and Fairness: Comments on the Ethical Foundations of "Just Compensation" Law,* 80 Harv. L. Rev. 1165 (1967); Sax, *Takings, Private Property and Public Rights,* 81 Yale L. J. 149 (1971); Sax, *Takings and the Police Power,* 74 Yale L. J. 36 (1964); Dunham, *Griggs v. Allegheny County in Perspective: Thirty Years of Supreme Court Expropriation Law,* 1962, Sup. Ct. Rev. 63; Kratovil & Harrison, *Eminent Domain—Policy and Concept,* 42 Calif. L. Rev. 596 (1954).

issue were to arise only infrequently, such is not likely to be the case in the environmental context. New interest in a wide variety of land use regulations[3] points to potential conflict on a broad front between society's desire to preserve certain resources or to regulate environmentally critical features of land, and the desire of private landowners to maximize the economic value of such land. While easy resolution of this conflict can hardly be expected, a brief review of the dominant themes in the judicial approach to the "taking" issue may furnish a basis for anticipating or suggesting directions for the future.

A. THE STANDARD JUDICIAL APPROACH: "NO SET FORMULA"

Among the earliest Supreme Court decisions construing the takings clause of the Fifth Amendment is the Court's decision in the latter part of the 19th century in *Mugler v. Kansas*.[4] The Court in that case upheld a Kansas ordinance forbidding the manufacture and sale of intoxicating liquors without requiring compensation of the existing brewery owners for the resulting ruin of their business. Nearly 100 years later, in *Goldblatt v. Town of Hempstead*,[5] the extent of the Court's progress in developing a consistent takings theory seemed aptly expressed in the Court's statement that "[t]here is no set formula to determine where regulation ends and taking begins."[6] Like *Mugler*, *Goldblatt* also upheld the challenged governmental regulation, which prohibited certain mining practices and required owners to fill mined areas, without providing compensation for the resulting economic loss.

The mine owners in *Pennsylvania Coal Co. v. Mahon*[7] on the other hand—perhaps the best known Supreme Court takings decision—were more fortunate. There the Court held invalid state legislation forbidding the mining of coal in a manner that would undercut the surface land on which homes, public buildings, and streets had been built. Since the mining companies had previously enjoyed the right to mine in such manner (and homeowners and the public had presumably purchased only surface rights), subsequent legislation, the Court held, could not undo the economic relationship to the disadvantage of one side without providing compensation for the resulting loss.

The absence of a "set formula" to explain these differences in result does not mean that no rational distinctions can be made. Indeed the greater danger is that too many and apparently conflicting formulas will be found to fill the resulting void.

Such, in fact, appears to be the current status of takings theory in the

[3]See the chapter on land use.
[4]123 U.S. 623 (1887).
[5]369 U.S. 590 (1962).
[6]*Id.* at 594.
[7]260 U.S. 393 (1922).

courts. Instead of a single formula, at least four theories for deciding when a "taking" occurs emerge from the court opinions, with no single theory providing either a consistent or acceptable explanation for the results in all cases. These four theories may be described as: the "physical invasion" theory; the "nuisance abatement" theory; the "diminution of value" theory: and the "balancing" (of public good v. individual loss) theory.[8] A brief review of the role these theories have played in the development of the judicial approach to the takings issue may help illustrate why the issue remains a troublesome one.

1. The Physical Invasion Theory

In some respects, the physical invasion theory is at once the most obvious test for taking, and at the same time the least satisfactory. The attractiveness of the theory lies in the fact that it seems to embody the paradigm case of governmental confiscation. Where public agents, for example, assume actual legal control over private property, for instance, by compelling transfer of title from the former owner to the government, a classic case of the use of the eminent domain power seems to be presented requiring compensation. The difficulty arises once one attempts to transform this theory from a *sufficient* "test for taking," into a *necessary* test. It takes little reflection to realize that actual transfer of title is not needed in order effectively to appropriate the use of a person's property. In an early Supreme Court decision, for example, *Pumpelly v. Green Bay Company*,[9] the Court agreed that a taking had occurred where the complainant's land had been flooded pursuant to state law providing for the construction of dams for the purpose of flood control. "It would be a very curious and unsatisfactory result," explained the Court:

> if . . . it shall be held that if the government refrains from the absolute conversion of real property to the uses of the public it can destroy its value entirely, can inflict irreparable and permanent injury to any extent, can, in effect, subject it to total destruction without making any compensation, because, in the narrowest sense of the word, it is not taken for the public use.[10]

At the very least, it seems, the essence of the classic case must lie, not in the actual transfer of title, but in the physical appropriation, by whatever means, of the right otherwise enjoyed by the owner to use and enjoy his property.

2. The Nuisance Abatement Theory

Once started down this path of reasoning, however, it is not easy to stop. It is not easy, for example, to explain why the appropriation of the

---

[8]Much of the discussion in the text draws on the identification and analysis of these four theories as presented in Sax, *Takings and the Police Power*, 74 *Yale L. J.* 36 (1964), and Michelman, *supra* note 2.

[9]80 U.S. (13 Wall.) 166 (1871).

[10]*Id.* at 177.

owner's right to control the use of his property must be the result of a physical intrusion.[11] The typical case of government impairment of a property owner's use opportunities, certainly in the modern context, arises from the use of the simple but effective technique of enacting legislation limiting the uses to which such land can be put.

Accordingly, three additional judicial theories have emerged for determining whether compensation is required in the case of regulations that do not result in actual physical invasions. The first theory, which might be called the nuisance abatement theory, is illustrated by *Mugler v. Kansas*, mentioned above. In explaining why compensation was not required in *Mugler*, in contrast to *Pumpelly*, Justice Harlan observed that in the former case the state was only acting to prohibit a publicly offending use of the property in question:

> The power which the States have of prohibiting such use by individuals of their property . . . cannot be burdened with the condition that the State must compensate such individual owners for pecuniary losses they may sustain, by reason of their not being permitted, by a noxious use of their property, to inflict injury upon the community. The exercise of the police power by the destruction of property which is itself a public nuisance, or the prohibition of its use in a particular way, whereby its value becomes depreciated, is very different from taking property for public use . . . In the one case, a nuisance only is abated; in the other, unoffending property is taken away from an innocent owner.[12]

This theory, also called the "noxious use theory"[13] or "private fault"[14] theory, expresses the idea that where private property is used in a manner that harms the general public, compensation is not required when the public reacts to protect itself from the nuisance-like use.[15]

The nuisance abatement theory has been relied on by courts to sustain a wide variety of regulations. Particularly where health or safety is involved, regulations requiring individuals to bear the expense of conforming to public standards in the area have been treated almost as if they

---

[11]The anomalies that result if one assumes that a physical invasion must accompany the restriction on property use are perhaps no where better illustrated than in the "inverse condemnation" cases involving airport noise. Those cases are explored at greater length in the chapter on noise. Like the water flooding complainant's land in *Pumpelly*, the noise of aircraft flying over one's land can reduce use opportunities to the point where compensation is required, as the Supreme Court held in *United States v. Causby*, 328 U.S. 256 (1946). But the aftermath of *Causby*, under the influence of the "physical invasion" theory, has produced a "fly-over, fly-by" distinction, that awards compensation in one case and denies it in another solely on the basis of whether actual penetration of an "owner's airspace" took place, even though the cases may otherwise be identical in terms of the impairment of the owner's ability to use or enjoy his property. See the chapter on noise.

[12]123 U.S. at 669.

[13]Sax, *supra* note 8, at 48.

[14]Michelman, *supra* note 2 at 1196.

[15]See E. Freund, *The Police Power* § 511 (1904).

enjoyed "a special presumption of constitutionality."[16] Cases supporting the uncompensated destruction of diseased trees,[17] animals,[18] and crops,[19] or upholding food and drug laws, occupational safety standards, fire regulations and the like[20] without compensating owners for the resulting expense are typical examples of the theory in operation.

The nuisance abatement theory is, however, subject to criticism to the extent that the application presupposes that the individual subject to the regulation is somehow to blame for the nuisance caused by his activities and hence is *for that reason* in no position to complain of the economic loss that mandatory abatement entails.[21] The problem with this line of reasoning is illustrated by Justice Sutherland's widely quoted statement that "a nuisance may be merely a right thing in the wrong place."[22] In many cases, the use that is being made of private property may have been lawful and inoffensive when begun, only to be turned into a "nuisance" because of changed conditions resulting from new growth or new use patterns in the surrounding area. A classic illustration is *Hadacheck v. Sebastian*,[23] where the complainant's brick manufacturing operation was drastically reduced in value as the result of a city ordinance forbidding the use of brick kilns in a residential neighborhood. The Supreme Court sustained the ordinance without requiring compensation even though whatever nuisance was caused from the smoke and fumes of the operation was the result of subsequent residential development significantly postdating the manufacturer's operation. To say who in such a case is "in the wrong place" and hence a "nuisance"—is to announce a result rather than to explain it.

The point is not that cases upholding land-use controls on a nuisance theory are wrongly decided, but only that some better rationale is needed to explain the result than one that denies compensation on the ground that a private owner is to blame for an activity that has become a "nuisance" to neighboring owners or the public. One such rationale, preferred by Professor Sax[24] suggests that compensation should never be required as a constitutional matter when the courts are acting, as in the above cases, solely in an "arbitral capacity" to resolve conflicting land use desires of private property owners. This suggestion will be explored briefly below.

[16] 1 United States Water Resources Council, Regulation of Flood Hazard Areas, 389 (1971).

[17] See, e.g., *Miller v. Schoene*, 276 U.S. 272 (1928); *State Plant Bd. v. Smith*, 110 So.2d 401 (Fla. 1959).

[18] See, e.g., *Jones v. State*, 240 Ind. 230, 163 N.E. 2d 605 (1960) (and cases cited).

[19] See, e.g. *Wallace v. Feehan*, 206 Ind. 522, 190 N.E. 438 (1934).

[20] See generally, United States Water Resources Council, *supra* note 16, at 389, and cases cited.

[21] Evidence of this presupposition at work is particularly clear in the so-called "grade crossing" cases, in which railroads have consistently been required to bear the expense of separating railroad tracks from intersecting highways. See, e.g., *Erie Railroad v. Board of Public Utility Comm'rs.*, 254 U.S. 394, 410–11 (1921); Sax, *supra* note 8, 49.

[22] *Village of Euclid v. Ambler Realty Co.*, 272 U.S. 365, 388 (1926).

[23] 239 U.S. 394 (1915).

[24] See Sax, *Takings, Private Property and Public Rights*, 81 *Yale L. J.* 149 (1971).

3. The Balancing Theory

A third taking theory (and a second formula for determining when regulation requires compensation) employs what might be called a general balancing test. Under this test competing interests, as evidenced by the particular facts of each case, are weighed against each other. On one side of the balance, presumably, would be the extent of the government's intrusion as measured by the economic or physical loss to the individual; on the other side would be the public benefit derived from the government action, including, for example the alleviation of a nuisance-like activity. A number of courts[25] and commentators[26] have explicitly embraced some such balancing test.

While this approach at least has the merit of being able to accommodate almost any example of alleged governmental taking, the doctrinal basis for the theory is somewhat questionable. Presumably the theory would make the need for compensation inversely proportional to the degree of public gain: the greater the gain, the less likely that a taking will be found and vice versa. But the public benefit to be gained from the action, while it may be relevant in deciding that government action is proper at all, does not seem obviously relevant to whether compensation is required.[27] Private property is not to be taken at all except "for a public purpose," and one might well argue that the more evident the public purpose, the more willing the public ought to be to bear the expense of realizing its interest, rather than shifting the burden entirely to a single individual.

Furthermore, the fact that the balancing theory is seldom applied in the converse case, to permit uncompensated physical appropriation where the public gain far outweighs the economic loss to the individual, also casts doubt on the validity of the theory's basic rationale.

4. The Diminution of Value Theory

The theory that seems to figure most prominently in judicial opinions on the taking issue centers the analysis on the extent of the economic loss that governmental action has caused to the complaining landowner. The persistence of the theory is perhaps explained by at least two factors. First, as noted above, discomfort with the logic of the physical invasion theory is most notable when cases otherwise identical in terms of impairment of the owner's use of his property are treated differently solely on the basis of whether a physical invasion occurred. Thus the natural step is to abandon physical invasion as a necessary test for taking, and to focus instead on what appears as the remaining crucial element: destruction of the economic value of the landowner's property, however it occurs.

---

[25]See, e.g., *Rochester Business Institute, Inc. v. City of Rochester*, 25 App. Div. 2d 97, 267 N.Y.S.2d 274 (1966); *La Salle Nat'l Bank v. Cook County*, 60 Ill. App. 2d 39, 51, 208 N.E. 2d 430, 436 (1965).

[26]See e.g., Kratovil & Harrison, *supra* note 2, at 609.

[27]See Michelman, *supra* note 2, at 1194.

Second, perhaps the most important prominent Supreme Court decision in this area, *Pennsylvania Coal Co. v. Mahon*,[28] seems to support the view that a drastic reduction in the economic value of property necessarily triggers the need for compensation. As noted above, the case involved a statute prohibiting the mining of coal in such a way as to cause the subsidence of surface structures. Justice Holmes explained the Court's decision that the coal companies were entitled to compensation for the resulting loss of mining rights as follows:

> One fact for consideration in determining [the limits of the police power] is the extent of the diminution. When it reaches a certain magnitude, in most if not all cases there must be an exercise of eminent domain and compensation to sustain the act. . . .
> The general rule, at least, is that while property may be regulated to a certain extent, if regulation goes too far it will be recognized as a taking.[29]

It should be noted that the diminution of value theory seems to serve at best only as a sufficient, not a necessary, test for taking. Thus, actual physical appropriation of land almost always remains a taking even though the intrusion is economically slight[30] Furthermore, even as a sufficient test for taking, the diminution of value theory is not easily reconciled with the "nuisance abatement" theory discussed above under which courts have not hesitated to uphold legislation prohibiting a "noxious" use, even though the result is virtual destruction of economic value. Indeed, Justice Brandeis' dissenting opinion in *Pennsylvania Coal* indicates that resolution of the taking issue in a particular case will often depend on which theory a court decides should take precedence. Apparently relying on the nuisance abatement theory, Justice Brandeis would have sustained the Pennsylvania statute:

> Every restriction upon the use of property imposed in the exercise of the police power deprives the owner of some right theretofore enjoyed, and is, in that sense, an abridgment by the State of rights in property without making compensation. But restriction imposed to protect the public health, safety or morals from dangers threatened is not a taking. The restriction here in question is merely the prohibition of a noxious use. . . . Whenever the use prohibited ceases to be noxious,—as it may because of further change in local or social conditions,—the restriction will have to be removed and the owner will again be free to enjoy his property as heretofore.[31]

---

[28]260 U.S. 393 (1922).

[29]*Id.* at 413, 415. Recent literature on the taking issue describes *Pennsylvania Coal* as a case employing a balancing test. See studies cited in note 59, *infra*. If that description were accurate, there would be much less need to worry about the case as a potential obstacle to needed land use regulation. But as the quoted passages in the text suggest—and as the contrasting approach of Justice Brandeis illustrates—Justice Holmes' opinion seems to leave no room for countervailing interests, however strong, to tip the balance against compensation, once the diminution in value has reached "a certain magnitude."

[30]See Michelman, *supra* note 2, at 1184–85, 1191.

[31]260 U.S. at 417.

Although the diminution of value theory has been criticized both on historical grounds and in terms of its basic rationale,[32] the most troublesome aspect of the theory is its failure to provide a clear guide to the magnitude of the harm that must be inflicted before compensation is required. Justice Holmes' explanation that a taking occurs when the diminution in value reaches "a certain magnitude" or when regulation goes "too far," leaves unresolved the critical issue of how much is too much. In consequence, a number of subsidiary formulas have been devised by lower courts. Thus cases fairly consistently agree that a taking does not occur merely because a landowner is not allowed to make the most profitable use of his land,[33] or is not allowed to realize speculative investment potential.[34] At the other end of the scale, regulations depriving property of all potential value or use are often condemned solely on the diminution of value theory.[35] Most cases, however, lie somewhere between these extremes, with the result that courts typically resort to a formula that awards and denies compensation depending on whether a "reasonable use" of the property remains in the face of the restricting legislation. Furthermore, a "reasonable use" in most cases seems to mean some economically profitable use, rather than any possible use.[36]

In addition to the practical problems of deciding whether an owner has been left with a "reasonable" remaining use, the diminution in value theory suffers from certain inherent definitional problems. As Justice Brandeis pointed out, dissenting in *Pennsylvania Coal,* the degree of loss will differ depending on whether one simply calculates the value of the coal rendered inaccessible, or compares that value with the total value of the mining companies' property. In the former case, one might conclude that the mining rights have been totally destroyed; in the latter case, one might conclude that the *relative* economic harm, and hence the owner's ability to bear the loss, is not so significant as to require compensation. These ambiguities in deciding what the particular "thing" is that has been adversely affected and in deciding what consequent proportion of its value is thus destroyed have led commentators to question the adequacy of the theory.[37]

B. THE "STANDARD APPROACH" IN THE MODERN CONTEXT: ILLUSTRATIVE RECENT CONTROVERSIES

As might be expected, the absence of a single theory to determine when regulation amounts to a "taking," has led to a parallel lack of uniformity among states in resolving the issue in essentially similar fact situations. A

[32]See Sax, *supra* note 8, at 50.

[33]See e.g., *Goldblatt v. Town of Hempstead,* 369 U.S. 590 (1962).

[34]260 U.S. at 417; see generally 1 Anderson, *The American Law of Zoning* §2.20 at 85 *et seq.*

[35]See *United States Water Resources Council supra* note 16, at 398 n.91 and cases cited.

[36]See, e.g., *Arverne Bay Construction Co. v. Thatcher,* 278 N.Y. 222, 15 N.E. 2d 587 (1938).

[37]See Michelman, *supra* note 1, at 1192; Sax, *supra* note 24, at 151–55.

good example is provided by the "wetlands" cases,[38] testing the validity of regulations restricting an owner's right to fill or otherwise develop low-lying marsh or coastal lands. Such restrictions, prompted both by flood control concerns and by a desire to preserve resources critical for the conservation and development of wildlife, often result in depriving the private owner of such land of all potential development value.

The tendency of some courts, in such cases, seems to be to require compensation solely on the diminution of value theory. The Supreme Court of Maine, for example, in *Maine v. Johnson*[39] held the State Wetlands Act invalid as applied to the particular land at issue on the basis of lower court findings that appellants' land absent the addition of fill "has no commercial value whatever."[40] Although the *Johnson* opinion also elaborates in some detail on the public interest in preserving the valuable marsh-land resource, such elaboration appears to be little more than window dressing in light of the court's reliance on a formula that automatically equates the extreme loss of commercial value with a constitutional taking.[41]

To similar effect is the New Jersey decision in *Morris County Land Improvement Co. v. Parsippany-Troy Hills*[42] holding invalid a meadow development zone as applied to certain swamp lands. Although the zoning legislation in that case allowed a wide variety of explicitly stated uses, the court noted that many of these uses were "public or *quasi*-public in nature, rather than of the type available to the ordinary private landowner as a reasonable means of obtaining a return from his property. . . ." In the court's view, "about the only practical use which can be made of property within the zone is a hunting or fishing preserve or a wildlife sanctuary, none of which can be considered productive." The court accordingly concluded that a taking had occurred under a theory requiring compensation where:

> the ordinance so restricts the use that the land cannot practically be utilized for any reasonable purpose or when the only permitted uses are those to which the property is not adapted or which are economically infeasible.[43]

Two recent Connecticut cases follow a similar pattern. In *Dooley v. Town Plan & Zoning Comm'n* of the Town of Fairfield[44] legislation placing land in a flood plain zone where no improvements were permitted was held invalid. The case admittedly involved an additional complicating factor: the land at issue had only recently been assessed with an $11,000 special levy for a sewage district, thus adding to the apparent harshness of the subse-

[38]See the chapter on wetlands.

[39]265 A.2d 711 (1970).

[40]*Id.* at 716.

[41]The continued validity of the decision in *Maine v. Johnson* may, however, be in doubt in light of the more recent decision of the State's supreme court upholding provisions of Maine's Site Location of Development Law. See in Re Spring Valley Development, Me., 300 A.2d 736, 3 ELR 20589 (1973).

[42]40 N.J. 539, 193 A.2d 232 (1963).

[43]*Id.* at 557, 193 A.2d at 242.

[44]151 Conn. 304, 197 A.2d 770 (1964).

quent land-use restriction. In *Bartlett v. Zoning Commission* of the Town of Old Lyme,[45] however, the court left little doubt that it was following a straightforward diminution of value theory. Tidal wetland restrictions in that case were held invalid on the basis of a finding that as a result of the restrictions "the plaintiff's use of his property is practically nonexistent."[46]

In contrast to these cases, decisions in Massachusetts and California, apparently employing a more flexible balancing test, have upheld similar wetland regulations despite the resulting destruction of commercial value. The Massachusetts court, in *Turnpike Realty Co. v. Town of Dedham*, explained its decision as follows:

> Although it is clear that the petitioner is substantially restricted in its use of the land, such restrictions must be balanced against the potential harm to the community from overdevelopment of a flood plain area.[47]

In *Candlestick Properties, Inc. v. San Francisco Bay C. & D. Comm'n.*[48] the California Court of Appeals reached a similar result in upholding the denial of a permit to fill bay lands, but the rationale for the result was less explicit. Complainant's evidence showed that the land in issue, which was submerged at high tide by the waters of San Francisco Bay, had been acquired in 1964 at a cost of $40,000 specifically "as a place to deposit fill from construction projects." Thus the land had no value "except as a place to deposit fill and as filled land."[49] Without disputing this evidence, the court nevertheless upheld the fill restriction, apparently relying on two considerations. First, the court noted the strong public interest in the restriction:

> [T]he Legislature has determined that the bay is the most valuable single natural resource of the entire region and changes in one part of the bay may also affect all other parts; that the present uncoordinated, haphazard manner in which the bay is being filled threatens the bay itself and is therefore inimical to the welfare of both present and future residents of the bay area; and that a regional approach is necessary to protect the public interest in the bay.[50]

Second, the court agreed that "an *undue* restriction" could amount to a taking, citing *Pennsylvania Coal Co. v. Mahon*,[51] but concluded that "it cannot be said that refusing to allow appellant to fill its bay amounts to an undue restriction on its use."[52]

[45]161 Conn. 24, 282 A.2d 907, 1 ELR 20177 (1971).

[46]*Id.* at 31, 282 A.2d at 910, 1 ELR at 20178.

[47] _____Mass._____, 284 N.E.2d 891, 900,3 ELR 20221,20224 (1972), *cert. den.* 409 U.S. 1108 (1973).

[48]11 Cal. App. 3d 557, 89 Cal. Rptr. 897, 3 ELR 20446 (1970).

[49]*Id.* at 562, 89 Cal. Rptr. at 899, 3 ELR 20447.

[50]*Id.* at 571, 89 Cal. Rptr. at 905, 3 ELR at 20447.

[51]260 U.S. 393 (1922).

[52]11 Cal. App.3d 572, 89 Cal. Rptr. at 906.

It is this latter conclusion that provides the contrast with the Connecticut and New Jersey decisions, noted above, and it is interesting to note how the California court attempted to distinguish both the decision in *Dooley* and in *Parsippany-Troy Hills.* In *Dooley,* the court explained:

> the restrictions placed upon the use of the plaintiff's land were so extensive that the land could be used for no other purpose than for a flood control district, with the result that the land was depreciated in value by 75%.[53]

In view of the undisputed evidence of the effect of the fill restriction on the value of the plaintiff's land in *Candlestick,* this attempt at distinction seems questionable. More to the point, perhaps, is the courts explanation of how the case differed from *Parsippany-Troy Hills:*

> The purpose of the regulations and restrictions imposed in the instant case is not merely to provide open spaces. Rather, they are designed to preserve the existing character of the bay *while it is determined how the bay should be developed in the future* [emphasis added].[54]

The *Candlestick* opinion thus seems to suggest three possible theories for upholding legislation despite extensive or complete destruction of economic value. The court may be saying: (1) that "reasonable remaining uses" are not to be measured solely in economic terms; (2) that however severe the restriction, it is not "undue" where the public interest is sufficiently great; (3) that a taking does not occur where a mere moratorium is placed on development, pending the completion of a comprehensive plan for rational and controlled future development of the area. In the last case, of course, resolution of the taking issue may simply have been postponed until the formulation of a more complete conservation and development plan. But under any of these theories, the "diminution of value" test of *Pennsylvania Coal* appears to have been modified significantly to allow the public interest in preserving existing features of the bay to outweigh the conflicting interest of the private owner in making an economically profitable use of his land.

C. UPDATING THE STANDARD APPROACH: THE RELEVANCE OF NEW ENVIRONMENTAL CONCERNS

It is not the purpose of this discussion to develop a single, consistent theory for dealing with the taking issue in all cases. Indeed, despite the criticisms that have been aimed at various judicial formulations, it may well be that no single formula is either possible or desirable. All such formulas, for example, may prove to be only extrapolations from what is basically an ethical judgment about the fairness of refusing to distribute across a broad base

[53]*Id.*
[54]*Id.*

the costs entailed in implementing certain public programs perceived to have positive net benefits.[55] As such, the taking clause, like the Due Process Clause and other constitutional expressions of broad social policy, may be expected to reflect changes in society in a way that allows doctrinal development to keep pace with shifting priorities in societal values. It is in this sense that the judicial approach to the taking clause bears re-examination in light of emerging environmental concerns.

The most obvious starting point for conducting such a re-examination is the concept of private property itself. It has never been the law, of course, that title to land automatically entitled the owner to use the land however he pleased. The common law of nuisance, for example, has long placed limits on the means by which one may realize economic gain from land. Property rights, in short, do not exist independently of the protections and responsibilities linked with such rights by the law. As those legal protections and responsibilities change to reflect new social and economic perceptions of society, so also does the concept of private property. It is not an exaggeration to state that in determining when a taking occurs a "definition and redefinition of the institution of private property is always at stake."[56]

With one exception, each of the four standard judicial taking theories described above should be able to accommodate new environmental concerns within this process of defining and re-defining "property." Thus, the physical invasion theory, to the extent that it serves as a sufficient test for taking, can be adjusted to recognize that air, noise, or water pollution can result in physical invasions just as surely as actual entry on land.[57] Similarly, the nuisance abatement theory has long recognized that public concern over pollution effects justifies restricting land use practices that threaten environmental values.[58] In like manner, the balancing theory's notion of the public good can easily be broadened to embrace concerns over pollution and the protection of natural resources as additional factors weighing in favor of particular land use regulations.

The single apparent exception is the diminution of value theory. Apparently endorsed by the leading, if somewhat dated, Supreme Court decision in *Pennsylvania Coal,* the idea that extreme reduction in the value of land results in a taking of property seems to leave little room for consideration of countervailing public interest. The question to be explored in the following pages is whether a rationale can be developed for rejecting in some cases the apparent automatic equation of destruction of commercial value with a constitutional taking.

1. Distinguishing "Regulation" from Taking

It is possible to view the development that extended compensation for restrictive regulations as well as for actual physical appropriations of prop-

---

[55]See generally Michelman, *supra* note 1.
[56]C. Haar, *Land Use Planning* 410 (1959).
[57]See text accompanying notes, 9–10, *supra*
[58]See *Hadacheck v. Sebastian,* 239 U.S. 394 (1915).

erty as the result of a refinement of what it means to take property rights. The upshot of that development, as noted above, has largely been to increase the occasions for compensation as distinctions between destruction by regulation and by direct takeover came to be discarded as superficial. At least one recent study suggests that this development is supported neither by history nor logic and considers whether courts might not do better to abandon *Pennsylvania Coal* and return to the "simple and unsophisticated principle" that a taking occurs only when the government physically appropriates property.[59]

While there is some evidence that this result may already have been reached in part, at least as far as the continued vitality of *Pennsylvania Coal* is concerned,[60]—the conclusion that regulation can never amount to a taking seems to sweep with a brush too broad for intellectual comfort. Although one may admit a wide range of disagreement over what is essential to the concept of "property," the mere fact that one can boast record title to a physical parcel of land is by itself the least important ingredient; it is the legal effect of such ownership, as reflected in one's ability to use and enjoy such land, that gives material content to the purely formal fact of ownership. Where the practical effect is to deprive an owner of all such possibilities for use of the land, it is not easy to see why different legal consequences should attach solely on the basis of whether the government chose to act by way of condemnation or by regulation.[61]

More promising than a categorical exclusion of all restrictive regulations from the purview of the takings clause is an approach that excludes only certain kinds of regulation. A good example of this approach is illustrated in a recent proposal[62] to redefine property rights in a way that takes account of the inextricable relationships between discretely owned parcels of land, and that accordingly limits any single owner's inherent "right" to use his land in ways that adversely affect others. According to this theory, when one person's use of his property has spillover effects that impose costs on other landowners (for example, the erosion effects of strip mining

---

[59]F. Bosselman, D. Callies, J. Banta, *The Taking Issue* 255 (1973) (study written for the Council on Environmental Quality); *see id.* at 238–55; Citizens' Advisory Comm. on Environmental Quality: Task Force on Land Use and Urban Growth, *The Use of Land* 174–75 (1973).

[60]See Sax, *supra* note 8, at 42–43 ("the opinion [in *Goldblatt v. Town of Hempstead,* 369 U.S. 590 (1962)] leaves some doubt about whether the Court is following, or repudiating, the Holmesian [diminution of value] doctrine").

[61]See *Arverne Bay Construction Co. v. Thatcher,* 278 N.Y. 222, 232, 15 N.E.2d 587, 592 (Ct. App. 1938) ("The only substantial difference . . . between restriction and actual taking, is that the restriction leaves the owner subject to the burden of payment of taxation, while outright confiscation would relieve him of that burden").
In fairness, it should be noted that an owner who retains legal title to land even though it cannot be commercially utilized may still enjoy some advantages over the owner who is forced to reliquish his land to the government through eminent domain. In the former case, entry on the land and use of the land in non-restricted ways still remains under the control of the private individual. In addition, the possibility that conditions may change to permit commercial uses, or that the permitted uses themselves may prove valuable (as in the case of a wildlife refuge) offers some support for a theory that would withhold compensation except in the case of outright confiscation.

[62]See Sax, *supra* note 24.

on lower-lying land) or that impinges on public rights (for example, the pollution of common resources such as air or water) neither owner can be said to have an a priori right to insist on his choice of property use; hence both owners should be treated alike with respect to compensation when one use or the other is restricted. When the government arbitrates in the case of such conflicting uses—for example, by imposing slope limitations on strip mining—compensation should not be constitutionally required for the mine owner's loss, any more than it would have been for the erosion losses suffered by adjoining landowners (or the water quality losses suffered by the more diffuse public) if the mining practices had been left unregulated.

This theory, while it has the merit of providing a ready solution to most of the present taking problems, is only slightly less broad than the previous theory. For in almost every case of current concern—wetlands preservation, airport noise, strip mining, billboard regulation, flood plain zoning—the issue will involve conflicting uses having spillover effects, with the result that any potential constitutional problem of compensation is eliminated whichever way the conflict is resolved.

In addition, it is not completely clear that the theory explains why current judicial emphasis on providing compensation where economic value has been severely destroyed is unsatisfactory. In the strip mining example, for instance, if one should decide to resolve the conflict in favor of the mining operator by leaving his operation unregulated, the spillover effects which adjoining landowners or the public would be forced to suffer as a result are not likely in the typical case to prevent all further reasonable or economic use of the land. If the converse is not the case, i.e., if regulation of the mining operation destroys all potential economic value, then to restore "relative positions of equality[63] seems to require that this choice be tempered by providing some compensation—thus placing the mining operator in a roughly similar position as would have been enjoyed by the competing landowners if the arbitration had gone the other way. While each landowner may be said to have an "equal" right to determine the use of his property, the effect of giving up that right in a particular case may have quite unequal consequences in terms of a landowner's remaining property rights. It is this relative inequality of the magnitude of the spillover effects, as seen from the viewpoint of the party that must bear them, that appears to give the diminution of value theory its initial plausibility.

2. The Nuisance Theory Revised

One need not resort to the theory that regulation can never (or seldom ever) amount to a taking in order to find a substantial body of judicial precedent for the proposition that in some cases regulation will not amount to a taking despite the diminution in value.

As noted earlier, the nuisance abatement theory has often functioned in the past as just such an exception to the rule that extreme loss in value

[63]*Id.* at 166 n.32.

results in a taking. A good example is provided by the case of *Hadacheck v. Sebastian*,[64] discussed above, in which the Supreme Court upheld an ordinance prohibiting the manufacture of bricks despite evidence that the property owner's land was diminished in value by over 90 per cent, from $800,000 to $60,000. This case was relied on by Justice Brandeis in his dissenting opinion in *Pennsylvania Coal.* Six years after *Pennsylvania Coal,* the Supreme Court in *Miller v. Schoene*[65] upheld a Virginia statute that required the destruction of a landowner's red cedar trees infected by cedar rust. The rust infection was not dangerous to the cedar trees, but was fatal to the fruit and foliage of nearby apple orchards. Relying on *Hadacheck* without even citing *Pennsylvania Coal,* the Court agreed that the paramount public concern justified the state's decision to protect apple trees even though it impaired the value of the complaining landowner's property. "Where the public interest is involved," the Court noted, "preferment of that interest over the property interest of the individual, *to the extent even of its destruction,* is one of the distinguishing characteristics of every exercise of the police power which affects property."[66] Thirty-four years later, the Court also cited *Hadacheck* as a precedent for its result in *Goldblatt v. Town of Hempstead.*[67] As described above, that case upheld prohibitions on mining activity that appeared to deprive the owner of all further economic use of his land.

The above cases indicate that there is considerable judicial precedent for upholding state regulation even where the effect is substantial impairment of economic value. The problem lies in articulating an underlying rationale for the nuisance abatement theory followed in these cases. As noted earlier in this chapter, the theory is sometimes tied to the notion that the landowner is somehow to blame for activities determined to be harmful and is for that reason in no position to complain of the loss in value when his activity is restricted. But the implication of fault is not essential to the theory. In all of these cases the same results can be reached simply by asserting the paramount public interest in preventing certain kinds of activities that are particularly likely to invade the interest of a significant segment of the public or of surrounding landowners. By thus shifting the focus to the relative priorities society has assigned to competing interests one need not rely on make-weight arguments about which of two or more landowners is primarily "at fault" for a problem.

Even with this articulation, however, a conceptual problem still exists in explaining just when the nuisance abatement theory should be applicable. Every legitimate exercise of the police power implicitly involves an assertion of paramount public interest in prohibiting certain private activities. If the nuisance abatement theory is to be used to determine when such assertions of public interest do not require compensation, it must be because the theory reflects more objective standards of society concerning

[64]239 U.S. 394 (1915).
[65]276 U.S. 272 (1928).
[66]*Id.* at 279, 280 [emphasis added].
[67]369 U.S. 590 (1962).

the rights that one can expect to accompany the ownership of property. In *Hadacheck v. Sebastian,* for example, the noise, smoke, and fumes emitted by the brick manufacturing operation corresponded fairly closely to the traditional kind of activity subject to abatement under common law theories of nuisance; thus to refuse to allow the concept of property to embrace the right to carry out such activities need not be viewed as doing violence to legitimate expectations about the rights that accompany property ownership. In contrast, application of the theory in *Mugler v. Kansas*[68] is somewhat more questionable. In that case, to label the brewery business a nuisance it seems, is little more than to announce a reordering of values that the complaining property owners could scarcely have anticipated when their businesses were established. This defect is avoided if the nuisance abatement theory is limited to cases where some objective standard limits the scope of property rights in accordance with implicit—if not yet legally embraced—expectations of society. The nuisance abatement theory then is a means of determining those types of cases in which an owner's expectations concerning the use of his land can be said to be unjustified, requiring him to take the risk that such uses will be subsequently restricted.[69] Under this approach, one avoids the objection that property has been redefined in new directions that could not have been anticipated.

The nuisance abatement theory, thus understood, could uphold a wide variety of land use regulations based on environmental concerns. Restriction of land use practices that entail obvious adverse pollution effects, threatening the safety and health of the public or adjoining landowners, for example (as in the case of many mining activities) would not normally require compensation regardless of the resulting economic impact. Whether the theory also has application outside of the pollution context is discussed in the following section.

3. The Critical Natural Features Theory

One recent approach, limiting the right to make profitable use of private land, builds on the above rationale of refusing to recognize as legitimate expectations of economic profit that are inconsistent with widely prevailing standards of society.

---

[68]123 U.S. 623 (1887).

[69]Whether the brickmaker in *Hadacheck* can in fact be expected to be on notice that his activities, "innocent" at the outset, are subject to later restriction may appear an historical question that limits the usefulness of the theory to cases where society's ordering of priorities has been made fairly clear. See Michelman, *supra* note 1, at 1242–45. However, where the effects of the activity in question have unquestionable potential for harm (the only question being whether subsequent development will place persons in sufficient proximity for the harm to be realized), subsequent regulation should not be viewed as upsetting legitimate expectations. It should not come as a total surprise to the prudent entrepreneur to think that activities with obviously harmful spillover effects may have to be insulated from other property owners through purchase of a buffer zone or be discontinued. Only where society subsequently discovers "harm" in activities previously thought innocent, as in *Mugler,* does the claim of unfair surprise have initial appeal. Even then, however, if one translates the "fairness" issue into the question whether the prudent investor, warned in advance of the fact that he must assume the risk of changes in society's values, would have significantly altered his investment decision, it is not clear that cases like *Mugler* should be differently decided.

As understanding of the interrelatedness of environmental concerns increases, so also does the identification of what might be called critical, "natural" features of the land, the alteration of which will drastically affect areas of vital public concern. The wetlands cases provide a good example. Population and urban expansion pressures have presented developers with opportunities to realize profits through expensive fill or reclamation techniques designed to overcome natural limitations in land. Such land, in its undeveloped state, serves a number of important functions, including flood control and ecological balance. To assume that one has an inherent right to make such alterations ignores or distorts an obvious relationship between such activity and interests of the public that have long existed, but that until recently, have been taken for granted. To declare in such cases that the public interest limits what would normally be accepted as property in a typical case of conflicting interests should not seem an undue restriction on the concept.

As with the nuisance abatement theory, the "critical natural features" theory does not depend on one's particular subjective view about what is or is not "natural" or on elevating the natural features of land to special protective status. The emphasis on the functions that particularly vital lands serve in their natural state is meant to explain why a declaration of paramount public interest, limiting the right to alter such features, need not be seen as overturning *legitimate* prior expectations of property owners. To require an owner to assume the risk of changing notions of property in the case of land that exhibits on its face, as it were, its publicly crucial nature seems a significantly lesser imposition than the risk assumed, for example, by the brewery owners in *Mugler v. Kansas* concerning possible changing public attitudes toward alcoholic beverages.

Judicial support for this theory can be found in the wetlands decision of the Wisconsin Supreme Court in *Just v. Marinette County.*[70] Faced with a taking challenge to prohibitions on the filling of land similar to the prohibitions that had led to conflicting results in other jurisdictions, the Wisconsin court upheld the restriction expressing dissatisfaction with "the basic rationale which permeates the decision that an owner has a right to use his property in any way and for any purpose he sees fit." Especially important to the court were the important public interests served by the land in its natural state:

> In the instant case we have a restriction on the use of a citizen's property, not to secure a benefit for the public, but to prevent a harm from the change in the natural character of the citizen's property. . . . What makes this case different from most condemnation or police power zoning cases is the interrelationship of the wetlands, the swamps and the natural environment of the shorelands to the purity of the water and to such natural resources as navigation, fishing, and scenic beauty. . . .
> Is the ownership of a parcel of land so absolute that man can change its nature to suit any of his purposes? An owner of land has no absolute and unlimited right to change the essential natural character of his land so as to use it for a purpose for which it was unsuited in its natural state and which

[70]56 Wis.2d 7, 201 N.W.2d 761, 3 ELR 20167 (1972).

injures the rights of others. The exercise of the police power in zoning must be reasonable and we think it is not an unreasonable exercise of that power to prevent harm to public rights by limiting the use of private property to its natural uses.

* * *

The Justs argue their property has been severely depreciated in value. But this depreciation of value is not based on the use of the land in its natural states but on what the land would be worth if it could be filled and used for the location of a dwelling. While loss of value is to be considered in determining whether a restriction is a constructive taking, value based upon changing the character of land at the expense of harm to public rights is not an essential factor or controlling.[71]

Just v. Marinette County thus stands as an explicit judicial recognition of an exception to the diminution of value theory in the case of regulations preserving publicly critical natural features of land.

[71]*Id.*, at 16–17, 201 N.W.2d at 767–71, 3 ELR at 20168.

Just v. Marinette County, Supreme Court of Wisconsin, 1972. 56 Wis.2d 7, 201 N.W.2d 761

Hallows, Chief Justice

Marinette County's Shoreland Zoning Ordinance Number 24 was adopted September 19, 1967, became effective October 9, 1967, and follows a model ordinance published by the Wisconsin Department of Resource Development in July of 1967. . . . The ordinance was designed to meet standards and criteria for shoreland regulation which the legislature required to be promulgated by the department of natural resources. . . . The legislation . . . authorizing the ordinance was enacted as a part of the Water Quality Act of 1965. . . .

Shorelands for the purpose of ordinances are defined . . . as lands within 1,000 feet of the normal high-water elevation of navigable lakes, ponds, or flowages and 300 feet from a navigable river or stream or to the landward side of the flood plain, whichever distance is greater. The state shoreland program is unique. All county shoreland zoning ordinances

Source: Reprinted from Hanks, Tarlock and Hanks' Cases and Materials on *Environmental Law and Policy,* 1975, Abridged Edition with permission of the West Publishing Company.

must be approved by the department of natural resources prior to their becoming effective. . . .

There can be no disagreement over the public purpose sought to be obtained by the ordinance. Its basic purpose is to protect navigable waters and the public rights therein from the degradation and deterioration which results from uncontrolled use and development of shorelands. In the Navigable Waters Protection Act, sec. 144.26, the purpose of the state's shoreland regulation program is stated as being to "aid in the fulfillment of the state's role as trustee of its navigable waters and to promote public health, safety, convenience and general welfare." In sec. 59.971(1), which grants authority for shoreland zoning to counties, the same purposes are reaffirmed. The Marinette county shoreland zoning ordinance in secs. 1.2 and 1.3 states the uncontrolled use of shorelands and pollution of navigable waters of Marinette county adversely affect public health, safety, convenience, and general welfare and impair the tax base.

The shoreland zoning ordinance divides the shorelands of Marinette county into general purpose districts, general recreation districts, and conservancy districts. A "conservancy" district is required by the statutory minimum standards and is defined in sec. 3.4 of the ordinance to include "all shorelands designated as swamps or marshes on the United States Geological Survey maps which have been designated as the Shoreland Zoning Map of Marinette County, Wisconsin or on the detailed Insert Shoreland Zoning Maps." The ordinance provides for permitted uses[1] and conditional uses.[2] One of the conditional uses requiring a permit under sec. 3.42(4) is the filling, drainage or dredging of wetlands according to the

[1]"3.41 Permitted Uses.
    (1) Harvesting of any wild crop such as marsh hay, ferns, moss, wild rice, berries, tree fruits and tree seeds.
    (2) Sustained yield forestry subject to the provisions of Section 5.0 relating to removal of shore cover.
    (3) Utilities such as, but not restricted to, telephone, telegraph and power transmission lines.
    (4) Hunting, fishing, preservation of scenic, historic and scientific areas and wildlife preserves.
    (5) Non-resident buildings used solely in conjunction with raising water fowl, minnows, and other similar lowland animals, fowl or fish.
    (6) Hiking trails and bridle paths.
    (7) Accessory uses.
    (8) Signs, subject to the restriction of Section 2.0."

[2]"3.42 Conditional Uses. The following uses are permitted upon issuance of a Conditional Use Permit as provided in Section 9.0 and issuance of a Department of Resource Development permit where required by Sections 30.11, 30.12, 30.19, 30.195 and 31.05 of the Wisconsin Statutes.
    (1) General farming provided farm animals shall be kept one hundred feet from any nonfarm residence.
    (2) Dams, power plants, flowages and ponds.
    (3) Relocation of any water course.
    (4) Filling, drainage or dredging of wetlands according to the provisions of Section 5.0 of this ordinance.
    (5) Removal of top soil or peat.
    (6) Cranberry bogs.
    (7) Piers, docks, boathouses."

provisions of sec. 5 of the ordinance. "Wetlands" are defined in sec. 2.29 as "(a)reas where ground water is at or near the surface much of the year or where any segment of plant cover is deemed an aquatic according to N. C. Fassett's 'Manual of Aquatic Plants.'" Section 5.42(2) of the ordinance requires a conditional-use permit for any filling or grading "Of any area which is within three hundred feet horizontal distance of a navigable water and which has surface drainage toward the water and on which there is: (a) Filling of more than five hundred square feet of any wetland which is contiguous to the water. . . . (d) Filling or grading of more than 2,000 square feet on slopes of twelve percent or less."

*   *   *

The land owned by the Justs is designated as swamps or marshes on the United States Geological Survey Map and is located within 1,000 feet of the normal high-water elevation of the lake. Thus, the property is included in a conservancy district and, by sec. 2.29 of the ordinance, classified as "wetlands." Consequently, in order to place more than 500 square feet of fill on this property, the Justs were required to obtain a conditional-use permit from the zoning administrator of the county and pay a fee of $20 or incur a forfeiture of $10 to $200 for each day of violation.

In February and March of 1968, six months after the ordinance became effective, Ronald Just, without securing a conditional-use permit, hauled 1,040 square yards of sand onto this property and filled an area approximately 20 feet wide commencing at the southwest corner and extending almost 600 feet north to the northwest corner near the shoreline, then easterly along the shoreline almost to the lot line. He stayed back from the pressure ridge about 20 feet. More than 500 square feet of this fill was upon wetlands located contiguous to the water and which had surface drainage toward the lake. The fill within 300 feet of the lake also was more than 2,000 square feet on a slope less than 12 percent. It is not seriously contended that the Justs did not violate the ordinance and the trial court correctly found a violation.

The real issue is whether the conservancy district provisions and the wetlands-filling restrictions are unconstitutional because they amount to a constructive taking of the Justs' land without compensation. Marinette county and the state of Wisconsin argue the restrictions of the conservancy district and wetlands provisions constitute a proper exercise of the police power of the state and do not so severely limit the use or depreciate the value of the land as to constitute a taking without compensation.

To state the issue in more meaningful terms, it is a conflict between the public interest in stopping the despoilation of natural resources, which our citizens until recently have taken as inevitable and for granted, and an owner's asserted right to use his property as he wishes. The protection of public rights may be accomplished by the exercise of the police power unless the damage to the property owner is too great and amounts to a confiscation. The securing or taking of a benefit not presently enjoyed by the public for its use is obtained by the government through its power of eminent domain. The distinction between the exercise of the police power and condemnation has been said to be a matter of degree of damage to the property owner. In the valid exercise of the police power reasonably restricting the use of property, the damage suffered by the owner is said to be incidental. However, where the restriction is so great the landowner ought not to bear such a burden for the public good, the restriction has been held to be a constructive taking even though the actual use or forbidden use has not been transferred to the government so as to be a taking in the traditional sense. . . . Whether a taking has occurred depends upon whether "the restriction practically or substantially renders the land useless for all reasonable purposes." . . . The loss caused the individual must be weighed to determine if it is more than he should bear. . . .

"[I]f the damage is such as to be suffered by many similarly situated and is in the nature of a restriction on the use to which land may be put and ought to be borne by the individual as a member of society for the good of the public safety, health or general welfare, it is said to be a reasonable exercise of the police power, but if the damage is so great to the individual that he ought not to bear it under contemporary standards, then courts are inclined to treat it as a 'taking' of the property or an unreasonable exercise of the police power."

Many years ago, Professor Freund stated in his work on The Police Power, sec. 511, at 546–547, "It may be said that the state takes property by eminent domain because it is useful to the public, and under the police power because it is harmful. . . . From this results the difference between the power of eminent domain and the police power, that the former recognizes a right to compensation, while the latter on principle does not." Thus the necessity for monetary compensation for loss suffered to an owner by police power restriction arises when restrictions are placed on property in order to create a public benefit rather than to prevent a public harm. . . .

This case causes us to reexamine the concepts of public benefit in contrast to public harm and the scope of an owner's right to use of his property. In the instant case we have a restriction on the use of a citizens' property, not to secure a benefit for the public, but to prevent a harm from the change in the natural character of the citizens' property. We start with the premise that lakes and rivers in their natural state are unpolluted and the pollution which now exists is man made. The state of Wisconsin under the trust doctrine has a duty to eradicate the present pollution and to prevent further pollution in its navigable waters. This is not, in a legal sense, a gain or a securing of a benefit by the maintaining of the natural *status quo* of the environment. What makes this case different from most condemnation or police power zoning cases is the interrelationship of the wetlands, the swamps and the natural environment of shorelands to the purity of the water and to such natural resources as navigation, fishing, and scenic beauty. Swamps and wetlands were once considered wasteland, undesirable, and not picturesque. But as the people became more sophisticated, an appreciation was acquired that swamps and wetlands serve a vital role in nature, are part of the balance of nature and are essential to the purity of the water in our lakes and streams. Swamps and wetlands are a necessary part of the ecological creation and now, even to the uninitiated, possess their own beauty in nature.

Is the ownership of a parcel of land so absolute that man can change its nature to suit any of his purposes? The great forests of our state were stripped on the theory man's ownership was unlimited. But in forestry, the land at least was used naturally, only the natural fruit of the land (the trees) were taken. The despoilage was in the failure to look to the future and provide for the reforestation of the land. An owner of land has no absolute and unlimited right to change the essential natural character of his land so as to use it for a purpose for which it was unsuited in its natural state and which injures the rights of others. The exercise of the police power in zoning must be reasonable and we think it is not an unreasonable exercise of that power to prevent harm to public rights by limiting the use of private property to its natural uses.

This is not a case where an owner is prevented from using his land for natural and indigenous uses. The uses consistent with the nature of the land are allowed and other uses recognized and still others permitted by special permit. The shoreland zoning ordinance prevents to some extent the changing of the natural character of the land within 1,000 feet of a navigable lake and 300 feet of a navigable river because of such land's interrelation to the contiguous water. The changing of wetlands and swamps to the damage of the general public by upsetting the natural environment and the natural relationship is not a reasonable use of that land which is protected from police power regulation. Changes and filling to some extent are permitted because the extent of such changes and fillings does not cause harm. We realize no case in Wisconsin has yet dealt with shoreland regulations and there are several cases in other states which seem to hold such regulations unconstitutional; but nothing this court has said or held in prior cases indicates that destroying the natural character of a swamp or a wetland so as to make that location available for human habitation is a reasonable use of that land when the new use, although of a more economical value to the owner, causes a harm to the general public.

Wisconsin has long held that laws and regulations to prevent pollution and to protect the waters of this state from degradation are valid police-power enactments. . . . The active public trust duty of the state of Wisconsin in respect to navigable waters requires the state not only to promote navigation but also to protect and preserve those waters for fishing, recreation, and scenic beauty. . . . To further this duty, the legislature may delegate authority to local units of the government, which the state did by requiring counties to pass shoreland zoning ordinances. . . .

This is not a case of an isolated swamp unrelated to a navigable lake or stream, the change of which would cause no harm to public rights. Lands adjacent to or near navigable waters exist in a special relationship to the state. They have been held subject to special taxation, . . . and are subject to the state public trust powers, . . . and since the Laws of 1935, ch. 303, counties have been authorized to create special zoning districts along waterways and zone them for restrictive conservancy purposes.[3] The restrictions in the Marinette county ordinance upon wetlands within 1,000 feet of Lake Noquebay which prevent the placing of excess fill upon such land without a permit is not confiscatory or unreasonable.

Cases wherein a confiscation was found cannot be relied upon by the Justs. In *State v. Herwig* (1962), 17 Wis.2d 442, 117 N.W.2d 335, a "taking" was found where a regulation which prohibited hunting on farmland had the effect of establishing a game refuge and resulted in an unnatural, concentrated foraging of the owner's land by waterfowl. In *State v. Becker*, . . . the court held void a law which established a wildlife refuge (and prohibited hunting) on private property. In *Benka v. Consolidated Water Power Co.* (1929), 198 Wis. 472, 224 N.W. 718, the court held if damages to plaintiff's property were in fact caused by flooding from a dam constructed by a public utility, those damages constituted a "taking" within the meaning of the condemnation statutes. In *Bino v. Hurley* (1956), 273 Wis. 10, 76 N.W.2d 571, the court held unconstitutional as a "taking" without compensation an ordinance which, in attempting to prevent pollution, prohibited the owners of land surrounding a lake from bathing, boating, or swimming in the lake. In *Piper v. Ekern* (1923), 180 Wis. 586, 593, 194 N.W. 159, 162, the court held a statute which limited the height of buildings surrounding the state capitol to be unnecessary for the public health, safety, or welfare and, thus, to constitute an unreasonable exercise of the police power. In all these cases the unreasonableness of the exercise of the police power lay in excessive restriction of the natural use of the land or rights in relation thereto.

Cases holding the exercise of police power to be reasonable likewise provide no assistance to Marinette county in their argument. . . .

The Justs rely on several cases from other jurisdictions which have held zoning regulations involving flood plain districts, flood basins and wetlands to be so confiscatory as to amount to a taking because the owners of the land were prevented from improving such property for residential or commercial purposes. While some of these cases may be distinguished on their facts, it is doubtful whether these differences go to the basic rationale which permeates the decision that an owner has a right to use his property in any way and for any purpose he sees fit. In *Dooley v. Town Plan & Zon. Comm. of Town of Fairfield* (1964), 151 Conn. 304, 197 A.2d 770, the court held the restriction on land located in a flood plain district prevented its being used for residential or business purposes and thus the restriction destroyed the economic value to the owner. The court recognized the land was needed for a public purpose as it was part of the area in which the tidal stream overflowed when abnormally high tides existed, but the property was half a mile from the ocean and therefore could not be used for marina or boathouse purposes. In *Morris County Land I. Co. v. Parsippany-Troy Hills*

---

[3]In *Jefferson County v. Timmel* (1952), 261 Wis. 39, 51 N.W.2d 518, the constitutionality of a conservancy district use restriction was upheld as being based on a valid exercise of police power. The purpose for this conservancy district, however, was for highway safety and not for the prevention of pollution and the protection of the public trust in navigable waters.

Tp. (1963), 40 N.J. 539, 193 A. 2d 232, a flood basin zoning ordinance was involved which required the controversial land to be retained in its natural state. The plaintiff owned 66 acres of a 1,500-acre swamp which was part of a river basin and acted as a natural detention basin for flood waters in times of very heavy rainfall. There was an extraneous issue that the freezing regulations were intended as a stop gap until such time as the government would buy the property under a flood-control project. However, the court took the view the zoning had an effect of preserving the land as an open space as a water-detention basin and only the government or the public would be benefited, to the complete damage of the owner.

In *State v. Johnson* (1970), Me., 265 A.2d 711, the Wetlands Act restricted the alteration and use of certain wetlands without permission. The act was a conservation measure enacted under the police power to protect the ecology of areas bordering the coastal waters. The plaintiff owned a small tract of a salt water marsh which was flooded at high tide. By filling, the land would be adapted for building purposes. The court held the restrictions against filling constituted a deprivation of a reasonable use of the owner's property and, thus, an unreasonable exercise of the police power. In *MacGibbon v. Board of Appeals of Duxbury* (1970), 356 Mass. 635, 255 N.E. 2d 347, the plaintiff owned seven acres of land which were under water about twice a month in a shoreland area. He was denied a permit to excavate and fill part of his property. The purpose of the ordinance was to preserve from despoilage natural features and resources such as salt marshes, wetlands, and ponds. The court took the view [that] the preservation of privately owned land in its natural, unspoiled state for the enjoyment and benefit of the public by preventing the owner from using it for any practical purpose was not within the limit and scope of the police power and the ordinance was not saved by the use of special permits.

It seems to us that filling a swamp not otherwise commercially usable is not in and of itself an existing use, which is prevented, but rather is the preparation for some future use which is not indigenous to a swamp. Too much stress is laid on the right of an owner to change commercially valueless land when that change does damage to the rights of the public. It is observed that a use of special permits is a means of control and accomplishing the purpose of the zoning ordinance as distinguished from the old concept of providing for variances. The special permit technique is now common practice and has met with judicial approval, and we think it is of some significance in considering whether or not a particular zoning ordinance is reasonable.

* * *

The Justs argue their property has been severely depreciated in value. But this depreciation of value is not based on the use of the land in its natural state but on what the land would be worth if it could be filled and used for the location of a dwelling. While loss of value is to be considered in determining whether a restriction is a constructive taking, value based upon changing the character of the land at the expense of harm to public rights is not an essential factor or controlling.

We are not unmindful of the warning in *Pennsylvania Coal Co. v. Mahon* (1922), 260 U.S. 393, 416, 43 S.Ct. 158, 160, 67 L.Ed. 322:

> . . . We are in danger of forgetting that a strong public desire to improve the public condition is not enough to warrant achieving the desire by a shorter cut than the constitutional way of paying for the change.

This observation refers to the improvement of the public condition, the securing of a benefit not presently enjoyed and to which the public is not entitled. The shoreland zoning ordinance preserves nature, the environment, and natural resources as they were created and to which the people have a present right. The ordinance does not create or improve the public condition but only preserves nature from the despoilage and harm resulting from the unrestricted activities of humans.

* * *

COST-BENEFIT ANALYSES

Since the late 1960s, the law of the United States has been that, before undertaking any project having a significant environmental impact, an environmental impact statement must be filed with the government. Companies, wanting to demonstrate objectively the acceptability of proposed projects, have produced impact statements that analyze the costs and benefits of the projects, and attempt to show that the benefits outweigh the costs. But the practice of constructing impact statements in terms of cost-benefit analyses has become controversial.

Consider briefly what a cost-benefit analysis is. A project is initially defined in terms of its goal, so the first step of the analysis is to state alternative means of achieving the goal. The second step is to state and compare the likely consequences of each means of achieving the goal. The third step is to assign a common quantitative measure, usually money, for defining the costs and benefits of each of the consequences. The fourth and final step is to adjust the definition of costs and benefits in the light of the accepted view that the earlier a benefit comes, the better, and the later a cost comes, the better.

Alasdair MacIntyre, Robert Socolow, and Alan Gewirth are all convinced that cost-benefit procedures are seriously inadequate. Each suggests different inadequacies. MacIntyre, discussing utility company price rates, tries to show how cost-benefit really fails on its own terms, how it fails to provide an objective, quantitative measure of value. Socolow argues that carrying out the procedure implies introducing arbitrary elements which reflect cultural biases and ignore environmental complexities. Gewirth, viewing the procedure socially in terms of environmental health, articulates traditional concerns for human rights that are not adequately accounted for in cost-benefit analysis.

Ralph Potter's essay shows how the perspectives of different disciplines (ecology, demography, economics, ethics) have led thinkers to approach population policy differently. He argues that an adequate procedure for determining environmental acceptability must incorporate these perspectives. The difficulty Potter finds concerning achieving an objective, quantitative analysis of the environmental impact of a project is that the assumptions from which one begins decisively influence the conclusions one reaches, no matter how one quantifies them. In other words, different statements of alternatives (step one of a cost-benefit analysis), according to Potter, already undermine the objectivity of the procedure.

Utilitarianism and Cost-Benefit Analysis: An Essay on the Relevance of Moral Philosophy to Bureaucratic Theory

Alasdair MacIntyre

INTRODUCTION

The practical world of business and government is haunted by unrecognized theoretical ghosts. One of the tasks of moral philosophy is to help us to recognize and, if possible, to exorcise such ghosts. For so long as philosophical theories in fact inform and guide the actions of men who take themselves to be hard headed, pragmatically oriented, free of theory, and guided by common sense, such theories enjoy an undeserved power. Being unrecognized they go uncriticized. At the same time the illusion is encouraged that philosophy is an irrelevant, abstract subject—part of the decoration of a cultured life perhaps, but unnecessary in and even distracting from the activities of the practical world. The truth is, however, that all nontrivial activity presupposes some philosophical point of view and that not to recognize this is to make oneself the ready victim of bad or at the very least inadequate philosophy.

Consider for example, the way in which the business executive or the civil servant characteristically defines and conceptualizes the activities of himself, his colleagues and his clients. He or she does so in a way which appears to exclude both moral and philosophical considerations from arising within his everyday decision-making tasks. Certainly some large moral considerations may have been involved in the executive's choice of a corporation; some might not be prepared to work for an armaments firm or in the making of pornographic movies. And certainly there may have been

Source: From *Values in the Electric Power Industry,* ed. Kenneth Sayre.

moral grounds for some of the legal constraints imposed by government—
the imposition of safety regulations, for example. But once the executive is
at work the aims of the public or private corporation must be taken as
given. Within the boundaries imposed by corporate goals and legal constraints the executive's own tasks characteristically appear to him as merely
technical. He has to calculate the most efficient, the most economical way of
mobilizing the existing resources to produce the benefits of power at the
lowest costs. The weighing of costs against benefits is not just his business, it
is business.

The business executive does not differ in this view of his task from
other bureaucrats. Bureaucracies have been conceived, since Weber, as
impersonal instruments for the realization of ends which characteristically
they themselves do not determine. A bureaucracy is set the task of achieving within the limits set by certain legal and physical constraints the most
efficient solution of the problems of realizing such ends with the means
available.

The impersonality of bureaucracy has two closely related aspects. The
first is that those who deal with a bureaucracy over time must be able to
have continuous relationships of an intelligible kind with it, no matter
which individuals within the bureaucracy retire, die or are replaced during
that relationship. Correspondence is correspondence with the organization
rather than with the individuals who dictate the letters. Hence the existence
of files or of computerized records is essential to bureaucratic organizations. From this aspect of impersonality a second emerges. Reasons cited as
explanations for or justifications of actions in correspondence or in other
external or internal transactions must hold as good reasons for the members of the organization independently of whoever actually on a particular
occasion enunciates them. Thus established and agreed criteria of sound
reasoning are presupposed in the successful functioning of all bureaucratic
organizations. This is the point at which their impersonality and their
commitment to means-ends rationality can be understood as two aspects of
the same phenomenon.

The presupposed agreement on ends allows all disagreement within
the organization to take place on questions of means, that is on the merits
of rival policies for achieving the agreed ends. If these arguments are to be
settlable, then there must also be preestablished methods both for isolating
all the relevant elements in each situation and for estimating the costs and
the benefits of proceeding by this route rather than that. In other words,
the norms of rationality, which on a Weberian or a neo-Weberian view of
bureaucracies must govern public discourse within bureaucracies and between bureaucracies and their masters, clients, customers, or other external agents, are such that the cost-benefit analysis provides the essential
normative form of argument.

The effect of this is that questions of alternative policies appear to
become settlable in the same way that relatively simple questions of fact are.
For the question of whether these particular means will or will not bring
about that particular end with less expenditure of this or that resource than
some other means is of course a question of fact.

The moral philosopher will at once recognize that the discourse of bureaucracy thus conceived reproduces the argumentative forms of utilitarianism. Not perhaps those of utilitarianism largely conceived as a morality capable of dealing with every area of life, but those reflecting acceptance of J. S. Mill's judgment upon "what a philosophy like Bentham's can do. It can teach the means of organizing and regulating the merely *business* part of the social arrangements." Poetry, music, friendship, and family life, as Mill sees it, may not be captured by the Benthamite calculus; but there is a part of life which may be so captured, and which therefore may be rendered calculable.

If it is correct that corporate activity embodies the argumentative forms of utilitarianism, then we ought to be able to identify the key features of utilitarianism, including its central errors and distortions, within corporate activity. The guide that I shall use to identify the argumentative forms of corporate activity will be the textbook versions of cost-benefit analysis, which not only form the mind of the corporate executive but provide paradigmatic examples from practice. The question is whether we discover in the texts the same lacunae and incoherences as in classical utilitarianism. First we must characterize these deficiencies.

UTILITARIANISM AND ITS DEFICIENCIES

The doctrines of classical utilitarianism appear to first sight simple and elegant. Every proposed course of action is to be subjected to the test: will it produce a greater balance of pleasure over pain, of happiness over unhappiness, of benefits over harms, than any alternative course of action? It is right to perform that action which will be productive of "the greatest happiness of the greatest number," which will have the greatest utility. In calculating the greatest happiness, everybody is to count for one and nobody for more than one. Utilitarianism sometimes has entangled itself, but perhaps need not entangle itself, in questions about the meaning of such words as "right" and "good." Bentham at least made no pretense that his doctrine was an analysis of what moral agents had hitherto meant in using such words; he proposed it instead as a rational substitute for the confusions and superstitions of earlier moral theory and it is as such that I shall examine it.

Two main versions of utilitarianism have been advanced: that which holds that the utilitarian test is a test of actions and that which holds that it is a test of rules. . . .

About any version of utilitarian doctrine five major questions arise. The first concerns the range of alternative courses of action which are to be subjected to the utilitarian test. For clearly at any moment an indefinitely large range of alternative courses of action are open to most agents. In practice I may consider a very limited set of alternatives: shall I use this money to paint my house or to educate my child? But perhaps I ought to weigh every proposed expenditure of energy, time or money against the benefit that might accrue from devoting it to the solution of world population problems or the invention of labor-saving devices or the discovery of new methods to teaching music to young children. . . . If I try to construct a list of this kind of indefinite length, all decision-making will in fact be paralyzed. I must therefore find some principle of restriction in the construction of my list of alternatives. But this principle cannot itself be utilitarian; for if it were to be justified by the test of beneficial and harmful consequences as against alternative proposed principles of restriction, we should have to find some principle of restriction in order to avoid paralysis by the construction of an indefinitely long list of principles of restriction. And so on.

Utilitarian tests therefore always presuppose the application of some prior non-utilitarian principle which sets limits upon the range of alternatives to be considered. But this is not all that they presuppose. Bentham believed that there was one single, simple concept of pleasure or of happiness. It did not matter what you called it.

Indeed Bentham believed that there were no less than fifty-eight synonyms for pleasure of which "happiness" is one. Nor is there any good which is not either pleasure itself or a means to pleasure. Moreover the difference between pleasures is only quantitative. Given these beliefs, the notion of summing pleasures on the one hand and pains on the other, in calculating which course of action will produce the greatest happiness of the greatest number, is not mysterious. But Bentham's beliefs are of course false and were recognized as false even by his immediate utilitarian heirs.

Consider for the moment only genuine pleasures. It is clear that the-pleasure-of-climbing-a-mountain, the-pleasure-of-listening-to-Bartok and the-pleasure-of-drinking-Guinness-stout are three very disputable things. There is not some one state to the production of which the climbing, the listening and the drinking are merely alternative means. Nor is there any scale on which they can be weighed against each other. But if this is true of pleasures, how much more complex must matters become when we seek to weigh against each other such goods as those of restoring health to the sick, of scientific enquiry or of friendship. A politician has to decide whether to propose spending a given sum of money on a new clinic for aged patients or on a new infant school; a student has to decide between embarking on a career as a musician or becoming an engineer. Both wish to promote the greatest happiness of the greatest number, but they are being called upon to decide between incommensurables—unless they can provide some prior scheme of values by means of which goods and evils, pleasures and pains, benefits and harms are to be ranked in some particular way. Such a method of rank-ordering will, however, have to be non-utilitarian. For like the principle which specified the range of alternatives to be considered, it has to be adopted before any utilitarian test can be applied.

Thirdly there is the question of whose assessment of harms and benefits is to be considered by the agent making his assessment. For it is clear not only that there are alternative methods of rank-ordering, but also that different types of people will adopt and argue for different methods. The old do not weigh harms and benefits in the same way as the young; the poor have a different perspective from the rich; the healthy and the sick often weigh pain and suffering differently. "Everybody is to count for one and nobody for more than one," declared Bentham; but others—Sir Karl Popper for one—have suggested that the relief of pain or suffering always should take precedence over the promotion of pleasure or happiness. So we have at least two contingently incompatible proposals immediately, for the outcome of Bentham's rule clearly will often conflict with the results of applying Popper's maxim.

Fourthly there is the question of what is to count as a consequence of a given action. We might be tempted to suppose this a very straightforward question, but it is not. For the apparently straightforward answer "All the predictable effects of my action are to be counted as consequences of my action" at once raises the question, "What are reasonable standards of prediction?" How much care and effort am I required to exert before I make my decision? Once again certain maxims must be adopted prior to the utilitarian test. But this is not the only difficulty which arises over the notion of a consequence. In the Anglo-Saxon legal tradition chains of cause-and-effect arising from an action are often thought to be modified when they pass through another responsible agent in such a way that the later effects are no longer held to be consequences of my action. I am a teacher grading a student's examination. I give him a well-deserved C−. The student who has hoped for an A goes home and in his anger beats his wife. Suppose that I could somehow or other have reasonably predicted this outcome; ought I to have counted the wife-beating as a consequence of my action in grading the paper? Ought I to have weighed this consequence against others before deciding on what grade to give the paper? Classical utilitarianism appears to be committed to the answer "Yes," the Anglo-Saxon legal tradition by and large to the answer "No." About what are they disagreeing? Obviously it is about the range of effects of an action for which the agent can be held responsible. Thus it turns out that some particular theory of responsibility must be adopted before we can have a criterion for deciding what effects are to count as consequences.

Fifthly, a decision must be made about the time-scale which is to be used in assessing consequences. Clearly if we adopt a longer time-scale we have to reckon with a much less predictable future than if we adopt a shorter one. Our assessment of long-term risks and of long-term probabilities is generally more liable to error than our assessment of short-term risks and probabilities. Moreover, it is not clear how we ought to weigh short-term harms and benefits against long-term contingencies; are our responsibilities the same to future generations as they are to the present one or to our own children? How far ought the present to be sacrificed to the future? Here again we have a range of questions to which non-utilitarian answers have to be given or at least presupposed before any utilitarian test can be applied.

Utilitarianism thus requires a background of beliefs and of evaluative commitments, a fact that has usually gone unnoticed by utilitarians themselves. They are able to apply the test of utility only because they have already implicitly decided that the world ought to be viewed in one way rather than another, that experience ought to be structured and evaluated in one way rather than another. The world which they inhabit is one of discrete variables, of a reasonably high degree of predictability; it is one in which questions of value have become questions of fact and in which the aim and the vindication of theory is its success in increasing our manipulative powers. The utilitarian vision of the world and the bureaucratic vision of the world match each other closely.

Yet this is not just a matter of resemblance; the bureaucratic world contains a number of devices for ensuring that thought, perception and action are organized in a utilitarian way. The most important of such devices in contemporary bureaucracy is probably the cost-benefit analysis.

COST-BENEFIT ANALYSIS AND BUREAUCRATIC DECISION-MAKING

The cost-benefit analysis is an instrument of practical reason, and it is one of the central features of practical reason that it operates under time constraints in a way that theoretical reason does not. Nothing counts as a solution of a practical problem which does not meet a required deadline; it is no good achieving a perfect solution for defeating Wellington at Waterloo on June 19, if the battle had to be fought on June 18. Hence problems cannot be left unsolved to await future solutions. But problems of a cost-benefit kind—of a utilitarian kind in general—can only be solved when all the elements of the problems are treated as belonging to the realm of the calculable and the predictable. Hence the executive is always under pressure to treat the social world as predictable and calculable and to ignore any arbitrariness involved in so doing. This pressure may operate in either of two opposite ways. It may appear in a tendency to restrict our operations to what is genuinely predictable and calculable; one manifestation of this will be a tendency to prefer short-term to long-term planning, since clearly the near future is generally more predictable than the more distant future. But the same pressure may equally appear in an opposite tendency to try to present all that we encounter as calculable and predictable, a tendency to overcome apparent difficulties in calculation by adopting *ad hoc* devices of various kinds. These conflicting pressures may appear in the way in which decisions are taken or evaluative commitments are made in any of the five areas which define the background of utilitarianism and which in a precisely parallel way define the background of cost-benefit analyses.

There is first of all the restriction of alternatives so that the benefits and the costs of doing this rather than that are weighed against one another, but neither alternative is assessed against an indeterminately large range of other alternatives. Yet every so often in corporate or governmental or private life the range of alternatives for which cost-benefit analyses are sought changes; and this change always signals a change in underlying evaluative commitments. Up to a certain point in the history of a marriage, divorce remains an unthinkable alternative; up to a certain point in the history of a foreign policy, embarking on an aggressive war remains an unthinkable alternative; up to a certain point in the history of a war, truce or withdrawal remains unthinkable. Corporate parallels are not difficult to think of. The history of publishing or of automobile manufacture abound with them. The one-volume novel or the cheap intellectually substantial paperback were once unthinkable; so was the car which could be advertised primarily for safety factors.

Corporate executives may respond to this by saying that what restricts the range of alternatives which they consider is simply profitability. They can attend only to those alternatives which in the shorter or longer run will yield their stockholders a competitive return in the market. What this reply fails to notice is that what is profitable is partly determined by the range of evaluative commitments shared in the community. Sir Allen had to *make* the intellectual paperback profitable for the very first time and for that a firm conviction about intellectual values was required. What attitude both automobile manufacturers and the public take to death on the roads *changes* what is profitable. Consumer markets are *made,* not just given. Underlying the restricted range of alternatives considered by corporate executives we may therefore find both covert evaluative commitments and also unspelled-out assumptions about human wants and needs.

* * *

Secondly, the use of cost-benefit analyses clearly presupposes a prior decision as to what is a cost and what a benefit; but more than that it presupposes some method of ordering costs and benefits so that what otherwise would be incommensurable becomes commensurable. How are we to weigh the benefits of slightly cheaper power against the loss forever of just one beautiful landscape? How are we to weigh the benefits of increased employment and lessened poverty in Detroit against a marginal increase in deaths from automobile accidents? Once somebody has to consider both factors within a cost-benefit analysis framework these questions have to be answered. Considerable ingenuity has in fact been exercised in answering them.

Consider for example how we may carry through a calculation where one of the costs we may have to take into account is the shortening of human life. One recent example occurred in the argument over whether the Anglo-French supersonic aircraft *Concorde* should be allowed to land at United States airports. It is reasonably clear that the greater the use of *Concorde* the greater—as a result of the effects on those layers of the atmosphere which filter the sun's rays—the number of cases of skin cancer. How are we to include such deaths in our calculations?

Writers on cost-benefit analysis techniques have devised four alternative methods for computing the cost of a person's life. One is that of discounting to the present the person's expected future earnings; a second is that of computing the losses to others from the person's death so as to calculate their present discounted value; a third is that of examining the value placed on an individual life by presently established social policies and practices, e.g., the benefits in increased motor traffic which society at the present moment is prepared to exchange for a higher fatal accident rate; and a fourth is to ask what value a person placed on his or her own life, by looking at the risks which that person is or was prepared to take and the insurance premiums which he or she was prepared to pay. Clearly, those four criteria will yield very different answers on occasion; the range of possible different answers to one and the same question that you can extract from the same techniques of cost-benefit analysis makes it clear that all the mathematical sophistication and rigor that may go into the modes of computation may be undermined by the arbitrariness (relative to the mathematics) of the choice to adopt one principle for quantifying rather than another. Thus there once more appears behind the ordered world of discrete, calculable, variable elements in which the cost-benefit analysis is at home, a range of relatively arbitrary decisions presupposed—and sometimes actually made—by the analyst himself.

Thirdly, once more as with utilitarianism in general, the application of cost-benefit analysis presupposes a decision as to *whose* values and preferences are to be taken into account in assessing costs and benefits. Indeed the choice of a method for weighing costs against benefits, the adoption of the type of principle discussed immediately above, will often involve equally a decision as to which voices are to be heard. Consider once again the different methods employed to estimate the cost of a human death. One of these considers the individual's own earnings, one the losses to others, one certain socially established norms, and one the individual's own risk-taking. The last is an attempt to give the individual the value which he sets on himself; the second gives him the value he has to others; the third the value he has in the eyes of "society"; the fourth perhaps the value that he has in the eyes of the taxation system. To adopt one of these methods rather than another is precisely to decide *who* is to decide what counts as a cost and what counts as a benefit.

Consider the range of possible decision-makers with whom a corporate executive might be concerned: his superiors, the consumers of his product, the stockholders, the labor force, the other members of his profession (if he is, say, a lawyer or an actuary), the community in which the corporation is cited, the government, and the public at large. What makes the question "Who decides?" so crucial is another feature of cost-benefit analyses. Very often, perhaps characteristically, neither future costs nor future benefits can be restricted to identifiable individuals. After the event we can say who died in the road deaths accompanying an increase in automobile traffic, or which children were deformed by the side effects of a new drug, or who in fact got skin cancer after an increase in use of higher-flying jet planes. But beforehand all that is predictable at best is what proportion of a given population will be harmed (or will benefit). It is a chance of harm or benefit which is assigned now to each member of the population. Therefore the question is: who should decide how the chances are distributed over a population?

There are some alien cultures where a family's ancestors are given an important voice in decision-making; so it is in traditional Vietnamese culture, for example. There are cultures where the old have a very special voice. In our own culture our explicit beliefs label the former as a superstition and our dominant practices show that we implicitly label the latter a superstition too. This is directly relevant to, for example, the policies of public utility companies. Light and heat are peculiarly important to old people; ought therefore the old to receive special consideration from public utility corporation executives in determining what is to count as a cost and what as a benefit? Implicitly or explicitly a decision will have been taken on this point whenever a cost-benefit analysis is offered in a relevant context.

Fourthly, the parallel with utilitarianism is maintained in the way in which the questions of what is to count as a consequence of some particular action or course of action arises for cost-benefit analyses. Any answer to this question, as I suggested earlier, presupposes a prior answer to the question: for what range of effects of his actions is an agent to be considered liable or responsible? What answer to this latter question is in fact presupposed by corporate practice? A necessary starting point is to recognize that in advanced societies today, and most notably in the United States, individuals often see their moral lives as parcelled out between the different roles which one and the same individual plays. Parts of his moral self are allocated to each sphere of activity, and within each sphere responsibilities—and therefore consequences—are understood in very different ways. So the individual *qua* father or husband has one role and one way of envisaging responsibilities and consequences; but *qua* consumer, *qua* citizen or *qua* corporate executive he may see matters quite differently. The effects of the division of the self are characteristically to exempt the individual in any one role from considering those responsibilities which he is prepared to acknowledge only too readily in other roles. The individual learns to confine different aspects of his evaluative commitments to different spheres. Consider in particular how this may define the situation of the executive in a public utility company. For what is to some degree present in the situation of many corporate managers in America is present in his situation in a highly explicit form. Public utility companies—and the Bell Telephone Company is in some ways the best example—from the outset accepted public governmental regulation as the price to be paid for the privilege of monopoly. The case for monopoly is quite simply that competition involves extremely expensive reduplication of equipment and—especially in the case of rival telephone companies, each of whom serves only a portion of the subscribers—grave inconvenience for consumers. But if monopoly is permitted, then the consumer must find elsewhere the protection which otherwise would (in theory, at least) be provided by competition. Hence the activities of public utility companies are to be regulated and restricted by government-designated agencies. The company's is the sphere of activity; the government's is the sphere of restriction. The executive himself inhabits both spheres: *qua* corporate executive he represents the company; *qua* citizen and consumer the government represents him. Parts of his self are allocated to each area.

* * *

Morally then the executive faces in at least two directions: towards the morality of restriction where it is the duty of others and not himself—or if you like, his duty *qua* citizen and not *qua* executive—to discipline his activities, and also towards the morality of service which defines a goal external to, but justifying his day to day activity. What do I mean when I call this goal external?

The power company executive is able at this point to avail himself of a picture of his activities which has nothing particular to do with his serving a public utility company, but is one common to many executives in many industries. This picture is one of a moral contract, prior to and providing warrant for all legal contracts, between an autonomous supplier and an autonomous client. Their autonomy entails that each is the sole authority as to his own needs and wants. The acts of production by the supplier are undertaken for the sake of the client's consumption. Everyone is both in one aspect supplier and in the other client. A simple model of economic value informs their exchanges (something very like a labor theory of value is presupposed). The moral contract has replaced the crude rule of *caveat emptor*. Autonomy also entails that the supplier has no responsibility for the use that the client makes of the goods which he supplies. Moreover, since the contract is between individuals, no transactions transcend one generation. The supplier is morally bound to give the client what *he* wants; for the nature of the client's wants and the consequences of the act of supply he is not answerable. To make him so would be to injure the autonomy necessary for such a contract.

Only one kind of moral distinction needs to be made by the supplier: that which divides off genuine goods from dubious commodities. . . . But once a businessman is assured of the goodness of what he supplies he has a sanction for what he does that leaves him free not to think about this aspect of his activity any more. In his dealings with consumers, in his investment policies, and in his dealings with his labor force he can press ahead exactly as he would do with any other product (except for technological considerations). The wants of the consumer for the good supplied are to be taken as given; whatever is asked for in the form of market demand will, so far as possible, be supplied. It is only as creators of demand that consumers appear in this picture.

It follows that the consequences of any course of action terminate for such an executive when the consumer has been successfully supplied. The further consequences of supplying demand—the trivialization of the culture by the major television networks, for example—are beyond the scope of any consideration by those who supply the electric power for such enterprises. Once again the cost-benefit analysis is not an evaluatively neutral instrument of choice.

The fifth and last parallel with utilitarianism concerns the time-scale on which costs and benefits are to be assessed. When we make a decision—implicitly or explicitly, recognizing it or failing to recognize it—about the time-span within which we are going to reckon up costs and benefits, at least three different kinds of consideration will affect our decision. The first of these concerns the fact that both types and rates of change for different cost and benefit factors may vary so that by choosing one time-length rather than another the relation of costs to benefits will appear quite differently. If I am deciding how to transport commodities from one place to another (by building a road, building a railway, maintaining a canal or whatever) changes in the price of land, the prices of raw materials, the size of the labor force, the demand for utilization of surplus carrying capacity, the technologies involved, the alternative uses to which each type of resource might be put, will all change in such a way that, even if I am a perfect predictor, the choice of dates within which costs and benefits are to be assessed may give strikingly different results. Of course in a private profit-seeking corporation the current rates of return expected on investment will place constraints on such a choice of dates; and in public corporations the need to vindicate policies within terms ultimately specified by electoral laws will set not dissimilar constraints. Nonetheless even within such limits a certain arbitrariness is likely to appear.

Secondly it is not just that the different factors in a situation will be subject to different types and different rates of change; they will also differ in the degree to which they are predictable. Three key types of unpredictability are likely to be generated in the relevant types of situation. One springs from the sheer complexity of so many of the relevant types of situation and their vulnerability to contingencies of an in-practice unpredictable kind: earthquakes, viruses, panics. A second springs from the systematic unpredictability of all innovation that involves radical conceptual invention. . . .

* * *

A less arbitrary consideration, but one perhaps no less difficult to handle, appears if we turn to the third factor impinging upon judgments about time-scales. This concerns the view taken by individuals of the existence, identity, interests and responsibilities through time of the organization for which they are working. Let me make an initial point about the interests of individuals. We know that individuals vary in the degree to which their identification of their own interests ranges beyond their individual selves and their present state in time. A man may see his interests as being those of a man with a future of a certain kind rather than a present of a certain kind. So a man may for considerations of interest vote for a measure which benefits the aged, although he himself is young, because it is in his family's interest that the aged be supported. Or he may vote for a tax measure which benefits forty-five-year-old married men with high incomes, although he himself is a low paid, unmarried twenty-five-year-old, because he votes on the basis of the interests of his predicted future self rather than his present self. As with individuals acting for themselves *qua* individuals, so also for individuals acting in their organizational roles. What time-span is assumed to be appropriate for determining costs and benefits will depend on how the organization's interests are envisaged through time and on how the interests of related institutions—the state, the local community, the profession or whatever—are envisaged through time. This becomes very clear if we look at the limiting case, that of organizations constructed and maintained only for some temporary purpose, such as a relief mission whose task is to feed and provide schooling for three thousand children for a period of four months.

The reason why the time-scale within which costs and benefits are to be assessed is much less arbitrary and debatable in such cases is *not* merely that the time within which the project is to be completed is specified; for even with projects whose duration is specified, costs and benefits may range in time far beyond the actual duration of the project. What limits the time-scale in a non-arbitrary way is rather the clear restraints placed on goals, tasks and resources in this kind of temporary organization and the consequent ease in identifying both the interests and the responsibilities of the organization. This limitation is, as it were, part of the legal or quasi-legal charter of the organization. But with permanent or at least long-term organizations the criteria for imputing responsibility for and defining interests in a variety of consequences are not assigned in this clear way; and the adoption of different time-scales for the assessment of costs and benefits may presuppose the adoption of different views of how organizational responsibility is to be imputed and how organizational interests are to be defined.

Consider the example of a university. What counts as a cost or a benefit to a university may—and, it is to be hoped, characteristically will—depend upon a distinction between the essential and long-term purposes which a university serves and the short-term *ad hoc* projects with which universities necessarily become involved. A university which undertakes remedial teaching of adolescents from deprived groups in a situation of social and educational crises, or which organizes some of its research in terms of the immediate practical needs of its community, may and often does pay costs in terms of the damage done to its contract with those long dead and those yet to be born in the distant future to whom it is committed to transmit in living form to the unborn the cultural tradition of the dead. A public utility company or a country club is committed to no such contract; and this means that the appropriate time-scale for assessing costs and benefits will be a different one from that appropriate to a university. But *any* time-scale may presuppose some view of its identity.

Note that I have written "may" and not "will." For those who inhabit organizations are often unclear and confused as to what precisely they are doing, and the implicit presuppositions of their actions may be similarly unclear. Sometimes what appears arbitrary in choice of time-scale just *is* arbitrary; but not always.

* * *

The moral structure underlying the corporate executive's thinking is one of which he remains almost entirely unaware. He does not recognize himself as a classical utilitarian; and he cannot therefore recognize that the presuppositions of classical utilitarianism which he shares—which the utilitarians themselves did not recognize—must go doubly unrecognized by himself and his colleagues. His vision of himself remains that of a man engaged in the exercise of a purely technical competence to whom moral concerns are at best marginal, engaging him rather *qua* citizen or *qua* consumer than *qua* executive. Does this false consciousness of the executive, whether in the private corporation or in government, itself have a function? It is plausible to suppose that it does. To consider what that function is, imagine what would occur if all these considerations became manifest rather than latent.

The executive would then be presented with a set of moral problems, or moral conflicts, on which he would have to make overt decisions, over which he would have to take sides in the course of his work. What sort of issues are these? The claims of the environment *versus* the claims of cheaper power, the claims of need (for example, of the old) against those of the urgent present, the claims of rival institutions—government, church, school—in certain respects, the claims of rival judgments of intelligence, integrity and courage. Now it is a crucial feature of our moral culture that we have no established way of deciding between radically different moral views. Moral arguments are in our culture generally unsettlable. This is not just a matter of one party to a dispute generally being unable to find any natural method to convince other contending parties. It is also the case that we seem unable to settle these matters within ourselves without a certain arbitrary taking of sides.

It follows that to allow moral issues to become overt and explicit is to create at least the risk of and more probably the fact of open and rationally unmanageable conflict both between executives and within each executive. The avoidance of such conflict necessitates two kinds of device. Where the recognition of moral considerations is avoidable they must be apportioned out between the different areas of the self and its social life, so that what is done and thought in one area will not impinge upon, let alone conflict with, what is done and thought in another. Boundaries must be drawn between areas of social action whose effectiveness will depend upon them not being recognized for what they are.

* * *

Failures of Discourse: Obstacles to the Integration of Environmental Values into Natural Resource Policy: A Reading of the Controversy Surrounding the Proposed Tocks Island Dam on the Delaware River

Robert H. Socolow

I. ANALYSES ARE NOT ABOUT WHAT PEOPLE CARE ABOUT

Major environmental decisions have a way of getting stuck and staying stuck. The discussions about whether to undertake substantial transformations of natural areas—to bring about new power plants, dams, airports, pipelines, deep water ports—have several pathologies in common. A cluster of detailed technical analyses accompanies the formulation of the program and its initial rush onto the stage; the proponents of the project imply, and generally believe, that all one could reasonably have expected has been done, both to justify the program and to anticipate its pitfalls. As after a carefully planned transplant, the reaction of rejection is slow in coming but grows relentlessly. The analyses are shown to be incomplete, and new analyses starting from different premises are eventually produced by those who wish to stop the program. But, contrary to what one might naively expect, the existence of disparate analyses does not help appreciably to resolve the debate. Rarely are the antagonists proud of their analyses; more rarely still are they moved by the analyses of their opponents. The combatants on both sides have been constrained by mandated rules of procedure as well as by the tactics of compromise. Understandably, the politicians in a position to determine the outcome conclude that their time is not well spent pondering the available analyses, even though they may commission still more of them.

The failure of technical studies to assist in the resolution of environmental controversies is part of a larger pattern of failures of discourse in problems that put major societal values at stake. Discussions of goals, of visions of the future, are enormously inhibited. Privately, goals will be talked about readily, as one discovers in even the most casual encounter with any of the participants. But the public debate is cloaked in a formality that excludes a large part of what people most care about.

Analyses are part of the formal debate. We should not be surprised to learn, therefore, that the disciplined analyses brought to bear on a current

Source: From *When Values Conflict: Essays on Environmental Analysis, Discourse and Decision,* Copyright 1981 American Academy of Arts and Sciences. Reprinted with permission from Ballinger Publishing Company.

societal dispute hardly ever do justice to the values at stake. Terribly little is asked of analysis, and analysts respond in a way that allows the potentialities of their disciplines to be undervalued. . . . There is a dynamic interaction between the demands made and the tools developed. It is not realistic to expect much refinement in tools to occur in the absence of a contemporaneous evolution in the rules of public discourse.

The land use debate I have most pondered, and the source of most of my generalizations, is the debate over whether to build a major rock-fill dam on the Delaware River at Tocks Island, thereby creating a 37-mile-long lake along the New Jersey-Pennsylvania border. The dam was proposed by the Corps of Engineers and was authorized by Congress in 1962. Although land has been acquired, and the National Park Service has arrived on the scene to administer the Delaware Water Gap National Recreation Area that is intended to surround the lake, construction has not yet begun. It may never begin. The likelihood of construction has diminished considerably during the period of our study (roughly 1972 to 1975). However, there is a well-known asymmetry: One can decide over and over not to build a dam; one only need decide *once* to begin construction, and there it is.

I happen to hope that the dam will not be built. Building the dam, it seems to me, would buttress an attitude of impudence toward our natural resources. Not building the dam, on the other hand, would stimulate the development of alternate technologies, intrinsically more respectful of nature, which are ever more urgently needed. Of all the arguments for and against the dam, this need to stimulate a reorientation of our technology is for me the single most compelling one. This essay, in part, seeks to imagine what a technology responsive to an environmental ethic would look like. The search for such a technology is one of the absent features of current analysis.

* * *

There are a wide variety of reasons why those concerned with affecting the outcome of a major land use issue are not envisioning (or at least are not expressing) many of the concerns that in fact move them and many of the options that in fact are open to them. Given the fact that virtually all the participants are dissatisfied with the way discourse currently proceeds, it seems worthwhile to make a substantial effort to understand some of the underlying reasons for these failures of discourse, and some of the possibilities for averting them.

II. BLUNT TOOLS AND SKEWED DISCOURSE

A. Golden Rules

The decision about whether to build Tocks Island Dam is widely perceived to be a choice among alternative conceptions of the region's future and, at a deeper but still articulated level, among alternative conceptions of man's appropriate relationship to nature. The tools that might have assisted in clarifying what the possible futures entail include cost-benefit analysis, which has been designed to facilitate comparisons between programs offering differing streams of future costs and benefits. Working with these tools . . . ought to lead to translations of dimly perceived preferences into relatively explicit strategies, and ought to reveal the incompatibility of some sets of aspirations and the compatibility of others. Current practice, however, follows a series of golden rules—prescriptions and routines that the analyst perceives to be a means of simplifying the tangle of options (and of staying out of trouble), but that prevent the analyst from taking full advantage of the capabilities the tools provide.

* * *

Discussions of the limitations of cost-benefit analysis nearly always emphasize uncertainties about the discount rate and contain caveats about the lack of sensitivity regarding who gets what. Only rarely do they call attention to the problem of drawing a boundary around the system being studied. As in idealized thermodynamics, the cost-benefit theory presupposes a system coupled with its surroundings in such a simple way that one can change the system without perceptibly affecting the surroundings. To do a sensible cost-benefit comparison of two alternative futures, one has to include in the "system" all the activities with which are associated large differences depending on which future is being considered.

If one is to compare a future with the Tocks Island Dam to one without it, even the dollar costs are such that one must include the incremental sewage treatment facilities required to coexist with a lake instead of a river, and the extra roads needed to bring the visitors to the recreation area, if lake-based recreation will indeed attract more visitors than river-based recreation. Both these costs, it turns out, are comparable to the cost of building the dam itself (several hundred million dollars). One may also have to include the uncompensated costs endured by the roughly 20,000 residents in the valley whom the reservoir project is displacing. But then what about including, on the other side of the balance sheet, the increases in property values expected if the dam is built? Does the series of new entries terminate, in the sense that one is finally considering effects (such as gross interregional migration?) that, even though large, are still effectively unchanged by the existence or nonexistence of the project? No analysis has convinced me that the series does terminate or converge in this sense.

Golden rules have been developed which shelter the practitioner of cost-benefit analysis from this uncertainty about boundaries. The analysis becomes stylized, like the folk art of an isolated village. Those costs and benefits which it is permissible to include in the analysis become codified, as do many of the procedures for evaluating their dollar magnitudes. The warping effect on discourse is substantial. It is hard not to introduce the project to a newcomer with: "The project has four intended benefits" (water supply, flood control, recreation, and electric power, in this instance).

The formal rules also carry weight in the detailed planning of a project. The Corps of Engineers continues to maintain that the "highest and best" use of the lake requires the provision of recreation facilities on its shores for 9.4 million visitors (actually, visitor-days) per year, in spite of the statement by two successive governors of New Jersey that they will approve the project only if the recreation facilities are scaled down to 40 percent of that figure. The Corps' persistence must be strongly affected by the way the analyses come out when the formal conventions are followed, for recreation comes to almost half the total annual benefits when the higher figure is used. Others in this volume comment on the extraordinary reduction in the problem's structure that occurs when the value of recreation is calculated by multiplying a fixed dollar value per visitor-day ($1.35) with a number of visitor-days per year, irrespective of who the visitors are, or how crowded the facilities are, or whether the same visitor spends several days or several visitors spend one day.[1] Here I wish to emphasize that these oddly formal rules do have real consequences—consequences such as extra roads being built through open country to provide the access needed to keep the park populated.

The rules of procedure that govern the planning process have yet further impact in restricting the search for alternatives. One of the rules, for example, is that, at a given site, either a multipurpose project or a single-purpose project is to be undertaken—and that, once this choice is made, *multipurpose projects are not to be compared with packages of single-purpose projects addressing the same needs.* Invoking this golden rule, the principal government agencies (the Corps of Engineers and the Delaware River Basin Commission) can dismiss a proposal without analysis if it addresses just one of the four intended benefits—even if another, companion proposal addresses the other three. Environmental critics of the Tocks Island Dam have advocated the use of "high-flow skimming" to provide increments to water supply equivalent to those the dam would produce. If one enlarged an existing reservoir (Round Valley) and perhaps built an additional small reservoir in a subsidiary valley, thus filling the reservoirs with Delaware water in high-flow months and emptying them in low-flow months, offstream storage would be achieved and the main stem of the Delaware would remain unblocked. This suggestion, to be sure, does nothing about main-stem flood control, but flood-plain zoning does. The package needs to be placed alongside the Tocks project. Yet high-flow skimming has been dismissed with a single comment: "This is not a multipurpose project."

When the routine procedures of a government agency are consistent with the perfunctory rejection of ideas emerging from outside its bureaucracy, "noise" is thereby built into the discourse between that agency and its

----

[1]The dollar values of alternate forms of recreation *are* distinguished; $1.35 is a weighted average of the forms of recreation Tocks will provide.

critics. The environmentalist critics have pushed the idea of highflow skimming harder (and with more success, perhaps, than the idea deserves), because of the inability of the government agencies involved to look at it squarely.

* * *

B. Acceptable Damage

The apparent thrust of engineering is to protect man and his works from nature's assaults. Bridges are to survive the highest winds, buildings are to stay warm on the coldest days. Dams, especially, are perceived as symbols of security, as protectors from both floods and droughts. "When water is stored behind a dam, it is there when you need it, like money in the bank," an old-timer told me. A dam's aura of invincibility derives, no doubt, from its sheer bulk, its monumentality. Yet the image is a most incomplete one, for the reservoir, which comes along with every dam, is the exemplar of compromise. How high should the reservoir be filled? Too high and a surprise flood will not be contained, too low and the reserve supply will be absent in a drought. From which of the multiple outlets, at varying heights, should water be withdrawn in late summer (when the reservoir is thermally stratified and the deep, cold water is laden with decaying organic matter)? One answer emerges if the goal is to "enhance" the fish life downstream, another if the goal is to remove nutrients that contribute to the eutrophication of the lake; the two goals are unlikely to be perfectly compatible. The hallmark of engineering is the trade-off and the artful compromise.

But people prefer appearance to reality. There is rarely any clamor to make trade-offs explicitly; it is enough for many that the compromises reached reflect professional judgment. Public discourse is thus dominated by solutions offered as risk-free. Among his colleagues, an administrator for the Federal Aviation Administration responsible for equipping private airports with traffic control equipment can admit to having a target figure in his head for "acceptable annual fatalities from general aviation operations." And military officers get used to thinking in terms of acceptable losses of troops and materiel. But neither the mayor whose town abuts the airport nor the President preparing the battle plan can use such language with his constituency. The larger the issue of public accountability (as opposed to professional accountability alone) looms in an official's mind, the less willing he becomes even to formulate a problem in terms of acceptable risk. These reflexes persist even when no lives are at stake: thus the desire to find a safe minimum flow so as not to think about tolerable levels of discomfort and dislocation.

Yet the usefulness of phrasing problems in terms of acceptable risk is probably nowhere so obvious as in problems that involve fitting man's activities onto a highly variable natural background. This has been recognized explicitly in some of the air pollution legislation, where standards are typically written in the form: the concentration of pollutant X shall not exceed C_o more than N times each year. The most compelling reason for drawing up probabilistic standards of this sort is to recognize and bend with the variability of atmospheric phenomena; atmospheric inversions, for example, will occur occasionally, with little notice, and will produce a buildup of pollution levels. It may be unreasonable to have so much pollution control equipment in place that on the occasion of the worst inversion on record, the pollution concentration C_o is not exceeded. Put another way, it may be possible to win community acceptance of a C_o that is lower as long as an occasional escape is permitted. Mathematically, having C_o and N to play with instead of just C_o (with N set equal to zero) gives the legislator and the community more options in terms of environmental planning.

The regulation of water use seems not to have manifested the same subtlety of design. Pollution targets are almost invariably set at specific values, rarely even adjusted for the time of the year.[2] Minimum river flows, as specified in rules and procedures without built-in escapes, determine the operation of reservoirs. New reservoirs are judged primarily in terms of their "safe yield." All these simplifications channel the imagination in similar ways. The safe yield of a reservoir is that rate of extraction of water from the reservoir which, under a recurrence of the most severe drought of record, could be sustained continuously. Usually the reservoir, at the extremum of the drought, lies nearly empty.[3] Attention is thus diverted from any consideration of riding with the punch, organizing one's affairs differently when the drought arrives, and leaving the reservoir with most of its water in it.[4]

From the standpoint of public health, there would seem to be no explanation for this distinction between air and water standards. The adverse health effects of air and water pollution are structurally similar: both involve no clear-cut level at which acute reactions ensue, no physiological warning that levels have become toxic, enormous variability among individuals (including certain groups that are especially susceptible), and uncertain synergisms. River flow is an even better example of stochastic (random) variability in nature than are the movements of cold and warm fronts of air. It is perplexing that environmental design reflecting this variability has not arisen. Perhaps the older traditions of water law and the concomitant self-images of the "water professionals" are historically inhibiting factors.

[2]For a detailed discussion of the remarkable oversimplification of the structure of the pollution problem in the planning for the cleanup of the Delaware estuary, see Bruce Ackerman, Susan Rose Ackerman, James W. Sawyer, Jr., and Dale W. Henderson, *The Uncertain Search for Environmental Quality* (New York: Free Press, 1974).

[3]If a reservoir is constrained by rules of operation to retain some minimum water level, this is incorporated into the calculation of its yield.

[4]The dissonance between the recreation and water supply objectives of the Tocks reservoir has figured prominently in its political history. In those years when "drawdown" of the reservoir would be necessary, mudflats would be exposed at its periphery and the opportunities for recreation correspondingly impaired. The Council on Environmental Quality has called particular attention to this problem, and to the problem of eutrophication, . . . in its reviews of the project.

The water professionals make continual use of the stochastic concept of the N-year storm, or flood, or drought—one whose severity should be exceeded, on the average, just once in N years. The concept is most often used in situations where N is large (50 or 100 or more) and a decision is to be made about how high to build a levee or how strong to make a mooring buoy. The concept unfortunately happens to be on least secure scientific footing when N is large, because of the shortness and uncertainty of the available hydrological record and the significance of unaccountable changes in topography. The concept is rarely used when N is small, say 10. It would be worth searching for a way of activating an interest in procedures where, say, one year in every ten (with the dates determined by nature), the planned interactions of man with river will be qualitatively different. If the river is ordinarily used for waste removal and for commercial fishing, for evaporative cooling and for drinking water, then during the summer and autumn months of a once-in-ten year of unusual low flow, either the wastes will be removed in a different way (or will be more highly treated or stored) or the commercial fishing will be suspended; and either the power production upstream will be cut back (or another form of cooling used) or the drinking water will be taken from somewhere else.

If one is willing to confront the costs of occasional disruption, one is led quite naturally to modify the usual analyses of the optimal timing of construction of water supply projects. When a positive discount rate is used to relate intertemporal preferences, the result, necessarily, is that it pays to delay any project somewhat beyond the time when it would be needed under the (usual) assumption that the historic worst drought will certainly befall the region the very year that the project is completed.[5]

Once acceptable damage becomes a legitimate subject for discourse, much of the fabric of water resource planning must be rewoven. Projects are deferred with a nonzero probability of their arriving too late; reservoir management proceeds under the expectation that in low rainfall periods there will be some compromise between drawdown and curtailment of consumption; and consumption is scanned for its lower and higher priority components. The cumulative effect of such a reweaving will be to weaken the insulation of society from natural events. Acceptable damage is disruption of routine at times beyond our choosing; it means brown lawns and fountains empty in droughts, closed highways and downed power lines in floods.

Nature modulating society: is this something we could ever get used to? The thrust of most of industrial society has been in the opposite direction: to reduce man's vulnerability to nature's excesses and, by extension, to reduce man's subordination to nature's variability. The starkest contrast in nature is *dead-alive*. Man has labored hard to be in control of that dichoto-

---

[5]These ideas have been worked out quantitatively, with a highly simplified model of the variable hydrology, in a significant but unpublished appendix to the Northeastern United States Water Supply Study of the Corps of Engineers, *Economic Analysis for Organization, Legal, and Public Finance Aspects of Regional Water Supply*, 1972. The appendix was prepared by the Institute of Public Administration, New York, N.Y., and, in particular, I believe, by Dr. Ruth Mack.

my to the largest extent possible; judging from the present concern with the treatment of the terminally ill, man may indeed be overdoing it. But there are lesser contrasts that industrial man has also felt it was his destiny to override, where it is even more certain that we are in sight of a boundary of reasonableness. *Light-dark:* The candle, the electric light, the night shift, the night ball game. *Cold-hot:* Clothing and housing, refrigeration, hot-house fruits and vegetables, air conditioning, heated patios in winter. *Wet-dry:* Boats, dikes, irrigation, umbrellas, humidifiers and dehumidifiers. One could go on—*grass-crabgrass*, overcome by herbicides, *grass-mud*, over-come by artificial turf (and plastic trees!). The shame of a city surprised by an early snowstorm, and of a town faced with a washed-out bridge—might that shame now have become excessive?

The vast majority of us are uncomfortable contemplating even the possibility of deliberately subjecting ourselves to the variability of nature. A representative of the Delaware River Basin Commission finds such a concept "not socially acceptable." Yet, . . . the possibility of *success* in insulating ourselves from nature is a horror it is time to confront. Have we indeed instructed the engineers to produce a technology such that no natural event, however rare, would require us to react? Did we really mean to do this?

C. Damage Limitation

When discussion of acceptable damage comes more naturally to the planners, more inventive approaches to *damage limitation* can be expected to follow. In recent years, there has been a start in this direction, promoted in considerable measure by The National Environmental Policy Act of 1970 (NEPA), which requires the examination of "nonstructural alternatives" to all federally assisted construction programs. The nonstructural alternatives to dams as a means of flood control include flood-plain zoning, carrot-and-stick flood damage insurance, and early warning systems. At least the first of these has figured prominently in the discourse in the State of New Jersey, whose legislature has passed a flood-plain zoning act as a direct result of a chain of argument originating with the proposal for the Tocks Island Dam.

The nonstructural alternatives to dams as a way of extending water supplies include, above all, strategies to improve water conservation, in-cluding metering and charging for water in a way which discriminates between consumptive and nonconsumptive uses and between high and low flow periods. Efforts along these lines have begun recently at the Delaware River Basin Commission. Indeed, part of the water resources community regards the Tocks Island Dam as an old-fashioned project precisely be-cause it fails, by and large, to incorporate the currently more fashionable nonstructural approach to the historic objectives of water management.

But damage limitation strategies are by no means limited to nonstruc-tural strategies. There are "engineering strategies" to minimize the dam-age of droughts and floods, which nonetheless may involve hardware in the cities instead of hardware in the wilderness. The new state buildings in downtown Trenton in the flood plain of the Delaware were built with their heating and cooling plants on higher floors so that flooding could be withstood. One damage limitation strategy for drought periods for Philadelphia might be to run a pipe upstream ten or even twenty miles, so that water could be taken from the Delaware in a region of lower salinity in the event of a severe drought; in normal times, the pipe would just lie there.[6] Another damage limitation strategy—one that would take much longer to implement and that might apply only to a new or rebuilt city—would be to maintain two parallel water systems, one for uses that require high quality water (drinking, cooking, bathing) and one for uses that can tolerate water of lower quality (many industrial uses, toilet flushing). In so doing, a city would substantially reduce the task of producing enough high quality water.[7] All these are "structural" or "engineering" solutions; conceivably, the system of parallel piping would be even more complex and costly than a system of dams and reservoirs. The difference, however, lies in the location at which the enterprise is carried out: engineering our urban complexes rather than our wilderness areas and landscapes. Those encouraging the search for nonstructural solutions are largely motivated by a desire to be more gentle to the natural environment; they should be reminded that the same end can often be achieved by a geographic transposition of the technological imagination.

If creative technology should one day return to the cities and there display an increased cybernetic emphasis, we will begin to raise our expectations of the machines around us. We will insist that they last longer, be easier to repair, and undergo a more satisfactory metamorphosis at the end of their lives. We will also learn to insist that our machines report to us more faithfully how they are functioning, so that we know when to repair them or replace them. Finally—and perhaps this is more controversial—we will come to insist that our machines allow us to increase our sensual contact with our natural surroundings.

Of all the impacts of the "energy crisis" of the 1973–74 winter, the most lasting, I predict, will be its impact on architecture. The downtown office building of the 1960s already stands as a metaphor for the whole society's desire for enforced independence from the natural setting: temperature, humidity, air exchange, and lighting are all controlled mechanically, independent of season, wind speed, or whether one is on the north or south side of the building. Neither materials nor design change as the location is moved in latitude by thousands of miles (In physicists' jargon, the building is invariant under ninety-degree rotations, displacements in space, and translations in time.) The notion of air conditioning a sealed office building on a mild day appears grotesque once one becomes aware that upstream from the power lines there are scarce resources whose ex-

[6]The earliest reference I know that presents this idea is the *Report on the Utilization of the Waters of the Delaware River Basin* (Malcolm Pirnie Engineers—Albright and Friel, September 1950).

[7]An analogous approach to the likely energy problems of the next two decades would seek a means to supply priority users of electrical energy (hospital facilities, refrigerators, elevators) even in situations of substantial brownout or blackout. As a colleague of mine put it, "invest in switching equipment."

traction and conversion are necessarily accompanied by environmental damage. The office building of the near future will have openable windows, fewer lights and more switches, north-facing walls very different from south-facing walls (the latter having awnings or comparable "soleil briser" projections), and east-facing walls different from west-facing walls if either east or west is the direction of the prevailing wind. It may also have solar energy collectors and water collectors on the roof and windmills mounted on the vertical edges. Less symmetry, more deliberate hassle, more life.

I could be wrong. The technology of the near future may instead be designed to refine our sensibilities still further in the directions of change of the past several decades: toward personal security, toward isolating ourselves from our machines, and toward being able to do everything everywhere. Cities connected by cars on rails that arrive empty at your home and leave you at work before they pick up another passenger, heavy cars to make the ride smooth. (The Personalized Rapid Transit systems on the drawing boards are usually presumed to operate under such constraints.) Junking consumer products at the first sign of breakdown. Recreation of all kinds available at all places and all times: outdoor iceskating rinks in the Caribbean, heated swimming pools (heated *lakes?*) for winter swimming in the Adirondacks.

It seems more likely to me that we are in the early stages of an intellectual and cultural sea change. Images of saturation of wants go only part of the way toward explaining why the near future should not be predictable by a straightforward extrapolation of the recent past. For part of what is involved is the development of new wants and the rediscovery of ancient ones. . . . An important class of new wants that is already palpable expresses a desire for interaction with "the only earth we have." These wants will call into being still uninvented technologies, public policies, and styles of discourse appropriate for such a resource-respectful new world.

III. THE SPECIAL PROBLEMS OF ECOLOGY

Biological information can be relatively easily tracked by the observer of decision making, in part because it is less emotionally charged than political or economic information, so people will talk about it, and in part because it is still novel, so people tend to have clear impressions of what they know and where they've learned it. Accordingly, the study of how biological information is processed in the course of making decisions about the use of natural resources ought to give insight into how other kinds of information are processed as well. . . .

* * *

A. Oysters

The fate of the Delaware Bay oyster is bound up with the dam. . . . The oyster beds, 150 miles downstream from the dam, are in a deteriorated condition relative to 50 years ago, and they are menaced by a predator known as the oyster drill. It is widely believed that the seasonal high flows of fresh water down the Delaware and into the Bay in April, May, and June are protecting the beds from further assault by the drill, because the oyster is able to tolerate less saline water than the oyster drill and hence gets rid of the drill druing that season.

Except for one year in 60, the lake behind the dam is supposed to be full before the spring months of high flow begin. Thus the natural flows (except flood flows, defined as flows in excess of 70,000 cfs) are expected to pass through the dam undiminished each spring. Between the dam and the oysters, however, water is expected to be withdrawn for out-of-basin shipment. The continuity of out-of-basin diversion provided by the reservoir constitutes a major justification for the dam. This diversion can only continue during the spring months at the expense of the water flow to the oysters. Thus, advocates of oysters and advocates of out-of-basin regional growth are potential adversaries.[8]

No one who understands this conflict of interest appears willing to break the news to those who don't. Once, searching vainly for an analysis of this conflict, I was told by a minor Corps functionary, "Who can put a price on the life of a fish?" Yet, within the Corps, it is clear that the over-constrained character of the oyster problem is recognized. With quintessential American optimism, however, the Corps it trying to find a way to *improve* the oyster beds, a way to get them back to their state of 50 years ago, or even better. The Corps is hoping to find a way to do this through a procedure of timed releases of fresh water, all through the year.

The presupposition of such a study is that man can improve on nature. Among conservation groups, however, the oyster issue has had a completely different symbolism. The oyster's dependence on an annual pulse of fresh water is regarded as an *indicator* of the dependence of an entire estuarine ecosystem on that same annual pulse. The life cycles of myriad organisms are tied to these seasonal fluctuations, and even if another way could be found to protect the oysters from the drill (by chemical or biological control, for example), there would still be other kinds of damage in the estuary if the fresh water pulse were removed. The presupposition here is that man can only diminish the quality of the natural environment by his intervention—that "nature knows best." Although logically inadequate as a guide to problems such as pollution control, in which one intervention of man is designed to reduce the consequences of another, the presupposition is nonetheless a touchstone for a large number of "preservationist" attitudes, which contravene the prevailing interventionist

•

---

[8]By the hydrologist's measure, the Tocks Island Dam, relative to its basin, is not big. To further even out the uneven flow would have required larger storage capacity, and the dam is *not* larger primarily to avoid either drowning or diking Port Jervis, 37 miles upstream. The construction of additional storage capacity on- or offstream should be expected if the goal continues to be to increase the "yield" (the minimum continuously deliverable flow) from the river valley; the yield is maximized only when the flow is completely evened out. Each future storage area will present the same trade-off problem: uneven flow for the oysters, steady withdrawal for man.

attitudes of most foresters, fisheries managers, and other environmental scientists.

So, whither has policy evolved in this new Age of Ecology? The Corps of Engineers now explores the ecological consequences of its projects. The Fish and Wildlife Service of the U.S. Government intervenes on man's behalf whenever either commercial fishing (oysters) or sports fishing (shad) is threatened. The Corps, in response, reformulates the task of protecting a fishing resource into the task of enhancing it. The Corps consults with leading biologists. It is a new Corps, a more and differently responsive bureaucracy, and, far more than previously, there is a biological dimension to decision making.

The economists tear their hair. What happened to costs and benefits and to the market—to transfer payments to the oystermen, for example, if their beds are destroyed, or payments *by* the oystermen if the beds are improved? There is nothing intangible or fragile about oystermen, so why should traditional methods of economic analysis suddenly be abandoned?[9]

The conservationists tear *their* hair. Their starting point is piety and self-doubt in the face of nature, and somehow it has gotten lost. To gain entry into the discourse, they talk about a cash crop; to avoid sounding softheaded, they fail to emphasize that, in their view, the "cash crop" is merely an indicator of the condition of a far more valuable ecosystem. The conservationists have separate languages for talking to one another, to politicians, and to their avowed opponents. Except when they talk to one another (and perhaps even then) they refrain all too often from articulating what really matters to them.

"Professionals," according to one definition, "don't back one another into corners." "I'd rather argue a point of procedure than a point of substance," another professional told me. Self-censorship is a tactic that keeps coalitions together and keeps opponents on speaking terms. But self-censorship, nonetheless, has considerable costs. Some of the costs are political. When a dialogue proceeds under false pretenses, its participants rapidly grow bitter; if after much effort you have scored a point, and your opponent acts as if the score is unchanged (because it really is), you want to quit. The Philadelphia office of the Corps now feels this way about the Environmental Defense Fund, and expresses a strong desire to keep its distance.

At another level, perhaps even more vital, the cost of the conservationist's failure to articulate what most troubles him is the loss of crucial information in the decision process. Many people outside the conservation groups assume that ecological insights are the property of conservationists and are up to them to introduce into the discourse. But what if they don't want to? Once, among conservationists planning strategy, I asked whether floods were beneficial to the life on the river banks. I was told to stop

---

[9]To be sure, there are intangible values at stake in the survival of the villages whose local economies are entirely dependent on the oysters, villages with pride, tradition, and people having untransferable skills. Such costs are like the costs of burying under water some of the historic farming villages upstream from Tocks, costs that the present-day cost-benefit analysis appears not to be equipped to incorporate.

wasting everyone's time; the answer was obviously yes, there was a good movie that showed why, and "this is not what one whispers in the governor's ear." Well, why *not* whisper this into the governor's ear? If the river banks will deteriorate, the governor should know it. If ecologists don't really know, but think they know how to find out, then the support of such research should get high priority.

The question, "Do ecologists really know anything useful?" is on many people's minds. The answer appears to be that, at the very least, they can distinguish among what they know with assurance, what they have hunches about, and what "pop" concepts they see no evidence for whatever. As long as their knowledge is not systematically incorporated into environmental discourse, the United States can continue unfolding its environmental programs and then folding them up again, acting as if only distributive issues and not "real" consequences (duck hunters' votes and not ducks) are at stake. Do estuarine ecosystems become less productive or just different when dams are built? I have the impression that most ecologists believe they know the answer to that one—that indeed a lot *can* be said about how an estuary is damaged when it is simplified; if so, the information may be too important to be left to the conservation groups to introduce.

The ecologists may not have welcome news (indeed, one of the first anthologies on ecology was called *The Subversive Science*), but they must be encouraged to speak, and they must be *questioned*. They have had something essential to say about DDT, and about predator control programs; in the process, we have all learned about food chains. By clarifying the importance of rhythms in nature, ecologists may cause us to rethink some of the practices that have grown up around the assumption that it is invariably to man's advantage to smooth out nature's peaks and valleys. To take a single example, the whole basis of the bartering between interests representing different river basins may be built on faulty ecological principles. The crux of this bartering is the concept that if you take water out of a basin when water is abundant, you must promise to return water to the basin (by releases from a reservoir) when water is scarce. . . . The result, if the agreement is respected, is that river flow is evened out. But a river that flows evenly is not a natural river, however convenient it may be to man; plants and animals, in countless well-understood ways, are keyed to the seasonal flow engendered by melting snow. By various yardsticks such as species diversity or production of desired species, the evening of flow could be judged to have deteriorated the river. The repayment with low-flow augmentation could be judged to have negative value.[10]

Ecologists may have something even more disturbing to say about the benefit nature derives from her most *extreme* variations, such as forest fires and floods, as opposed to her regular seasonal variations. If redwoods have depended on periodic forest fires to clear away the understory, and if

---

[10]A system of values that elevates man's convenience is flawed in other ways: . . . the very enterprise of bringing some of nature's rhythms under deliberate control takes something important from our experience of the world.

mangroves have depended on floods to propagate to new locations, what is man to make of such information? The benefits of nature's excesses come as a surprise to those of us who grew up in a culture that emphasized that what was destructive in nature it was man's responsibility to tame (like his temper). The benefits of seasonal flow are less difficult to appreciate; after all, we have our own daily and monthly clocks built in.

IV. IF I LEARN TO LISTEN, YOU MAY LEARN TO CONVERSE

* * *

A. Models and Data Must Be Located in More Helpful Places

A moderate amount of science and an enormous amount of data usually pertain to a given policy decision related to natural resources. In the case of the Tocks Island Dam, historical flows of the Delaware at several gauging stations are available stretching back many decades. The historical record can be restated in stochastic form (giving the probability of recurrence of various degrees of flooding and drought, among other things) and can be "rerun" on a computer with any desired assumption about reservoir releases, out-of-basin shipments, consumptive losses, and so forth. The water professionals agree with one another to a very large extent concerning how their analytical tools should be used, and the approach they take is not particularly dependent on who the client is: anyone's preferred strategy for management of the river's water flows would be analyzed in essentially the same way. Not only are the data base and the analytical procedures common property resources; so too are the problems of uncertain and missing data, of extrapolation, and of oversimplification in modelling.

One might expect analysts occasionally to be encouraged to assume a neutral stance and to generate an array of results flowing from deliberately varied starting assumptions representative of several conflicting points of view. But this does not in fact happen. One reason, I believe, is that expertise is so widely presumed to be the captive of the adversaries. The model of the court of law is devastating: we have come to expect an insanity trial to produce a psychiatrist for the defense and a psychiatrist for the prosecution. Some environmental expert is presumed to be available who will come out with any answer for which a combatant is willing to pay. The analyst's results are presumed to be little more than the packaging of opinion and sentiment.

Although such attitudes are more often accurate than one might wish, they represent a significant exaggeration. And the costs of such attitudes are high indeed. Not only does a common ground among adversaries fail to be established, but, perhaps just as serious, a constituency for nurturing the data base and the analytic techniques fails to develop. No one in a position to do anything about it cares whether measurements are made or not. Yet almost inevitably, because new issues keep arising, critical data are missing. After years of consultants' reports pleading for the taking of data on the flow of nutrients into the river. . . , such a program is still not underway, in spite of the fact (or perhaps because of the fact) that the politically most troublesome technical issue in the current Tocks debate— the likelihood of eutrophication of the reservoir behind the dam—largely depends for its resolution on the availability of such data.

The most unfortunate cost of excessively disparaging the technical tools is the discouragement of sustained efforts to generate alternatives. When a computer stores large blocks of historical flow data and a few elementary routing routines, it cries out to be played with. Questions of the "What If" variety, the seeds of all inventive proposals, are all but certain to germinate if such an invitation is accepted. Yet, today, the ground is not fertile. No one wants to hear. No one has such play as his work.

It is worth looking hard for ways to activate the better use of the relevant "hard science" in policy making. One obvious possibility would be to dissociate the experts from the historic adversaries, in at least a few institutions. Suppose that, in each major river basin, a facility could be established and nurtured which at the least would house the hydrological capability I have just described as well as, presumably, comparable demographic, social, economic, and ecological data banks and software. It is conceivable that, over time and abetted by the staff of such a facility (who would of course seek to justify their existence), the facility would find ways to be useful to a wide range of clients. At such a Center for the Delaware River Basin, the Greater New Jersey Chamber of Commerce, Trout Unlimited, the City of New York, the Environmental Defense Fund, all could come to refine their preferences.

The staff of such a facility would press for further data gathering and model development, and might logically take responsibility for this enterprise. But monitoring the modelers must also be accomplished somehow. There is a market in elaborate computer models today, and it resembles the market in dangerous toys; there is something a little unsavory about sellers and buyers alike.

The seller may have initially developed his model for a research problem to which it was relatively well suited, and the buyer may have begun with a policy problem an appropriate model could clarify. But bargains are struck when there is no match possible. Perhaps the necessary input data do not exist; perhaps the model has structural limitations (inadequate grid size, dimensionality, time dependence); perhaps the positivist character of the output is certain to blind the recipient to its defects. At an earlier time, before computers, it was harder to lose track of a model's uncertainties and imperfections. The water professionals resorted to physical analog models, scaled and distorted, equipped with faucets, wave generators, bottom rougheners, and other hardware. But today's numerical models are often not significantly better in fact at prediction, especially when they are run under a constraint of "modest cost." It is worth thinking about how to structure a center for modeling so that it has incentives to be candid about its models' shortcomings.

The structuring of improved environmental discourse poses other problems of institutional design that can only be touched on here: sources of financial support for the facility, the merits of embedding the facility within a university or national laboratory, its relation to existing facilities, and the confidentiality of both the data and the assistance rendered the clients. The facility should almost surely retain a "service" character, like the Library of Congress, rather than becoming itself the generator of policy. The best (most thorough, most inventive) analysis will usually be demanded only by those who have a stake in the outcome (whether bureaucratic, financial, or emotional), and it would surely be unwise (even if possible) to create a facility that becomes so smart that all the initiative passes to it.

Even those with no initial stake in the outcome can often be helpful: they ask usefully awkward questions. One would like to build in a role for them. I have twice been part of a group of such outsiders, and in each case we left behind us a considerable alteration in perceptions.

In a 1969 summer study run by the National Academy of Sciences, a group of us worked quietly in California trying to understand the raging debate over whether a jetport should be built near the northern boundary of Everglades National Park, in Florida. The conservationists and the land developers flew across the country to talk to us. We discovered that both groups had a working hypothesis that if one was for something, the other ought to be against it. But, in fact, there was an outcome *both* had reason to fear, on different grounds, and so could unite to prevent: the drainage of the interior. The water flowing slowly southward through the inland region containing the jetport site not only prolonged the wet season in the Everglades, establishing critical rhythms for the entire ecosystem, but also played an essential role in protecting coastal fresh water supplies, so that coastal land development and inland drainage were incompatible over the long term. The developers, in particular, had not appreciated the scale of planning that limits to fresh water resources demanded. By emphasizing the opportunity costs of a future of unplanned regional development, our report (along with several others) led state and federal officials to reappraise the value of "undeveloped" land. A consequence of that reappraisal has been the creation by the federal government of the Big Cypress Swamp Water Conservation Area, a development which, at the time of our study two years before, had seemed unwise both to the conservationists and to the developers—extravagant to the former, an infringement on property rights to the latter. Another consequence has been the relocation of the jetport 30 miles to the northeast.

A similar reappraisal of the value of undeveloped land occurred as a consequence of the 1970 National Academy of Sciences summer study of plans to extend Kennedy International Airport into Jamaica Bay. The attitude of public officials to the Bay as a recreational resource, other than for bird watching and nature study, was well expressed by the head of the

New York City Department of Parks and Cultural Affairs when he said, "If you put your foot in that water, it will come out bones." Accepting the assumption that the objectives of an extensive program of water pollution control already underway would be fulfilled, our group emphasized a possible future in which Jamaica Bay would be intensively used by the people of Brooklyn and Queens for water sports. By suggesting modifications of a plan for the extension of regional subways that would permit access to the Jamaica Bay shore, and by suggesting locations and estimating costs of shoreline beaches, we were able to help those involved in the future of the area to imagine new alternatives. A consequence of such altered perceptions has been the redesign of the Gateway National Recreation Area: it now includes the shore of Jamaica Bay, where previously the boundary had been drawn at the water's edge.

The moral of these two stories, for me, is that no group of analysts, however constituted, should ever imagine that their work—whether it focuses on the "science" of a dispute or its politics—can proceed apart from the debate, for it always becomes part of the debate. As Laurence Tribe observes in his essay, "any analysis must become part of the process it has helped to shape." This is the classic conundrum of the observer and the observed embodied in Heisenberg's Uncertainty Principle, and it assures that the work of the analyst of land use disputes will have consequences—in the unfolding of that dispute and other disputes. I would rather commend to analysts the assumption that *everyone* is listening and will go on listening. Like Lord Keynes, I would expect that "madmen in authority, who hear voices in the air, are distilling their frenzy from some academic scribbler of a few years back. . . . Soon or late, it is ideas, not vested interests, which are dangerous for good or evil."

B. What We Should Hear Before We Say the Discourse is Good Enough

*   *   *

. . . Men can now move mountains, melt icecaps, turn rivers around. Their power to assault leads to competing images of nature as victim and nature as ward. In either case, nature is politicized.

Doing nothing has now become a judgment: the act of not implementing a technology to modify a natural phenomenon is politically and morally different from the act of leaving nature alone at a time of innocence. Apparently, Fidel Castro, following a devastating hurricane over Cuba, went on the radio to accuse the United States *not* of seeding the hurricane in a way that went awry, but of *failing* to seed the huricane, knowing that it would hit his country.[11]

Suppose a decision is made not to build the dam, and the following year an immense crack develops in the Kittatiny Ridge, rocks begin to tumble into the valley, the river becomes plugged, and a lake build up

[11]I owe the story, as well as the basic thought in this paragraph, to Edith Brown Weiss.

behind the plug. Does the Corps restore the navigable waterway?[12] That the river should have standing in such a decision seems appropriate. But if I were the guardian for the Delaware, I would be perplexed. I would not want my ward to drown Port Jervis and other human settlements on her banks. I would expect to see some abridgement of her prerogatives. Why should I assume that my river is a savage? Might not a river *like* the idea of being helpful to man? It is not obvious to me that the end result of an enlargement of rights must be an enlargement of selfishness.[13]

The problem of rocks falling into the river was posed in a discussion between dam builders and dam stoppers at a university, a setting that permits some of the usual rules of discourse to be suspended. I look forward to the day when it is usual to have more open, more self-critical, even more playful discourse. I do not argue on grounds of efficiency alone; I rely on more than the enhanced potential for resolution of conflict. Such arguments from efficiency are not self-evident; if one knows one's neighbors better, one may want *less* to compromise with them. Improvements in discourse can be better justified in terms of higher ends than the instrumental one of "solving" the problem at hand. The new discourse would manifest a fuller expression of the diversity of preferences and emotional commitments of the participants. It would enhance the sensitivities of both participants and bystanders to the complex, tragicomic process of self-definition a culture goes through when it seeks to resolve any of its hard problems. It seems worth pursuing for its own sake.

---

[12]The Corps of Engineers, in its environmental impact statement, considered the possibility of taking the *dam* apart at a later time. The two relevant paragraphs are extraordinary enough to merit full quotation:

With the exception of a large permanent rock face at the left abutment, occupation of the area by the project facilities does not in general constitute an irreversible or irretrievable commitment of resources.

The major resource commitments are less enduring and of restorable character. In areas of local protection works the natural stream banks will be lost and replaced with flood walls and levees. The corridor of relocated U.S. 209 due to grade adjustments requiring cut and fill represents an artificial land modification. These features could be removed and the area completely restored to its pre-project uses, should future generations find that such removal and restoration could serve some greater public economic or social good. The construction of the basic dam embankment although very massive does not preclude its alteration or removal. While truly a major undertaking, this change could be made for a compelling (and as yet unknown) future need.

[13]As Lawrence Tribe argues in his essay, "recognizing rights in a previously rightless entity is entirely consistent with acknowledging circumstances in which such rights might be overridden. . . ." My point goes a bit further: it is that recognizing rights does not preclude imposing responsibilities.

Human Rights and the Prevention of Cancer

Alan Gewirth

Every person has a basic human right not to have cancer inflicted on him by the action of other persons. I shall call this right the RNIC (the Right to the Non-Infliction of Cancer). Since it is a species of the right not to be killed or severely injured, the RNIC is perhaps too obvious to need any justificatory argument. Nevertheless, it raises questions of interpretation that have an important bearing both on the ascription of responsibility and on the requirements of social policy.

Closely related to the RNIC is a further right, which I shall call the right of informed control. Each person has a right to have informed control over the conditions relevant to the possible infliction of cancer on himself. This is also a basic human right not only because of its connection with well-being but also because informed control is a component of freedom, which is a necessary condition of action and of successful action.[1]

I

To understand the RNIC, we must consider what it is to inflict cancer on other persons, who is responsible for this infliction, and how it can be prevented. . . .

According to current estimates, 80% to 90% of all cancers are caused by the controllable actions of human beings. In the case of cigarette smoking the victims may be held to inflict the cancer on themselves. But in very many cases, it is other persons who cause the victims to get cancer, and it is to such cases that the RNIC directly applies. . . .

Serious efforts to prevent these cancers must be determined by the specific principles that underlie the RNIC and the right of informed control. First, if we know which substances are causally related to cancer, then exposure to these substances must be prohibited or carefully regulated. Second, every effort must be made to acquire the relevant knowledge and to publicize the results. Hence a major part of the causal and moral responsibility for inflicting various cancers can be attributed to manufacturers, employers, and sellers of various products who control the situations in which the cancers are caused if these persons are made aware of the causal connections and do nothing to stop the actions and policies, in the industrial processes and in marketing, which lead to the cancerous effects. A

[1]On the grounding of human rights in freedom and well-being as the necessary conditions of human action, see my *Reason and Morality* (Chicago, 1978), pp. 63–103. In chapters 2 and 4, I also explain the distinction between "basic" and other human rights.

Source: Reprinted with deletions by permission of the author and the *American Philosophical Quarterly*, 17, no. 2 (April 1980), 117–25.

secondary responsibility can also be attributed to government officials, ranging from legislators to administrators charged with enforcing already existing laws, if, while having knowledge of these carcinogenic dangers, they do not take adequate steps to prevent them.

The basis of this responsibility is similar to that which applies to other forms of killing. The general prohibition against killing innocent humans extends not only to murder but also to manslaughter and other kinds of homicide, including those that stem from advertently negligent and other actions whose likely or foreseeable outcome is the death of their recipients. The general point is that if someone knows or has good reasons to believe that actions or policies under his control operate to cause cancer in other persons, then if he continues these actions or policies, he is in the position of inflicting cancer on these other persons, and he violates a basic human right: he is both causally and morally responsible for the resulting deaths and other serious harms. I shall refer to this as the *informed control criterion* for attributing responsibility.

This criterion is distinct from the criterion of intentionality. To be responsible for inflicting lethal harms, a person need not intend or desire to produce such harms, either as an end or as a means. It is sufficient if the harms come about as an unintended but foreseeable and controllable effect of what he does. For since he knows or has good reasons to believe that actions or policies under his control will lead to the harms in question, he can control whether the harms will occur, so that it is within his power to prevent or at least lessen the probability of their occurrence by ceasing to engage in these actions. . . .

There is a problem about the informed control criterion for attributing responsibility. Consider, for example, the case of automobile manufacturers. They know, on the basis of statistics accumulated over many years, that a certain percentage of the cars they make and sell will be involved in highway deaths and crippling injuries. Hence, since the actions and policies of making automobiles are under the manufacturers' control, why can't we say that they too are causally and morally responsible for inflicting these deaths and injuries on the victims and hence violate their basic human rights? . . .

To answer these questions, I shall refer to a certain principle about the attribution of legal and moral responsibility, which, paraphrasing Hart and Honoré, I shall call the "principle of the intervening action."[2] The point of this principle is that when there is a causal connection between some person A's doing some action X and some other person C's incurring a certain harm Z, this causal connection is "negatived" or removed if, between X and Z, there intervenes some other action Y of some person B who knows the relevant circumstances of his action and who intends to produce Z or who produces Z through recklessness. For example, suppose Ames negligently leaves open an elevator shaft—call this action X—and Carson falls through the shaft and is severely injured—call this harm Z.

---

[2]See H. L. A. Hart and A. M. Honoré, *Causation in the Law* (Oxford, 1959), pp. 128 ff, 195 ff, 292 ff.

According to the principle, the causal connection between X and Z is negatived or removed, so far as moral and legal responsibility is concerned, if some other person Bates, who knows the elevator is not there, intentionally or recklessly entices Carson to step into the elevator shaft. Here it is Bates's intervening action Y that is the direct cause of Carson's falling through the elevator shaft and suffering the harm Z, and for purposes of assigning responsibility this action Y removes or "negatives" the causal connection between X and Z, and hence also removes Ames's responsibility for the injuries suffered by Carson. The reason for this removal is that Bates's intervening action Y of enticing Carson to step into the absent elevator is the more direct or proximate cause of his getting hurt, and unlike Ames's negligence, Bates's action is the sufficient condition of the injury as it actually occurred. Even if Bates does not intentionally bring about the injury, he is still culpable according to the informed control criterion, for he knows that the elevator is not there and he controls the sequence of events whereby Carson is injured.

The principle of the intervening action enables us to see the difference between the case of the producers of carcinogens and the cases of the automobile manufacturers. . . . When the automobile manufacturers turn out cars, this does not itself usually cause or explain the suffering of injuries by the drivers and car occupants. There intervenes the reckless car operation of the drivers—their going too fast, not using seat belts, driving while drunk, and so forth, all of which are under the drivers' own direct and informed control. . . . Thus it was not the auto manufacturers . . . who can correctly be held to have inflicted the respective injuries, but rather the drivers, . . . so that, on the informed control criterion, the causal and moral responsibility lies with them.

In the case of the producers of most carcinogens, on the other hand (omitting for now the manufacturers of cigarettes), there is no similar intervening action between their production or marketing activities and the incurring of cancer. The workers, consumers, and other persons affected do not actively and knowingly contribute to their getting cancer in the ways in which the drivers . . . actively and knowingly contribute to the ensuing injuries. To be sure, the workers work and the consumers eat and so forth, and these actions are under their respective control. But such actions are part of the normal course of everyday life; they do not involve new intervening actions that go outside the presumed normal cause-effect sequences on the part of persons who are informed about the carcinogenic properties of the substances they use; hence, their actions do not break or "negative" the causal connection between the exposure to carcinogens and the getting of cancer. It is for this reason that these cancers may correctly be said to be other-inflicted, i.e., inflicted on the victims by other persons, the manufacturers or distributors, who hence are guilty of violating the RNIC, as against the self-inflicted cancers that result from such actions as cigarette smoking, or the self-inflicted injuries that result from reckless car-driving.

It may still be contended that part of the causal and moral responsibility for inflicting cancer on workers and consumers rests with the victims themselves, in that they have at least a prudential obligation to use due caution just as motorists do. There is indeed some merit in this contention; but it is important to note its limits. The contention may be viewed as resting in part on the hoary maxim *caveat emptor*. Since workers and consumers are buyers or takers of offers made by employers, distributors, and so forth, the maxim says that it is these buyers who must exercise proper caution in accepting the offers.

While the maxim has much plausibility as a counsel of prudence, it has serious limitations when viewed morally. We can especially see this if we look at a general point about the moral principle which is at the basis of a civilized society. This is a principle of mutual trust, of mutual respect for certain basic rights: that persons will not, in the normal course of life, knowingly inflict physical harm on one another, that they will abstain from such harms insofar as it is in their power to do so, insofar as they can informedly control their relevant conduct. The normal course of life, in a society like ours, includes hiring persons for work and selling substances for use, including consumption of food and other materials. Hence, when workers agree to work for others and when consumers agree to buy various products, they have a right to assume, on the basis of this moral principle, that the work and the products will not be physically harmful to them in ways beyond their normal ability to control, or at least, if there is knowledge or good reason to believe that the products are harmful, as in the case of cigarettes, that full knowledge and publicity will be given to this fact. Failing this knowledge and publicity, the primary responsibility for inflicting cancer on workers and buyers, and thereby violating a basic human right, rests with the employers and producers, since it is they who knowingly offer the conditions of work and the products for sale. What is especially serious about this infliction, by contrast with cases to which the principle of the intervening action applies, is that there is not the same opportunity on the part of the victims to control, with relevant knowledge, the causal factors that proximately impose the cancerous harms on them, so that their own right of informed control is violated.

The most direct requirement that the RNIC lays on the responsible agents is simply that they cease and desist from these lethal policies. This requirement must be enforced by the state because of the pervasiveness and seriousness of the harms in question, especially where the actual or potential victims lack the power and the knowledge to enforce the requirement themselves, and because the voluntary cooperation of the agents in stopping such infliction cannot be assumed. Whether this enforcement takes the form of an outright ban on the use of certain substances or the setting of standards that specify the levels at which various potential carcinogens may be used, in either case there must be appropriate sanctions or penalties for the violators. In addition, sufficient information must be made available so that all persons potentially affected may be able to help to control the conditions that affect them so severely. Thus both the state and the various employers, manufacturers, and distributors are the respondents of the RNIC, and their correlative duties have to an eminent degree the moral seriousness and coercibility that go with all basic human rights. . . .

II

I have thus far presented the RNIC as an absolute right not to have cancer inflicted on one by the action of other persons. . . .

* * *

III

Let us now turn to a(n) area of probabilism that may be invoked to mitigate the absoluteness of the RNIC's prohibition against inflicting cancer, and that has been implicitly present in my preceding discussion. This area bears . . . on a weighing of certain values in reaction to those probabilities. The weighing in question is concerned with the relation between the benefits obtained by prohibiting carcinogenic exposures and the costs of such prohibitions; or alternatively with the relation between the benefits obtained by accepting certain risks of cancer and the costs of accepting those risks. It is here a matter of the cost-benefit analysis dearly beloved of economists, which is simply the contemporary version of the pleasure-pain calculus long pursued by utilitarians.

In view of the extreme importance for human well-being of preventing cancer, and the human right to the non-infliction of cancer, how can the avoidance of such infliction be legitimately subjected to a cost-benefit analysis whereby its benefits are weighed against various costs? The better to understand this question, let us compare the problem of preventing cancer with such a situation as where coal miners are trapped in a mine by an explosion. So long as there is any hope of rescuing the miners, all possible means are used to effect a rescue. Except where other human lives are at stake, questions of cost are deemed irrelevant, and so too is the number of miners; lesser efforts would not be made to rescue one miner than to rescue fifty, except insofar as less equipment might be needed to rescue the one. The basis of such unlimited effort to save human lives is that the right of an innocent person to continue to live is normally regarded as absolute, being limited only by the right to life of other persons, and human life is considered to be priceless, in the literal sense of being without price: it is incommensurable with, cannot be measured in terms of, money or any other material goods that might be needed to preserve the life or lives that are endangered.

There are obvious dissimilarities between such a situation and the prevention of cancer. In the former case the lethal danger is actual and immediate, not potential and remote; it is a danger to determinate individuals, not to some general percentage or statistical frequency out of a much larger, less determinate population; and the life-saving operations that are called for are similarly determinate and immediate. Partly because of these differences and partly for other reasons, economists and others have engaged in the cost-benefit analyses mentioned before. There is, after all, time for calculation, and the calculation bears especially on how much, from among the total values both of the individuals directly concerned and of society at large, it is worth spending in order to avoid the risks of cancer and other lethal harms.

*   *   *

Accepting for the present at least the possibility of such a procedure, we may ask how the money value of a human life is to be estimated. Economists have answered this question in different ways, but the way that is most favoured is based on the familiar idea of a Pareto improvement.[3] According to this, one allocation of resources is an improvement over another if it involves at least one person's being made better off while no person is made worse off. The criterion of being made better off consists simply in the preferences of the person concerned, so that if some person prefers allocation X to allocation Y, then he is made better off by X than by Y. And if no person prefers Y to X, then the change from X to Y is a Pareto improvement. Thus if some person A is willing to accept some life-risking situation R on payment to him of a certain sum of money S by another person B who is willing to make this payment, then A's having R and S together is to that extent a Pareto improvement over the situation or allocation where he does not have R and S. On this view, the monetary value of A's life to himself is measured by the minimum sum of money he is willing to accept to compensate for the risk of losing his life in some activity or other.

There is a direct application of this Pareto criterion to the case of cancer, especially as this is incurred by industrial workers in various occupations. According to the criterion, the risk of cancer may be imposed on some worker in some job if he is willing to accept that risk on payment to him of a certain sum of money. Since he prefers a situation where he works at some carcinogenically risky job and hence earns money to a situation where he has no job at all, or since he prefers a carcinogenically riskier job at more pay to a less risky job at less pay, while in each case no one else is made worse off, it follows that the former situation is in each case a Pareto improvement over the latter. Hence, in contrast to the earlier position whereby human life is priceless and the RNIC is an absolute right, according to this new position human life turns out to have a price, and the right to the non-infliction of cancer is now limited not only by unavoidable deficiencies of knowledge but also by the willingness of potential victims to accept financial compensation.

*   *   *

The Pareto criterion's applicability is . . . dubious over a wide range of cases because of a difficulty bearing on distributive justice. Since the

[3]Cf. E. J. Mishan, "Evaluation of Life and Limb: A Theoretical Approach," *Journal of Political Economy* 79 (1971): 687–705; M. W. Jones-Lee, *The Value of Life: An Economic Analysis* (Chicago, 1976), chaps. 1–3.

poorer a person is the greater is the marginal utility for him of a given sum of money, whereas the opposite is true the richer a person is, the poor are willing to accept much greater risks for considerably less money. Thus, in effect, they and their relative poverty are exploited as a way of getting them to do dangerous work far beyond what others will accept. While this is, of course, a very old story, it casts doubt on the economists' model of citizens' sovereignty where workers "voluntarily" accept compensation for risks and thereby show that they consider themselves to be better off than they would be without the risks and the compensation. For many workers are in effect confronted with a forced choice, since the alternative to their taking the risky job with its slightly added compensation is their not having any job at all. Where workers and others do not have the power to ward off such risks by themselves, it is an indispensable function of government to protect such persons from having to make such forced choices, and hence to protect their right both to the non-infliction of cancer and to the non-imposition of serious risks of cancer. This function can be generalized to the more extensive duty of the supportive state to try to provide opportunities and means of knowledge and well-being so as to reduce the vulnerability of poorer persons to such coercive alternatives. In this and other respects, the prevention of other-inflicted cancers merges into more general issues of the distribution of power and wealth in a society.

A quite central difficulty with this application of cost-benefit analysis is that human life or health is not a commodity to be bought, sold, or bid for on the market. Thus the Pareto criterion is mistaken in principle insofar as it assumes that any great risk of death can be compensated for by any amount of money. There are important differences in this regard between engaging in carcinogenic work risks, on the one hand, and buying life insurance, driving cars, or doing aerial acrobatic stunts, on the other. Even though in buying life insurance one implicitly places a certain monetary value on one's life, this is different from undertaking the risk of carcinogenic work for pay. In buying life insurance one recognizes that death is inevitable for everyone sooner or later, and one does not thereby voluntarily incur the serious risk of death. But to undertake the risk of cancer by one's work is not itself inevitable, so that the compensation involves putting a market price on one's life in the context of a controllable, avoidable choice. In addition, the worker in a carcinogenic industry usually does not have the same kind of control over his degree of risk as does the driver of a car or an aerial acrobat. Hence the case for outright prohibition of more than minimal risk in the former case is much stronger than it is with regard to auto driving or aerial acrobatics despite the dangers of death common to these kinds of cases.

A further issue about the economic valuation of human life bears on who does the valuing. It is one thing for a person to put a money value on his own life where he has a relatively unforced choice between alternative ways of life and work. It is another thing for other persons to put this money valuation on his life, as is done when the benefits of making jobs less risky and hence prolonging workers' lives are weighed against alternative uses of public money, such as building new roads or ball parks. In such cases the worker and his life are made economic objects vulnerable to the preferences or choices of other persons rather than of himself. The very possibility of making such choices on such grounds represents a drastic lowering of public morality.

A related criticism must be made of the suggestion that the Pareto criterion should be applied to tax firms or manufacturers so as to encourage them to remove or lower the levels at which their workers are exposed to cancer.[4] For a firm may choose or prefer to pay the tax rather than remove the risk, while passing the tax on to its customers and, under conditions of oligopoly, suffering little or no financial drain. Such payment would be small comfort to the workers who continue to be exposed to the lethal dangers. This taxational incentive approach also has the severe difficulty previously noted, that it makes persons' lives and health matters of bargaining or purchase rather than viewing them as basic goods and rights not subject to such cost-benefit calculation.

*   *   *

I conclude, then, that the probabilistic issues of the carcinogenic cause-effect relations and cost-benefit analysis do not materially affect the conclusion drawn earlier. So far as the moral responsibility of agents is concerned, the Right to the Non-Infliction of Cancer is an absolute human right, and it requires the most determined efforts both to ascertain when such infliction is likely to occur and to take all possible steps to prevent it, and thereby to make its respondents fulfill their correlative duties.

[4]See Albert L. Nichols and Richard Zeckhauser, "Government Comes to the Workplace: An Assessment of OSHA," *The Public Interest* 49 (fall 1977): 64 ff.

The Simple Structure of the Population Debate: The Logic of the Ecology Movement

Ralph B. Potter

Our purpose is to understand the contribution that members of the ecology movement have made to public debate concerning population policy in the United States. Such understanding can come only from an analysis of the structure of arguments as they are put forward in the context of polemic confrontation with alternative views. It is not helpful to describe a single viewpoint in isolation from the alternative positions with which it

Source: From *Population Policy and Ethics* (ed. Veatch), New York: Irvington Pub., 1975.

must contend in the public arena. Similar "values" may be invoked by various protagonists in the population debate. But it would be deceptive to suppose that similar terms bear the same meaning when they are used by different contestants. The significance of appeals to "justice," "freedom," "well-being," or "security/survival" can be determined only by analysis of the function they perform within the framework of a comprehensive approach to questions of population policy. Hence, we must step back momentarily from detailed consideration of the particular arguments put forward by members of the ecology movement and consider the structure of the entire debate within which arguments are designed and put forward to overcome specific counterarguments advanced by opponents. We need to isolate the major alternative policy goals that determine the emphases and priorities of different approaches.

* * *

In spite of the great diversity of focus and perspective, a common formulation of "the population problem" can be stated as follows: In certain parts of the world, the pressure of population factors of size, rate of growth, or distribution is so severe that it may prove to be impossible to develop or maintain a level of resources necessary to sustain a good life for all persons through time.

This common formulation contains four variable elements, each of which has come to serve as the primary point of attack determining the fundamental strategy of four alternative approaches to the population problem. In attempting to alleviate population problems, policy can be aimed, in the first instance, at:

1. Increasing the level of available resources
2. Decreasing, halting, or reversing the rate of population increase
3. Redefining what is necessary to sustain a good life
4. Limiting the range of access to the good life by excluding some and denying the requirement that the full measure of resources necessary to sustain a good life must be available "for all persons through time"

Stating the issue crudely, with the aid of the metaphor of the "banquet of life," we can (1) provide more, (2) invite fewer guests, (3) require each to get along with a smaller share, or (4) exclude some from access to the common table. The issues can be seen primarily as questions of resource development, demographic trends, standards of living, or questions of distributive justice. In each case different disciplines become primary. But any persistent reflection upon the issues must eventually come to grips with all four types of consideration.

In order to understand the position of ecologists, or any other participants in the population debate, it is necessary to begin analysis with the consideration of which of these goals, or which combination of them, constitute the primary aim of policy suggestions. Many disputants attempt to bolster their position with the aid of any argument that holds promise of convincing prospective allies. The population debate has not yet been conducted with the patience, persistence and precision necessary to winnow out collateral arguments that may prove incompatible when advanced simultaneously by a single spokesman. To avoid quibbling, and to insure that the debate is joined at the most crucial level, it is necessary to "get behind" particular propositions to lay bare the simplest structure of reasoning within the stark polemic context, so that we may comprehend what contestants are actually "trying to do" as they assemble ostensibly telling points from here and there. It is important to know which of the four major variables of the population problem they take to be the most promising point of attack.

In practice, the logic of the population debate exhibits a peculiar reversal: what is most important is which of these four possible emphases of policy a particular participant takes to be most inflexible, admitting of no significant degree of change, to be simply accepted as "given." Reasoning begins by the exclusion of certain options. Certain elements of the situation are perceived as "given," fixed, incapable of yielding to any manipulation through policy. The tendency is for practitioners within each discipline or field to be highly conservative in their assessment of the possibilities of adaptation within the area of their own primary interest. Since they see factors within the field of their special competence as "given," the burden of change is thrown into other areas where there must be some "give," allowing adjustment.

Several areas can be taken to be given at once. Fourteen distinct subtypes can emerge from such combinations. When two or three areas are taken to admit of no adaptation, an obvious pressure for change is placed upon the remaining variables. The population debate can best be read as a search for some "give" by those who hold different views concerning what must be accepted as "given." The typical pattern of debate begins with specialists in one area asserting, on the basis of their professional authority, that matters can change but little within their own area. They then proceed to offer recommendations for modifications with respect to one or more of the remaining variables. Next, they must address rebuttals to contending experts who insist that the suggested changes within *their* bailiwick is impossible or unlikely. Individual arguments must be interpreted within this polemical context.

There are two recurring "moves" or phases in the debate; first, members of a discipline must forestall instrusions by those who would seek to find some "give" within a realm that is taken to be given; second, an attack must be launched against "conservatives" who, on the authority of their expertise in their own discipline, resist changes proposed in the areas to which the original defenders would shift the burden of adaptation. Careful analysis of the pattern of debate can make it possible to pinpoint the intersections at which collisions between representatives of different disciplines are likely to take place.

1. Ecologists and economists are most likely to collide over the feasibility of *increasing the supply of available resources* to a level necessary to sustain a good life for all persons through time. To those who would suggest that human needs are fairly stable and human wants greatly ex-

pandable, so that anticipated increases in numbers must be accompanied by a rise in the supply of resources available for consumption, members of the ecology movement have replied that the ecosystem that supports all life on earth cannot long tolerate significantly intensified exploitation. If patterns of consumption remain constant, the level of resources cannot be significantly increased over a period of time without incurring long-term damage to the ecological basis that sustains life. The sanction for the ecologists' rejection of hopes that science and technology will provide an ever increasing bounty of goods through the more intensive exploitation of the finite resources of the earth is their understanding of the objective reality of scientific natural laws which set limits that men cannot evade or forever ignore. Survival itself is menaced by those who foolishly seek to impose burdens beyond what the "carrying capacity of the earth" can bear. Garrett Hardin proposes the formula, "population × prosperity = pollution." An increase in pollution is incompatible with human survival. Hence, there must be "give" elsewhere in the interrelated system of factors constituting the population problem: the population must be reduced, the level of prosperity must diminish, or some must be excluded from access to an equal share to the supply of resources. "Injustice is preferable to total ruin." (Hardin, 1968, p. 1247) "Survival" is the value to which constant appeal is made by ecologists. Survival must be predicated upon restraint from further abuse of the ecosystem. The limits of the given ecosystem make it impossible to "solve" the population problem by continually expanding the supply of resources necessary to sustain present patterns of consumption for all the members of an expanding population.

2. A second appealing solution to the population problem would be to bring about a *reduction or reversal in the rate of population increase*. Growth rates are determined by only three factors: birth, death, and migration. If migration is eliminated as a significant consideration when the problem is viewed in widest perspective, only two options are left: an increase in the death rate or a decrease in the birth rate. Most prefer to direct policy towards the accomplishment of a lower rate of birth.

That which is taken as "given" by demographers and other social scientists who concern themselves professionally with the study of patterns of fertility is the prolific tendency of human beings to increase in numbers, a tendency rooted in the formidable power of human reproduction urged on by biological drives, and reinforced and channeled by cultural traditions and definitions of social roles that may have served evolutionary purposes well in more tenuous demographic settings but that are now held by many to be dysfunctional in a period of rapid population increase.

Demographers may seem to represent an exception to the conservative bias noted among specialists who seek to divert the pressure for change into areas other than their own. Demographers seem to be certain that fertility rates constitute the crucial variable in the population problem and generally welcome the attention their realm of expertise has received. But this much is true of virtually every type of specialist. It is not doubt that their field is crucial but the conviction that they have accurately delimited the extent to which change is possible within their field apart from the destruction of fundamental values that marks the conservatism of the expert. Demographers have generally espoused the value of freedom; they have assumed and favored the value of self-determination of individual actors capable of adapting their procreative behavior in light of their own perception of their own best interests within evolving circumstances. That which they take to be "given"—the prolific tendency to reproduce—has been recognized to be variable from person to person and group to group. Some want to reproduce more than others. The reduction of unwanted fertility, the removal of the barriers of ignorance and social control that prevent the realization of self-determination in the realm of procreation, can be seen as a triumph for freedom, a vindication of the libertarian tradition that has marked the family planning movement and has served as the frequently implicit ethical foundation of the thought of most demographers.

The moral dynamism of the family planning movement has been generated out of the value of freedom. In an earlier, different demographic circumstance, the movement asserted the value of the freedom of the family to determine its own size in opposition to the obligation to give weight to the demographic needs of the wider community alleged by both secular nationalists and ecclesiastical natalists. As concern about the problem of "overpopulation" has increased, the gospel of "responsible parenthood," with its emphasis upon the voluntary, purposeful choice of family size and spacing by autonomous family units armed with the knowledge and means of effective birth control, has gained new converts. Some have been slow to notice that concern about the population problem has been grafted onto a movement previously existing within middle-class, Protestant circles in Scandinavia and Anglo-Saxon lands which is grounded in libertarian principles establishing the autonomy of the family unit and the natural right of each family to decide for itself, in light of its own perception of its own interest, the number and spacing of its offspring. This highly individualistic, nearly atomistic approach to freedom has ironically come under attack just at the moment of its apparent triumph, as some observers foresee that a logic that begins with the autonomy of individuals and families can be invoked to vindicate the right to bear any number of offspring and thus intensify demographic dangers within a system containing a finite supply of resources.

Ecologists pursue a different path of reasoning that brings them into direct collision with the individualistic, libertarian tradition of demographers steeped in the ethos of the family planning movement. Starting with projections of the limited supply of resources available on board the "Spaceship Earth," Paul Ehrlich, the most prominent spokesman for the ecological movement, asserts: "What must be done is to determine how much 'good' should be available for each person. Then just how many people can enjoy that much 'good' on a permanent basis can be determined, at least in theory. That number of people would then be one 'optimum' population size for our finite planet." (Ehrlich and Harriman, 1971, p. 12ff) Thought begins, not with acknowledgment of the freedom that must be accorded to individual families, but with a view of ecological reality, a projection of the supply of resources that can be generated through time without destruction or deterioration of the ecosystem's life-sustaining elements. Survival is the first value. The conditions of survival are set by the ecological realities best known to ecologists. Once the parameters of possible provision are known, the second step is to determine what sized share of the available resources each person must command in order to lead a decent life. An interpretation of what constitutes "well-being" must here be inserted into the population policy equation. Next, one must divide the total supply of resources available under the given ecological limits by the amount necessary to sustain the welfare of each person in order to derive the optimum size of population. Paul Ehrlich's more recent renditions of the ecologist's procedure for thinking about population issues reflect a strong egalitarian sense of justice demanding that goods be equitably distributed to all members of the human community. There can be no justifiable basis for excluding some from equal access to a full share in the common supply. Indeed, strenuous remedial measures must be initiated to undo existing inequities.

Thus, in thinking about population issues, ecologists such as Ehrlich start from an assessment of the prospects of *survival* as defined by their understanding of the capacities of the ecosystem. They apply a conception of *welfare* to derive the divisor necessary for the estimation of optimal population size in relation to the projected capacity to produce needed resources. Considerations of *justice* enter in to impose an obligation of equity in the distribution of that which is necessary to sustain a good life for all persons through time. Only after the demands of survival, welfare, and justice have been considered do ecologists treat of *freedom,* that value which is the starting point of the demographers and social scientists imbued with the ideology of the family planning movement. The depth of the division between the two movements is profound. Their differences are rooted in opposite priorities of method used in thinking about the moral dilemmas of population policy. Ecologists are prone to appear as "totalitarians" to those formed in the libertarian tradition; family planners can be seen as naive and dangerous proponents of a brand of freedom that may bring destruction to those whose life is to be understood as a journey upon a finite and fragile, and already overcrowded, Spaceship.

The infusion into the population debate of the stream of ecological thought that sees the limits upon the carrying capacity of the ecosystems of the earth as severe and imminent has created unanticipated moral dilemmas for those who have emphasized the reduction or reversal of the rate of population increase as the "answer" to the population question. Heretofore, the reduction of unwanted fertility could be seen as consonant with the value of individual freedom and autonomy. But, when the possible exercise of such freedom can be seen as an occasion for license that may bring ecological disaster if the cumulative effects of individual decisions lead to a level of population incompatible with the continued provision of resources necessary to sustain a decent existence for all through time, there are those who assert that, not only unwanted, but also wanted fertility must be reduced. If the level of needs and wants is held roughly constant, while the limits of the production of resources can expand little, or not at all, and insistence upon distribute justice forbids the exclusion of some citizens, here or abroad, from equal access to such goods as are available, some "give" must be sought through the restraint of the freedom of parents to procreate beyond that which would produce an "optimal level of population."

That which is "given" for the demographer is the capacity and desire to procreate. Where wanted fertility exceeds that which is held to be tolerable, the demographer is forced to move out beyond the narrower limits of his precise specialty to search for the biological, psychological, social, economic, and cultural determinants of differential fertility, in the hope that it may be possible to manipulate some aspects of the context confronting prospective parents so that they may be induced to diminish their rate of reproduction with the least possible direct restraint upon their freedom. The demographer, like other specialists, is basically conservative within his own field. He does not anticipate that the given factor of man's capacity and desire to procreate will suddenly change, apart from significant adjustments in the other factors of the population equation. He is thus forced, like others, to address himself to issues beyond the boundaries of his own immediate discipline, assessing the effects that changes in the level of resources, definitions of the good life, or ideals of justice may have upon levels of fertility. Change in levels and patterns of reproduction is made contingent upon changes in social structure, cultural ideals, or legal and economic sanctions.

3. A third approach to the solution of the population problem would be to bring about a widespread readjustment in the *definition of what is necessary to sustain a good life.* The professional conservatism of those attuned to the discipline of economics is reflected in a propensity to take as "given" a constant level of human needs and the capacity for human wants to expand. If the desire to maintain or improve a given standard of living is held constant, while a population committed to equitable distribution increases, the supply of resources available must be steadily increased. The link between the fear of falling, or the hope of rising, in economic and social status and the determination of family size has been recognized by population theorists for centuries (See Eversly, 1959, p. 65 and passim). Men are determined not merely to sustain a bare subsistence, but to maintain a style of life held by habit and convention to be suitable for them. It is not simply "survival" that they prize, but their own understanding of what constitutes "well-being" for themselves and others. Economists point to the tenacity with which such expectations are held, and are thereby led to look for possibilities of adjustment elsewhere among the variables of the population equation.

Other participants in the population debate are disposed to discover considerable "give" within the definition of what is necessary to sustain a good life. They point to the existence of a gap between that which is needed for bare subsistence and that which is anticipated as the accustomed standard of living. This gap is filled in by subjective expectations, buttressed by social conventions adjusted to role and status. But the existence of the gap suggests an opening through which leverage can be exerted to press down the corporate and individual level of demands for goods to be consumed. People can learn to expect less and to get along on a smaller share of the resources of the earth.

Four ways of redefining what is necessary to sustain a good life can be distinguished. First, it is possible simply to *moderate wants*, to maintain or lower the overall level of consumption by accepting a smaller share per capita of the outpouring of a system of production basically unchanged in the substance of its offerings. Secondly, Hippies and others testify to the possibility of *modifying the content* of the ideals of the good life by reducing dependence upon consumer goods and stressing the noncompetitive elements of the common life. Although minimal requirements for nutrition place an ultimate limit upon the prospects of a thoroughgoing modification of expectations, a decline in the total demand for certain ecologically costly products could come about through a recasting of the pattern of expectations of consumers. Third, Marxists summon believers to accept a *delay* in the fulfillment of their desires for higher rates of consumption until the day that a revolutionary reordering of society can bring forth a flourishing of science and technology and a more equitable distribution of goods that will enable a larger population to be sustained in plenty. Fourth, Roman Catholics and others may affirm not only an ascetic ideal for some that would modify wants, but also a common *obligation to sacrifice* even one's fair and moderate share for the sake of sharing, in the name of brotherhood and equality, with those who are presently deprived. A lower level of consumption should be voluntarily accepted, if not as a witness to the disordered priorities of modern life, at least as a natural obligation to facilitate the attainment of a decent, if modest, standard for all men.

Paul Ehrlich, as a representative of the ecology movement, combines insistence upon the moderation and modification of expectations concerning what is necessary for the good life with encouragement of a spirit of sacrifice and self-denial in the acquisition of material things. Ehrlich calls for "new economists" who will "develop a sophisticated economics of stability and find new ways of defining and evaluating utility. . . . Economics must become a science in which the competition is to find ways to satisfy human needs that minimize environmental impact while maximizing human well-being." (Ehrlich and Harriman, 1971, p. 128) A "spaceman economy" must replace the "cowboy economy."

> The key to new life styles is a shift of emphasis from material to human values. We must reduce our material wants to a level which can be sustained by a stable population over a long period of time. (Ehrlich and Harriman, 1971, p. 124)

We must modify the desires inculcated by "a blind science and technology and a berserk econo-centric culture" and take a new direction "away from competition, materialism and consumerism" by renewing elements in our cultural tradition, such as the "ideals of fairness, honesty, generosity, compassion and love," which may foster a spirit of community and cooperation enabling men to "understand that life can no longer be considered a competitive game." (Ehrlich and Harriman, 1971, pp. 126–30) "There are, in fact, enormous intrinsic advantages and joys in simplifying our life-style." (Ehrlich and Harriman, 1971, p. 125)

Demands must be immediately moderated and soon modified. Ehrlich is interesting as one who has started the difficult task of thinking through the ultimately inescapable but frequently evaded question of what style of life is compatible with continued existence under the circumstances he envisions for the future. Progress towards a new ideal of individual and communal existence is encouraged both by the push of disastrous ecological circumstances and the pull of a positive utopian vision of human fulfillment. Ehrlich is certain that "there's no way we can go on the way we're going now." (Ehrlich, 1970, p. 55) The crisis is upon us; "we haven't got a generation—we only have a few years." (Ehrlich and Harriman, 1971, p. 145) "The choice is basically new men or no men." (Ehrlich and Harriman, 1971, p. 138) In such a crisis, sacrifice is called for.

> But whether or not we decide to make sacrifices, the population-environment problem in the United States is going to cause a decline in any genuinely human standard of living. (Ehrlich, 1970, p. 55)

A "genuinely human standard of living" cannot be measured by the economists' tool of the Gross National Product, which "most assuredly *is not* a measure of the standard of living or quality of life of the people." (Ehrlich and Harriman, 1971, p. 59) Indeed, "it is becoming increasingly obvious that without dramatic changes in our society in the future there will continue to be a negative correlation between the GNP and the QOL (Quality of Life)." (Ehrlich and Harriman, 1971, p. 60)

> Even without a major disaster, our lives seem doomed to become nastier, shorter and more brutish as a result of our unceasing pursuit of a "high standard of living," which is simply not a rational measure of what's desirable in life.
> In essence, we need to turn the whole system down and start concentrating on what life's really about. (Ehrlich, 1970, pp. 55)

*   *   *

The dilemma of Spaceship ethics, as of other ethical systems of earlier ages, is how to reconcile harmony with individual fulfillment in freedom. "Our end must be a life of satisfaction for each individual; our means must be free self-expression of the individual compatible with the rights of all other human beings." (Ehrlich and Harriman, 1971, p. 125) "As an ultimate goal, the culture of the new men must provide a maximum number of options to pursue one's own interests and a minimum number of assigned tasks." (Ehrlich and Harriman, 1971, p. 125) "Diversity of experience and an appreciation for differences must be encouraged at every step." (Ehrlich and Harriman, 1971, p. 125) Competition for material goods is a constant threat to the harmony of fellow voyagers on Spaceship Earth." Somehow, our society must replace its present emphasis on materialism and consumerism. We must begin to concentrate on maximizing the growth of each individual spirit, rather than each individual bank account." (Ehrlich and Harriman, 1971, p. 126)

> There is abundant evidence from both within and outside of Western culture that human beings do live extremely satisfying lives with a minimum of material possessions. Intellectual activity, art, music, sexual pleasure, good food, good friends, stimulating conversation, sports, hunting, fishing and gardening are just some examples of pleasures requiring a minimum of physical trappings. (Ehrlich and Harriman, 1971, p. 125)

Emphasis upon simpler joys may reduce the ecologically costly demand for massive supplies of certain manufactured items. But the process of ethical and political reasoning has not yet proceeded to the point of specifying who shall have access, on what basis, to the still scarce means necessary for the fulfillment even of the less materialistic joys of a simpler, ecologically aware life style. How will access to land for gardening, fields and streams for hunting, instruments for music, travel to friends be alloted by adherents of the Spaceship ethic? It is assumed that the quality of life "is intimately related to the number of options open to each individual." (Ehrlich and Harriman, 1971, p. 82) But the manner of apportioning these options and adjusting them with the possibly incompatible desires of others remains vague.

The value of freedom is affirmed, but its substance remains uncertain until the outline of specific restraints are filled in. "Each individual human being must have a maximum of freedom, limited only by the boundaries where his freedoms may encroach on others." (Ehrlich and Harriman, 1971, p. 14) The formula remains vague:

> The operative word is "fulfillment." The goals of society must center on each individual's leading the life he or she wishes to while also insuring that society functions well and that its collective goals are met. (Ehrlich and Harriman, 1971, p. 138)

Freedom is a very ambiguous concept in the Spaceman ethic. To preserve certain options, others must be closed.

> If one assumes, as we do, that the Quality of Life is intimately related to the number of options open to each individual, it can be argued that development will always lead ultimately to a lowered Quality of Life; that the restrictions imposed by industrialization will always eventually counterbalance the freedoms opened up. Clearly, though, society must restrict certain options, such as extreme materialism, in order to maximize the number which remain open. (Ehrlich and Harriman, 1971, p. 82)

Not everyone can be left free to define wherein his own freedom lies. "People aren't sufficiently aware that their freedoms are rapidly disappear-

ing *because* there are more and more people." (Ehrlich, 1970, p. 55) Some
freedoms will have to be restrained for the sake of freedom. Driven by a
sense of crisis, by a certainty that "we're all doomed if we don't control
population growth" (Ehrlich, 1970, p. 55), Ehrlich reveals a deep am-
bivalence concerning the limits of freedom. The present proliferation of
people erodes the number of options open now and in the future. A sharp
decline in the birth rate is necessary for the preservation of the freedoms
he prizes as constituting the substance of a good life. But, given the self-
interest and lack of awareness of most prospective parents, it is unlikely
that strictly voluntary programs of birth control will have significant demographic impact. If such voluntary programs do not suffice, "compulsory
Government control of births is a virtual certainty." (Ehrlich, 1970, p. 55)
But this in turn entails an increase in bureaucratic intervention in our lives
and a resultant loss of the freedom that was to be preserved.

It is no wonder that in such an impasse a heavy emphasis comes to be
placed upon the possibilities of persuasion, propaganda, education, and
the power of example as means that hold promise of insuring the conditions of freedom to choose among existing options in the determination of
one's life style without seeming to violate that very freedom en route. The
dilemma of freedom remains unresolved. Freedom to choose one's style of
life is essential to a decent human existence. But "the world ecosystem in
aggregate should be thought of as a gigantic commons" (Ehrlich and Harri
man, 1971, p. 114) and, in the words of Garrett Hardin, "Freedom in a
commons brings ruin to all." (Hardin, 1972, p. 254) Ehrlich concedes that
"appeals for the voluntary exercise of restraint in relation to the commons
have proven notoriously ineffective." (Ehrlich and Hardin, 1971, p. 114)
He alludes to Hardin's summons for "mutual coercion, mutually agreed
upon." The possibility of compulsory measures of population control in-
stituted by governmental authority is discussed in very general terms as the
last resort to which recourse must be made if less coercive measures fail.
But no persistent, penetrating examination of the political and moral as
pects of compulsory measures is offered. Upon each mention of the issue,
discussion reverts quickly to hopeful assertions of the power of educational
processes that will make the public aware of its plight and willing voluntarily to take measures to forestall both ecological disaster and the politically distasteful imposition of coercive sanctions.

* * *

4. The fourth major approach to the population problem is to exclude certain categories of people from full participation in the division of
resources. In his book, *The Population Bomb,* published in 1968, Paul
Ehrlich seemed to endorse schemes that, by making receipt of aid contingent upon the implementation of vigorous population control policies
possibly unacceptable to leaders and peoples in underdeveloped nations,
might, in effect, abandon large numbers of persons to a misery sealed for
them by the improvident actions of their forebears. Ehrlich then reported
that he was "sometimes astounded at the attitudes of Americans who are

horrified at the prospect of our government insisting on population control as the price of food aid." In the 1971 volume, *How To Be a Survivor*, the topic is treated more delicately with the observation that "any direct food aid must be given in ways which do not make people dependent on imported food (thus discouraging local agriculture)" (p. 98). In the latter volume the central axiom of the Spaceship ethic is that the limited supply of goods available upon the fragile ship must be divided equitably. The implication is drawn that nations whose "overdevelopment" has enabled them to extract, exploit, extort, and consume a disproportionate share of the world's supply of goods must undergo a process of "de-development," converting to a less rapacious, ecologically sound economy. Underdeveloped nations, in turn, must be granted massive infusions of aid to enable them to reach a level of "semi-development" at which they may become agriculturally, but not industrially, self-sufficient.

> It is perfectly clear that development of the underdeveloped countries into industrialized countries modeled on today's overdeveloped countries is impossible. The phenomenal amounts of raw materials required to do the job may not exist at all, and the environment could not endure the trauma of their extraction and use if they do. (Ehrlich and Harriman, 1971, p. 81)

Justice demands that the underdeveloped nations receive compensation for foregoing claims that the principle of equality would ordinarily entitle them to make against the common supply of resources. The differential in the degree of industrialization will probably be permanent:

> Therefore, underdeveloped countries will be foregoing much-desired industrialization in order to keep the planet habitable, a sacrifice much to the benefit of the overdeveloped countries also. The overdeveloped countries should be willing to be taxed to pay for this service performed by the underdeveloped countries for the life-support systems. This tax could take the form of changes in the international trade system so that it strongly *favored* underdeveloped countries, rather than discriminating against them as the present system does. (Ehrlich and Harriman, 1971, p. 86)

Justice finds expression in the idea of stewardship. "All nations must come to view nonrenewable resources as being held in trust for all mankind, present and future. And all mankind must have a say in their use." (Ehrlich and Harriman, 1971, p. 116) The demands of equity in distribution have been flagrantly violated within American society as well as in the relations between over- and underdeveloped nations. We have built up an enormous "debt to the poor" that must be repaid through fundamental changes in the pattern and mechanisms of distribution. The central principle is clear and simple: "Spaceship Earth must function as a single entity." (Ehrlich and Harriman, 1971, p. 113)

Massive changes are needed in American social, economic, and political life, in the system of international trade and relations, in the underlying understanding of what life is really about. But how are such changes going to come to pass? In the writings of Paul Ehrlich there is a constant undercurrent of puzzlement concerning this fundamental question. "The de-development of the United States will be a big project indeed, but it can be accomplished to everyone's benefit if we have the will. The 'will' is the most important element." (Ehrlich and Harriman, 1971, p. 60) Among nations, as among individuals, the power of example is stressed.

> . . . population control aid flowing from overdeveloped to underdeveloped countries will only have a chance of success *once the overdeveloped countries have started to control their own populations and have ceased their exploitation of the underdeveloped countries.* Until that time, knowledgeable people in the under-developed countries will simply view any attempt to control their populations as one more imperialistic-racist plot and will oppose it at every turn. (Ehrlich and Harriman, 1971, p. 56ff)

The task that must be accomplished at home and abroad includes the educating of leaders and citizens in the rudiments of ecological wisdom. But Ehrlich has discerned that much more than the transmission of information is entailed in the equipping of men to live harmoniously upon Spaceship Earth.

> The essentials of the science of ecology won't be hard for this well-educated society to learn; the hard part will be learning to live differently than we do now—to conserve rather than to consume, to abstain rather than to indulge, to share rather than to hoard, to realize that the welfare of others is indis-tinguishable from our own. (Ehrlich, 1970, p. 55)

Everything is made to hinge upon the emergence of "a new breed of men" who "might attempt to control their affairs for the common good. But we would be among the first to proclaim that without the new men no structural change will function." (Ehrlich and Harriman, 1971, p. 104) Christians who have mused about the paucity of saints, communists whose schemes await the evolution of the "new socialist man," and observers of utopian schemes of all sorts may be startled and dismayed by such a conclu-sion. If human destiny hinges upon the structural reforms Ehrlich has outlined and the reforms hinge upon the emergence of a new breed of man, those who cannot sustain hope for such a cultural mutation should find themselves on the brink of despair. They may escape despair through the loophole of uncertainty. The ecological eschaton cannot be assigned a fixed date.

> Ecologists cannot predict exactly when or how the world ecosystem—the life-support system of our spaceship—will break down. However, we can guaran-tee that, if our present course is continued, sooner or later *it will break down.* Preliminary signs make "sooner" seem more likely than "later." (Ehrlich and Harriman, 1971, p. 6)

In the absence of very immediate and definite threats vividly and confidently portrayed as severely impinging directly upon that which one values intensely, it is difficult to induce men to relinquish voluntarily the habits and goods to which they have become accustomed. Recognition of this social-psychological insight places a severe strain upon academic ecologists, expected by the conventions of their university training to speak quietly and temperately, but driven by the need to awaken the public to take steps to avert the oncoming doom, to speak loudly and dramatically. There is no way they can make their point without appearing to some to be extravagant. Ironically, there is no way they can enter into the leisurely, harmonious existence they recommend without abandoning the mission to which they've been called.

*   *   *

REFERENCES

EHRLICH, PAUL.   1968. *The Population Bomb.* New York: Ballantine Books.

EHRLICH, PAUL, AND EHRLICH, ANNE.   1970. *Population, Resources, Environment.* San Francisco: W. H. Freeman.

EHRLICH, PAUL.   1970. "Playboy interview: Dr. Paul Ehrlich." *Playboy Magazine,* August. pp. 55 ff.

EHRLICH, PAUL, AND HARRIMAN, RICHARD L.   1971. *How to Be a Survivor.* New York: Ballantine Books.

EVERSLY, D. E. C.   1959. *Social Theories of Fertility and the Malthusian Debate.* Oxford: Clarendon Press.

HARDIN, GARRETT.   1968. "The Tragedy of the Commons, 1972." In *Exploring New Ethics for Survival.* New York: The Viking Press.

INDIVIDUAL VERSUS COLLECTIVE CHOICE

Individual liberty and utilitarian efficiency are prominent, fundamental values in American society. Much public policy is founded on one or the other of them. A free enterprise system postulates that the efficiency for which individuals will strive, when they have the liberty to act as they choose, will work to the benefit of the consuming public, which will in a free marketplace have more opportunities to get what it wants. But several discrepancies between this ideal and reality have been recognized. William Blackstone poses a conflict between liberty, efficiency, and the rights of individuals not to be harmed by others. If the liberties of chemical manufacturers and the efficiency of the free market are not to be compromised, what guarantees do consumers have that they are not somehow being poisoned by new chemicals too expensive and too complicated to test adequately before marketing? What kind of regulation, if any, is appropriate in the name of environmental health?

Donald Scherer argues that the pressures of a free enterprise system may force well-intentioned competitors to violate the integrity of the natural systems on which they and others depend. Moreover, such problems also arise in social systems. Thomas Schelling reminds us of the immense value of coordinated actions and of the power of social norms, when simple and widely practiced, to achieve such coordination. But how does the environment, both social and natural, endure the costs when no simple coordination can be found and adopted?

Environmental problems also result from the diversity of values reflected in human desires. The aggregate of a people's preference may compromise the world in which each person wants to live. As Mark Sagoff argues, the consumer preferences one exhibits in behavior may contradict one's view of the kind of community of which one wants to be a citizen. Sagoff suggests that, as markets are designed to reflect consumer preferences, the legislative arena in a democracy is designed to reflect citizen deliberation and self-definition. The prevalence of market mechanisms in American society, including the use of cost-benefit analysis for determining public policies, Sagoff argues, tilts the balance away from people and their reasoned decisions toward consumers and their expressed preferences.

On Rights and Responsibilities Pertaining to Toxic Substances and Trade Secrecy

William T. Blackstone

INTRODUCTION

There is general consensus that much of the population of this country and many workers are being exposed to innumerable toxic substances in their air, water, and food; and that new chemical agents are being synthesized and put into use with inadequate testing for harmful effects. A solution to this problem is urgent. In this paper I want to try to move us closer to a solution by discussing the question of rights and responsibilities of individuals, industry and government pertaining to toxic substances and trade secrecy doctrine, which was developed to protect unjust misappropriation. My primary concern is with the ethical issues at stake, not with existing trade secrecy law and its proper boundaries. But the latter can be assessed only within some given ethical framework.

There are grave conflicts of rights and conflicts of interest at stake in the development and use of new chemicals, chemical processes, and chemical products. There are the rights and interests of workers and the general public who often benefit enormously from new products but who also are often exposed to health hazards, unbeknownst to them. There are the rights and interests of corporations and enterprises, with great investments of capital and property rights in chemical products. Non-disclosure of product composition and product processing methods is often seen to be in the economic interests of these industries and, hence, a justifiable trade secret. There are also the rights and interests of future generations who may be dramatically, and negatively, affected by the development and use of chemical products. Some would go even further and argue that non-human species and nature herself have rights which must be respected and considered, rights which cannot be reduced to a purely anthropocentric value framework. Plainly, the complexity of the question of rights and

Source: Reprinted with permission from *The Southern Journal of Philosophy*, vol. 16, 1978, 589–603.

responsibilities vis-à-vis the development and use of toxic chemicals increases as one's interpretation of the scope of the rights and interests at stake increases.

The issue is made even more difficult because of the complexity of the facts and causal chains involved, the lack of knowledge of those causal connections in many cases, and the absence of communication of knowledge when the knowledge does exist. As pointed out in the Congressional Hearings on this issue, ". . . there have been few studies on the potential toxic effects of new chemicals, processes and products. Very little is known about the additive or synergistic effects to more than one chemical substance. The limited knowledge that is available about the effects of chemicals is often difficult to locate, for there is no central data source for retrieving and disseminating information about hazardous chemicals."[1] Questions of adequate health standards involving the manufacture and use of such products are difficult to answer. Often we do not know the dangers involved; nor, consequently, what sort of regulation or safety precaution is desirable.

* * *

My concern in this paper is not with the complexity of facts. That must be granted. Nor is it with the discovery of facts. That is beyond any competence of mine. I want simply to talk in a general way about the rights and responsibilities of consumers, manufacturers, and government concerning this issue. I presuppose no specific facts, only the general description of the problem and the discussion of the dangers of the use of toxic substances as found in the literature.

My procedure will be (1) to say a few things about the concept of a right, including alternative definitions of a right. (2) Then I will present brief accounts of several models or theories of rights. I refer here to moral rights and the models I will sketch are (a) the utilitarian model, (b) what I will call the liberal-pluralist model, and (c) the libertarian model. These models are by no means intended to be exhaustive.[2] (3) With these models before us, it will be possible to see the different implications entailed on the general role or responsibility of government and the rights of individuals within each model. We should be able to glean a *general* conclusion from each theory on the proper response of government to the issue at hand.

* * *

[1]94th Congress, 2d Session; House Report No. 94-1688, "Chemical Dangers in the Workplace," Thirty-fourth Report by the Committee on Governmental Operations, U.S. Government Printing Office, Washington, D. C. (1976) p. 6.

[2]We will not address the issue of existing *legal* rights and responsibilities of manufacturers and of government. At least part of that is plain by simply reading legislative acts pertaining to this issue. See, for example, the Occupational Safety and Health Act of 1970; cited on p. 14 of House Report No. 94-1688.

THE CONCEPT OF RIGHTS

First, we must recognize that if one possesses a right, one possesses a powerful moral commodity. (If the right is a legal one, it is even more powerful.) For unlike the morally desirable or the morally good, a right implies a correlative duty, obligation or responsibility on the part of someone to accord the possessor of the right a certain mode of treatment (though not all duties or obligations imply rights).[3] In legal contexts the possessor of a right can demand a certain remedy if his right is violated.

Aside from this logical feature of the notion of a right, which is commonly agreed upon, there are important differences among philosophers on the definition of a right. H. L. A. Hart, for example, defines a right as belonging "to that branch of morality which is specifically concerned to determine when one person's freedom may be limited by another's. . . . [T]o have a right entails having a moral justification for limiting the freedom of another person and for determining how he should act."[4] This definition of a right fits many, perhaps most, of our uses of this concept. For most rights involve limitations of freedom. But not all rights involve such limitations—unless the concept of freedom is stretched very far, perhaps beyond recognition. Welfare rights, for example, do not seem to fit Hart's definition. For this reason it may be that Joel Feinberg's definition is more adequate in terms of our use of the notion of a right. Feinberg states: "To have a right is to have a claim against someone whose recognition as valid is called for by some set of governing rules or moral principles."[5] Note that Feinberg does not define a right as narrowly as does Hart. Rights are valid claims within a set of rules or principles. This definition includes justified restrictions on the freedom of others, but it does not exclude the possibility of other sorts of justified claims as well. Feinberg's definition of a right leaves open wider grounds for rights and responsibilities. The scope of justified rights-claims depends on the scope of the governing rules or moral principles accepted. (Of course, factual or empirical states of affairs also constitute part of the grounds for any justified rights-claim.) If those principles include not just freedom or liberty but also security and welfare, for example, then the scope of rights and responsibilities for both individuals and governments is much broader than in a framework of principles which emphasized only freedom or liberty as a value.

* * *

[3] For discussion, see W. T. Blackstone, "Human Rights and Human Dignity," *Philosophy Forum*, 9 (1970).

[4] H. L. H. Hart, "Are There Any Natural Rights?" *Philosophical Review* 64 (1955).

[5] Joel Feinberg, "The Nature and Value of Rights," *Journal of Value Inquiry* 4 (1970) p. 250.

THE UTILITARIAN MODEL

The utilitarian requires that laws and public policy be so formulated that they maximize the greatest happiness of the greatest number. He also subscribes to the principles of equality and justice, which require that equal consideration be given to each person's interests or happiness in the calculation of consequences ("Each is to count as one and no more than one"). But equality and justice are conceived as subsidiary maxims under the principle of utility, receiving their justification from the latter. That is, the ultimate grounds for the equal consideration of each person's interests is that this principle or policies based on it do in fact maximize overall welfare or happiness. All rights rooted in the principle of equality and justice are rules adopted because of their instrumental effects, that is, rules which maximize the good or happiness of the greatest number.

If previously adopted rules, principles, or rights can be shown to be harmful (or policies based upon them), then the utilitarian maintains that those rights should be overridden, altered, or wiped off the books. Rights are not natural or inalienable or absolute. They are tools for maximizing human welfare. It follows that when the conditions of human life change, conditions which affect human welfare, then rights themselves may properly be changed. In fact, we are morally required to change them to maximize human welfare.

There are variants of utilitarianism, the best known of which are act-utilitarianism and rule-utilitarianism.[6] In the former, the principle of utility is directly applied to all decisions. In the latter, rules are applied and the rules are in turn justified by reference to utility. But basically, rights are rule-utilitarian devices. What bothers many persons about this model (the act-utilitarian version is seen as the more objectionable) is the easy, facile way in which rights can be overridden or taken away by the state. The framework of decision-making is what is often called cost-benefit analysis. Given some method for assessing costs and benefits (and the whole business of interpersonal comparison of satisfactions and interests is problem-laden), the utilitarian permits the alteration or demise of rights, if it can be shown that the costs outweigh the benefits of the recognition of those rights. This allows, some philosophers believe, for the easy rationalization of state intrusion into our lives and the denial of basic individual rights.

If utilitarianism is inadequate as a total theory of rights or philosophy of government, this fact by no means entails that utilitarian arguments carry no weight. Also, it should be noted that if one appeals to the utilitarian framework, it could justify either a minimal state or greater state intrusion and control, depending on the facts of human life which bear on the maximization of human welfare and on one's assessment of those facts. Depending on those facts and that assessment, the utilitarian model could justify wide restrictions on property rights and on the use (or abuse) of environmental resources. And this includes, of course, restrictions on the

[6]For an analysis of utilitarianism, see David Lyons, *Forms and Limits of Utilitarianism.* Oxford (1965).

development and use of chemical products which impact on the welfare of humans.

THE LIBERAL-PLURALIST MODEL

A different model of rights, one which rejects the value reductionism of the utilitarian and the purely cost-benefit decision procedure which accompanies it, is what might be called the liberal-pluralist model. Under this model there are several kinds of values, none of which are reducible to the other—liberty, equality, welfare, security, utility and so on. Each of these values is a locus of human interests and human needs and a ground for different kinds of rights. The philosophical basis for these rights differ a great deal amongst liberal theorists. Some appeal to God, some to natural law, some to natural rights, some to a social contract base, and so on. But they agree generally on the sorts of human interests, needs, and rights which are to be prized. They differ further on the hierarchical ordering of the interests or rights prized and, consequently, on the way in which they should be restricted or qualified in cases of conflicts of rights. John Rawls, for example, has an explicit lexical ordering of principles, with liberty receiving priority over equality and welfare.[7] Isaiah Berlin denies that we can have that sort of moral geometry. Conflicts of rights, interests, and values require a "balancing" process for Berlin, but there is no arithmetical precision possible in arriving at a balance.[8]

Conflicts arise, furthermore, not only *between* general principles like liberty, equality, welfare, security and utility but also *within* particular principles. One type of liberty may conflict with another—the right to free speech, for example, with the right to a fair trial. Types of equality may conflict. The right to equal treatment, in the sense of the uniform application of the same meritocratic standards of access to positions (employment, admissions, etc.), may conflict with other types of equality—economic equality, for example. Some persons, because of past discrimination, may not be able to meet those meritocratic standards and they continue to suffer economic inequality as a result. These conflicts *within* principles also require some kind of "balancing." Resolution of conflicts of values or conflicts *between* principles and conflicts *within* principles depend on the values and principles adopted and the priorities chosen. A liberal of the Rawlsian type offers principles and priorities of one sort; other liberals offer quite different priorities.[9]

---

[7]See John Rawls, *A Theory of Justice*, Harvard University Press, Cambridge, Mass., 1971.

[8]Isaiah Berlin, "Equality," *Proceedings of the Aristotelian Society* 56 (1955–6).

[9]Not only the ordering of principles but the explicit formulation of the principles in the ordered theory are points of contention. Many liberals stress welfare rights, for example, along with basic liberties. But they differ on how far the state should go in looking after the *welfare* of citizens. Some advocate only minimal standards; others, like Rawls, would extend welfare rights greatly. His "difference" principle requires that no inequalities of wealth be permitted which do not raise the standard of living of those at the bottom of the economic ladder. This may permit great inequalities but the burden of proof is placed on him who advocates the inequalities.

The point I am trying to make here is that different liberals strike the balance between conflicting values and conflicting rights in different ways. Reasonable men may disagree on the right balance. But when one of these values—equality, liberty, welfare or security—is overemphasized at the expense of the others, the result is various forms of extremism. Security and welfare can be pressed at the expense of liberty and equality; and equality can be pressed so far that liberty is lost.[10] Some maintain that the extension of equality from the legal and political spheres to social and economic spheres results in the demise of liberty. For the state, in order to provide social and economic equality, must intrude further and further into our lives A society, some claim, which operated on Rawls' "difference principle" would require massive state control of the economy and, ultimately, of our individual lives; for his theory of justice requires not only that the state transfer or redistribute income so that all enjoy a minimally satisfactory life but that the minimum be progressively increased until we reach that point when any further increase lessens the standard of those at the bottom (by decreasing the amount of goods and services available for distribution). Some would claim that this is an extreme form of egalitarianism, for the price to be paid in terms of liberty is too high. Others would say that the very liberties which we cherish are meaningless unless certain basic social and economic conditions for each are satisfied.

Where can the line be drawn? Which is the right "blend"? The right balance? There may be no final answer to these questions. Surely all decisions involving conflicts of values and rights must be made in contexts where, hopefully, knowledge of facts, of what is lost and gained, is clear. But the traditional liberal has given preference to liberty. Without liberty, humans cannot be human. Their capacities as rational and free beings are muted. I agree with this view, but we must not forget that the ideal of liberty is that of equal liberty for all. It is not "license," Locke tells us. And equal liberty for all may require more than the absence of arbitrary intrusion, which some have called "negative freedom." In particular, as the conditions required for the nurture and sustenance of life change, it may require the provision of at least minimal economic conditions for those who are unable to satisfy those conditions for themselves. Some philosophers have called this "positive freedom."[11] The principle of equal liberty requires different decisions or policies under different circumstances, as Locke seemed to be aware in qualifying the right to property in the way he did.

For the liberal-pluralist there is no escaping the complexity of ethical, political and legal life: several irreducible value principles must be contextually applied; value trade-offs must be made when those principles conflict; and further trade-offs and priorities must be made when rights or rules internal to one principle conflict. Concerning the topic of this paper, or at least one aspect of it, namely, what is the proper role of government

[10]For an analysis and discussion of these conflicts, see W. T. Blackstone, ed., *The Concept of Equality*, Minneapolis, 1969.

[11]See W. T. Blackstone, "The Concept of Political Freedom," *Social Theory and Practice* 2 (1973).

concerning the regulation of the development and use of chemical products, the liberal-pluralist must contextually apply his several principles—liberty, welfare, security, equality, utility, and so on. He must ask what the impact of such regulation (or non-regulation) would be. Then he must look for the right blend, the right balance between the responsibility of government to prevent disaster or harm, that is, to look after the general welfare, and the responsibility to preserve and protect basic rights and freedoms. When any given right or its exercise threatens the welfare or rights of others, what is generally called for is some qualification in the right, not its utter obliteration. To avoid certain kinds of environmental destruction and threats to human life, for example, certain traditional property rights must be qualified or restricted. This does not entail that property rights must be completely taken away. It requires only that they operate within some new rules designed to prevent health hazards and the destruction of the environment which are essential to the well-being, even the existence, of all of us.[12]

THE LIBERTARIAN MODEL

Let us briefly note one more model of rights and responsibilities, the libertarian model. This model emphasizes a value—that of liberty—which is dear to our moral and political traditions in the West. And, yet, many would argue that the libertarian model of rights takes the principle of liberty to extremes in the same way in which some egalitarians who press for sameness, uniformity and identity of treatment, indeed, for a kind of "leveling" of society, have taken the principle of equality to extremes. Let me briefly characterize this model and point to the implications of it for the problem at hand.

The objective of the libertarian is a society and a government ". . . in which coercion of some [men] by others is reduced as much as possible. . . ."[13] Individual freedom is his fundamental value. Each person is permitted to do whatever he wants as long as he does not harm others or violate their rights to non-interference. The rights to non-interference include the rights not to be coerced, killed, defrauded and imprisoned and the rights not to have one's property stolen by others or appropriated by the state. When the role of the state goes beyond the protection of these negative freedoms or rights, it oversteps its proper grounds. Objectives like national defense and the protection of persons and property, which require court systems, police agencies, prisons, armies, navies, air forces and so on are legitimate state purposes. But other state purposes—the alleviation of poverty, the effort to assure equal opportunity for all, the creation of a public system of education, a public health delivery system and the

[12]For discussion, see W. T. Blackstone, "Ethics and Ecology," in W. T. Blackstone, ed., *Philosophy and Environmental Crisis,* University of Georgia Press, Athens, Georgia, 1974.

[13]F. A. Havek, *The Constitution of Liberty,* Chicago, 1960, p. 11.

like—are illegitimate purposes. These ends should all be pursued within private, voluntary frameworks. Plainly, much of what the modern state engages in is rendered illegitimate by the standards of the libertarian.

The ideal of maximal freedom and individual autonomy is best expressed, the libertarian asserts, in a market economy where people engage in the voluntary exchange of goods and services. The role of the state is to enforce the rules required for the system of voluntary exchange. It is not that of imposing a system of exchange, that is, some pattern of distribution or redistribution of goods and services. When it engages in the latter, it violates individual rights or "entitlements," to use Nozick's term. Property rights are always rooted in past circumstances or actions of people and those circumstances and actions "create differential entitlements or differential deserts to things."[14] When the state, no matter how good its intention or objective, appropriates one's property and transfers it to someone else, it violates basic individual rights—as long as one's property was justly acquired or justly transferred to one, and no rectifactory measures are required by justice.

Given the magnitude of past injustice and the requirements of rectification and given the limitations on just property acquisition to which some libertarians agree,[15] even the libertarian framework might justify far more government intrusion or intervention than appears at first blush. For there have been huge past injustices which would require massive state action and redistribution to rectify, and current conditions of property acquisition, given the "Lockean proviso,"[16] may call for far more restrictions than in the days of Locke. Further, even if liberty is restricted to the negative freedoms listed above, considerable state action (of a welfare sort) may be required to assure *equal liberty* for all.

Thus, the line delimiting state action may not be so narrow or so sharp as some libertarians believe, even on their own value presuppositions. Concerning the topic of this paper, the role of the government in the development and use of chemical products, the libertarian framework may justify considerable regulatory efforts, even without explicit reference to values other than liberty, e.g., welfare, security, equality, utility and the like.

MODELS OF RIGHTS AND THE ROLE OF GOVERNMENT

I have sketched these three models to indicate that the scope of rights and responsibilities—moral, political, and legal—vary considerably from one

[14]Robert Nozick, *Anarchy, State, and Utopia*, Basic Books, New York, 1974, p. 155.

[15]Robert Nozick, *op. cit.*, accepts what he calls the "Lockean proviso," that there be "enough and as good left in common for others." See Chap. V, *Locke's Second Treatise on Civil Government.*

[16]See note 15 above.

model to the next.[17] Of course, as indicated earlier, each of these models also is susceptible to variations. There are forms and types of utilitarianism, as David Lyons points out. Amongst subscribers to what I called the liberal-pluralist framework, there are different hierarchies of values, rules, and principles. And libertarians formulate the principle of liberty or the framework for the instantiation of liberty in somewhat different ways. Still, it is helpful to see the core stances of these models, for it permits us to see some of the fundamental rationales for government regulation or deregulation.

Is an act-utilitarian, cost-benefit model an adequate framework within which to decide whether government should regulate or not? Is the libertarian framework of rights and responsibilities adequate? It seems to me that any adequate ethical theory or philosophy of government must be concerned with both liberty and maximizing human welfare. But both the emphasis on individual liberty and the emphasis on utility or cost-benefit analysis can be carried to extremes. The cost-benefit emphasis can and has been used to override fundamental rights of individuals; and the emphasis on individual liberty can be pushed so far that the welfare and security of millions (persons who cannot look after themselves in a purely competitive scheme and consumers who cannot be aware of the dangers of certain products) is ignored. I believe the liberal-pluralist model to be a far more adequate framework for specifying rights and responsibilities. That model includes utility. It includes freedom. But it also requires that those basic values be "balanced" against other values like equality, welfare, and security.

As I indicated at the start, I do not propose to discuss the question of whether a given framework of principles can be rationally proven to be superior to others or objectively true; or whether there is a particular ordering or balancing of values which can be demonstrated to all rational minds. . . . But the value pluralism which I have described seems plainly to be the framework which we have embraced in this country. That framework gives a certain priority to liberty. It does not give the absolute status to liberty which the libertarian demands. But there is a presumption in favor of liberty. We place the burden of proof on him who would restrict or regulate. At least, it seems to me, that is our ideological commitment, whether it works out that way in practice or not. And it seems to me that it often does *not* work out in practice this way. The burden of proof is often shifted from the regulator to the regulatee. That, I think, is unfortunate, except in those cases where regulation is demonstrably and invariably in the public interest.

[17]Differences in frameworks or models, however . . . , do not always entail that subscribers to the different frameworks will always disagree on a given issue, say, a regulatory question. They may disagree on certain factual matters and that disagreement, conjoined with differences in their normative frameworks may lead to *agreement* in any given evaluation. Or, even if they see the facts concerning a given problem in the same way, two different normative frameworks may entail the same evaluative conclusion but for different reasons. The utilitarian, for example, may endorse a policy or regulation because he thinks it will maximize human welfare. A liberal theorist may endorse the same regulation because he thinks it protects the right to life or the right to property. So we cannot simplistically assume that different frameworks of principles automatically entail different evaluative conclusions.

Although freedom or liberty is perhaps our basic value; although we give primary concern to the avoidance of arbitrary intrusion and to rights of non-interference; although our philosophical assumption is that the state exists for the individual, not vice-versa, and that the individual, not the state, is the best judge of what is in his interest and welfare and, further, that the best way of assuring individual and societal welfare is through a system of voluntary exchange between individuals or groups—the free enterprise system; although we are committed to the view that government can never justifiably dictate to the individual what is in his interests and how he should live; although we recognize that excessive government control and regulation is a threat to democracy itself; and although we recognize that such regulation can kill the autonomy, initiative and creativity which has produced perhaps the highest standard of living in the world—in spite of all of this primary emphasis on freedom, we also from the very beginning have recognized that certain kinds of regulations and controls are necessary. Laissez-faire has always included some justifiable restrictions. The questions have always been where, for what purpose, and how much.

In those critical areas which vitally affect the safety, security, well-being and rights of us all, those areas where a completely autonomous market system might detrimentally affect the interests of all consumers, government regulation has been seen as absolutely necessary. Thus, utilities, transportation, banking, energy-production, the communications industry, food and drugs, and so on have been heavily regulated because such was seen to be required for the common good. . . .

. . . In what contexts are we willing to trade off some liberty for security? How much liberty are we willing to trade off for how much security or welfare? There is no simple answer to these questions. A rational approach always requires attention to highly context-dependent facts. We must apply our value commitments or principles and priorities to the facts in each context.

RIGHTS, RESPONSIBILITIES AND TOXIC SUBSTANCES

This brings us finally to the main concern of this paper. What sort of trade-offs, how much freedom, how much regulation is rational or justifiable in contexts in which the rapid growth, development and use of chemical products composed partly of toxic substances pose a threat to human health, to the environment, and to future generations? There is little doubt about this threat. But the threat to human welfare and to the environment varies from one context of chemical use to another. What is desirable, if we accept the priority-on-liberty interpretation of the liberal-pluralist model (though the same sort of approach may be justified on utilitarian grounds as well), is a balancing of values in which we adopt the minimum kinds of control required to protect human welfare and the environment. Without that protection there can be little significant human freedom. Certain material conditions are necessary for the sustenance of life and the exercise of choice.

The principle which emerges from this balancing might be formulated in this way: "Impose only those minimal controls necessary to protect human welfare and the environment" (this includes the interests of future generations); or, put negatively, "impose only the minimum controls necessary to prevent harm to present and future generations and to the environment which sustains all of life." If this principle is acceptable, then we must ask "What is the best means of applying this principle?"

At least three possibilities suggest themselves: (1) Is the best means a system of voluntary controls, one in which the chemical industry regulates itself? If so, what means would the industry use? (2) Is government regulation the best means? And, if so, what are the most effective means of government regulation? (3) Is a joint system of voluntary controls plus government controls the best system for instantiating the principle above?

One's answer here must depend, it seems to me, on one's assessment of certain facts—several kinds of facts: (1) What is the extent of the danger of the development and use of certain chemical products to human welfare, the environment and future generations? (2) Does the chemical industry have a viable professional code of ethics which, if applied, would solve the problems? (3) Would the chemical industry be willing to enforce that code, should it be viable? (4) Are there effective industry-wide means of enforcing the code, assuming the willingness to do so?

Now I do not have the answers to these questions. The answer to (1) will surely be dependent on context and product. Some products pose little or no danger; others, a great deal. With others, we simply do not know. The effects of certain chemical products—their carcinogenic effects, their impact on man's genes, their effect on the biosphere generally—we simply do not know; or, we do not discover those effects until long after use. There is no escaping some sort of risk; but we now know enough about the threat of some chemical products to be aware that very careful controls are required. The dangers are simply too great to permit simple market forces to operate. (2) I know nothing about the existence or content of a professional code of ethics for the chemical industry as a whole.[18] But such a code should surely include careful guidelines and tests involving the effects of any chemical products on humans and on the environment. It should also include a doctrine of informed consent, a requirement that the producer disclose to the public and to the consumer the constituents of any product with toxic effects or risks of any kind; further, that all workers in chemical industries be informed of any kind of risks involved in production.[19]

[18]If there is such it should receive very careful analysis for strengths and weaknesses. I recently examined the American Psychological Association's Code of Ethics for the use of humans in experimental research for such strengths and weaknesses. See W. T. Blackstone, "The American Psychological Association Code of Ethics for Research Involving Human Participants: An Appraisal," *The Southern Journal of Philosophy* 13 (1975).

[19]For discussion of the doctrine of informed consent, see W. T. Blackstone, "Reflections on Informed Consent," in G. Dorsey, ed., *Equality and Freedom: International and Comparative Jurisprudence*, Oceana Publications, and A. W. Sijthoff, The Netherlands, 1977.

I cannot say how far the right to informed consent or to disclosure of contents should be pressed. Obviously, both the testing of products for effects and disclosure of contents have large economic consequences. At least some of the trade secrecy which characterizes the industry would be affected by a code of ethics or any regulatory scheme which protected these rights. Whatever tests, whatever disclosure is required to protect the rights and interests of the consumer, the quality of the environment and future generations should be required. (Admittedly, this is no easy matter to determine, especially when one adds the effects on future generations.) This is not to say that an industry or corporation has no right to confidentiality or trade secrecy concerning both the contents of products and processing methods. It is to say that those rights must be qualified or restricted when they conflict with the rights and interests of the consumer or of society as a whole. That sort of restriction on property rights and liberty is fully justified by the commonly accepted value commitments of our society and the pluralistic model described above.

The justifiability and desirability of restrictions on the development and use of chemical products leaves open the question of the best means to do it—whether it should be voluntary controls, government controls, or some combination of both. If the answers to (2), (3), and (4) were affirmative, then a prima facie case would exist for a purely voluntary, industry-imposed system of restrictions. But it may be that affirmative answers to (2), (3), and (4) are not justified—that there is no viable professional code of ethics in the chemical industry, that the industry is not willing to enforce one, and that it does not have the means of enforcement. Some in fact have suggested that this is so, and, further, that the primary concern for profit in the industry militates against the development of such a voluntary enforced code.

What then? Unless such a code is developed and enforced by industry, government has no alternative but to step into the breach and impose regulations. . . . [G]iven the magnitude of the current threat to human welfare and the environment under our current regulatory system, greater centralized control and coordination and higher costs appear to be rational value trade-offs.

The Game of Games

Donald Scherer

The purposes of this paper are to characterize a common pattern of resource depletion,[1] to explicate and contrast three proposed responses to the pattern, and to provide criteria for evaluating proposals to restructure the pattern so that resource depletion will not eventuate. To these ends, I present a stylized narrative history of contemporary farming practices exemplifying prevalent patterns of resource use. I shall argue that the pattern involves a sequence, which I shall represent in terms of a series of game theoretical matrices. Garrett Hardin (mis)characterizes the kind of pattern I have in mind as a Tragedy of the Commons. He calls the pattern tragic because he sees its outcome as inevitable (1). The entire sequence, however, is a complex structure which occurs only if a conjunction of natural and social conditions is met. Accordingly, in the latter half of the paper I shall discuss three prominently mentioned proposals for truncating the sequence. The focus of my discussion will be on the questions (a) which necessary conditions of resource depletion does each solution attempt to negate? (b) what does each solution require for its success? and (c) what sorts of natural and social consequences does each solution-path produce or facilitate? Although I regularly recur to my example, I also generalize regularly to emphasize the scope of the pattern I am discussing.

Imagine the farmers who have farmed a river valley over the course of the preceding generation. They have bought seeds, fertilizers, pesticides and herbicides from supply companies. The trade of the farmers created profits for the companies, and using the supplies of the companies yielded profits for the farmers. Adam Smith theorized that such relationships work to the profit of each of the parties: "When everyone chooses, intending only his own good, resources are used by those who can use them most efficiently, and, though no part of their intention, through that efficiency the whole society benefits as if guided by an invisible hand" (9).

In initial stages of the use of a set of resources, it is typical that the prominent components of that set will be abundant, with the twin results that their use will be priced cheaply and that economic factors will not motivate conservationist practices. This tolerance for resource inefficiency provides a period of time in which the opportunity exists for an efficiency of operation to be developed within a new industry that prevents or greatly reduces resource waste. The advantage Adam Smith and contemporary free market theorists claim for the invisible hand is that it encourages efficient resource use and discourages waste.

We can schematize Smith's thoughts and this initial stage of a resource history as follows. Imagine both the farmers and the farm suppliers deciding between two courses of action, one involving less time, money, ability and effort, and the other more. Each chooses the latter on the grounds that the greater investment of inexpensive, available resources will probably

---

[1]Brevity prevents my presenting the similar claims one can make about pollution.

yield the greater profit. But in fact each profits additionally because of the other's choice.

Game 1

SUPPLIERS

	less	more
	1 3	
less 1	2	
	2 4	
more 3	4	

FARMERS (less / more) on left side.

The relationship within each of the two groups in the game complicates this profitable arrangement. Consider an individual farmer. As his yields have increased, so have his neighbors'. Such an increased supply of farm produce may cause decreased farmer profit in a free market unless the market expands. (The export of feed grains is significant here.) Hence, although the farmers and suppliers are benefitting each other, they compete among themselves, owing to the relatively inelastic demand for their products. Each is led to act so as to improve his chances and profits in the competition. Accordingly, when each farm supplier attempts to outdo the other in the development of new fertilizers, seeds, etc., the farmers bear the suppliers' development costs in the hope of competing successfully. Consequently, the farmers increase their indebtedness to banks by buying more expensive supplies and purchasing farm equipment which must be used for several years of crops before the investment will repay itself. While competition will force some farmers and suppliers to intensify their efforts, others will have sufficient capital developed from earlier times that they will act not out of compulsion but in the desire to capitalize through expansion.

Let us represent this intensification of competition between farmers and between farm suppliers as an ordinal relationship between the old game and the new game which evolves from it.

Game 2

SUPPLIERS

	less	more
	2 4	
less 2	3	
	3 5	
more 4	5	

Superficially, the development from Game 1 to Game 2 represents pure progress. Classically, economists have defined this progress by noting that the numbers in both games represent net profits. Given that net profit in Game 2 exceeds that for Game 1, the intensity of competition has proved beneficial, and the costs necessary to secure the profits are irrelevant.

The higher costs, however, bring three dangers. First, while externalities are often understood in terms of cost to non-participants in the game, the definition of an externality as a cost not borne in the market is broad enough to include later costs to participants in the game. It is estimated, for example, that of the sixteen inches of top soil the average Iowa farmer had 30 years ago, only eight remain today. Clearly soil erosion has become potentially tragic.

Second, to the extent that intensification involves amortization of expenses, the participants are no longer judging simply that the game is presently likely to be profitable. Instead they must also decide that the game is likely to remain profitable long enough that investment costs will be recoupable through later rounds of the game.

Third, the judgment of long-term profitability is further complicated by the issue of delayed costs already implicit in the recognition that the availability of top soil eventually affects farmers' yields. If a resource is available beyond the amount in which it is presently useful, little economic motivation exists to conserve. Indeed any expense of conservation is unrewarded by increased short-term profit. Waste consequently becomes a habit, and if it is necessary at a later time to break the habit, breaking it will be difficult not only psychologically but also economically if breaking it involves increased expense. Such expense obviously compounds whatever other factors may be undermining a previous judgment of the soundness of amortizing one's future.

Clearly these are ominous developments. They suggest what, historically, has often proved to be the case, namely, that the game has reached its historical high-profit point. Garrett Hardin is famous for asserting that if resources are owned, then the owners will not use their resources in such a way as to destroy them (2).[2] He speaks of a Tragedy of the Commons because he believes resource depletion results from people's having *common*, rather than private, rights to parcels of resources. The history of homesteading, culminating in the Dust Bowl, however, is one of several decisive counterexamples to this view. Empirically, Agriculture Department statistics show both increased erosion due to the plowing of marginal lands and decreased fertility of the land owing to reduction in such vital conservation practices as rotating crops and allowing lands periodically to remain fallow. Each farmer is in the position of reasoning that if he does not dangerously intensify his land use, he will be unable to produce a crop sufficient to generate the income required to repay his creditors. Unpredictable variations in weather then prove catastrophic. When parties have made investments in properties great enough that it becomes true both (1) that they cannot free capital for alternative investments and (2) that com-

---

[2]"The Tragedy of the Commons as a food basket is averted by private property" (p. 1245).

petition to make their present investments profitable forces them to use their resources in such a way as would certainly destroy those resources in the long term, then destruction of resources in the short term will inevitably occur as the unintended result of assuming risks perceived as unavoidable. The mere fact that the practices the farmer adopts cannot be continued indefinitely will not suffice even as a rational deterrent to a risky short-term policy.

Thus modern farming would appear to be approaching a point reached in the Dust Bowl and in the use of many other resources, beaver (1820's and 30's), buffalo (1865–84) and timberland (different pre-twentieth century times in different regions). The point all these games reached can be schematized in the following diagram:

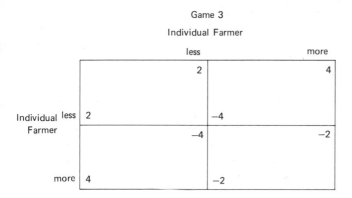

Game 3 is a losing game: when each player acts self-interestedly, the result is that all players lose. The problem I have attempted to outline is the apparent inevitability of the sequence from the initial exploitation of an abundant resource to the evolution of a game in which the players cause losses both for those outside of the game and for themselves.

Can we analyze the "inevitability," not of the entire sequence, but simply of Game 3? My conclusion, as I have examined the attempts of others in this matter, is that the analyses regularly reflect the sort of solution a particular author proceeds to advocate. Thus Hobbes, champion of a strong monarch says,

> If a covenant be made wherein neither of the parties perform presently but trust one another, in the condition of mere nature, which is a condition of war of every man against every man, upon any reasonable suspicion, it is void; but if there be a common power set over them both, with right and force sufficient to compel performance, it is not void. For he that performs first has no assurance the other will perform after, because the bonds of words are too weak to bridle men's ambition, avarice, anger, and other passions without the fear of some coercive power which in the condition of mere nature, where all men are equal and judges of the justness of their own fears, cannot possibly

be supposed. And therefore he which performs first does but betray himself to his enemy, contrary to the right he can never abandon of defending his life and means of living (3).

While Garrett Hardin somewhat confuses matters by framing the issue as a tragedy of the "commons," he does clarify that coercion need not imply prohibition:

> We are willing to say "Thou shalt not rob banks," without providing for exceptions. But temperance also can be created by coercion. Taxing is a good coercive device. To keep downtown shoppers temperate in their use of parking space we introduce parking meters for short periods, and traffic fines for longer ones. We need not actually forbid a citizen to park as long as he wants to; we need merely make it increasingly expensive for him to do so. Not prohibition, but carefully biased options are what we offer him. A Madison Avenue man might call this persuasion; I prefer the greater candor of the word coercion (1).

In another passage Hardin calls his strategy "mutual coercion, mutually agreed upon." In Game-theoretical terms this amounts to making II sufficiently less attractive that it no longer dominates I.

		I	II	
		1	$2-n$	
I	1		-2	$n \geq 1$
		-2	$-1-n$	
II	$2-n$		$-1-n$	

The other broad alternative is to increase the attractiveness of I.

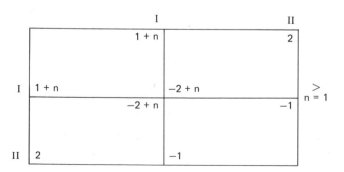

		I	II	
		$1+n$	2	
I	$1+n$		$-2+n$	$n \geq 1$
		$-2+n$	-1	
II	2		-1	

Two very distinct approaches to this strategy are prevalent in environmental thought. One possibility is that cooperation may come to be seen as having an intrinsic value of its own. Then, if this intrinsic value is added to the smaller (I, I) self-interested advantage persons can obtain by jointly choosing I, then the sum may be greater than the value to be gained, if gain there be, on choice II. Schumacher, whose name is most frequently associated with this line of thought, is most popularly known for the idea that "small is beautiful" (8). Schumacher was himself, however, aware of economies, as well as diseconomies, of scale and not at all pleased with the title *Small Is Beautiful.* Rather the center of Schumacher's concern with smallness is that small social groupings can be selective and can thereby promote *community solidarity.* As Schelling notes, community solidarity is a basis of trust and an alternative to coercion for avoiding Tragedies of the Commons (7).

Similarly, Sagoff proposes the formation of common intentions, e.g., national purposes (historical precedence: convenanting as God's people, manifest destiny) for providing the sense and substance of direction, community and trust (5). On a smaller scale, community trust operated significantly on wagon trains west in the nineteenth century. What Sagoff's proposal brings into focus is the fact that all successful solutions to the Tragedies of the Commons require some basis of trust. If persons are not to be coerced into trust, Hobbes would argue that there can be no adequate basis for trust. But historically, social solidarity has, at various times and in various communities, been a viable alternative.

The choice of I, however does not have to rest upon the intrinsically appreciated value of cooperation. Alternatively, I may be chosen because of the instrumental value of cooperation (7). This is what Schelling (6) calls "as-if altruism." This means that persons *behave* just as they would if they were altruistic, but their intentions are self-interested, rather than altruistic.

Perhaps an example will clarify both as-if altruism and its differences from the other two strategies. Suppose a city's freeways are very congested with automobile traffic at the rush hour. The roadway, to which all motorists have a common, equal right, is "overgrazed." "Mutual coercion mutually agreed upon" would have us make the driving of so many private automobiles less attractive, for example by charging a very high gas tax in the city or more directly by making the road a toll road. If the cost of driving the road became high enough, presumably many would be coerced into not driving their private cars on it. The "small is beautiful" approach can be presented in both its "small" and its "large" format. If the city could be decentralized, transportation distances would be reduced and the greater conviviality of, e.g., bicycle travel would become more feasible (4). If the city must remain large, without decentralization, then bicycles may be infeasible but the "small is beautiful" strategy would look to the possibilities that (a) the workers in a large plant might be collectively proud that, with all their car pools, they need only a small parking lot, and (b) the members of the car pools could enjoy the companionship of co-workers as an alternative to isolation as the only passenger in their own private vehicle. Finally, as-if altruism would promote the creation of special lanes on the freeway just for buses and cars with at least four passengers. Then self-interested persons who wish to transport themselves more efficiently would join car pools and ride buses, behaving altruistically, but not necessarily for altruistic reasons. Rather, their motivation might be the self-interested one of efficient transportation.

"As-if altruism" and "mutual coercion, mutually agreed upon" are both solutions which modify the course of action in one's self-interest. It is in this point of agreement that they contrast with the "small is beautiful" strategies, which attempt to stimulate communal interests. What I want to emphasize now is how different the two former strategies are. The use of coercion introduces a new constraint, a constraint, that is, beyond the limits of resource depletion and pollution accumulation, for that matter. Some political constraint is employed so that parties who act in an environmentally irresponsible way will be unable to diffuse the costs of their actions. The new cost of fines, taxes, permits and the like can be used to offset any self-advantages of their impacts upon the environment.

"As-if altruism" works quite differently. What makes an as-if altruistic solution feasible is, in the first place, unused capacity in the natural-social system for resource delivery. For example, electric utilities have substantial unused generator capacity on weekends and at night. The second requirement of an as-if altruistic solution is the possibility of creating a social structure which shifts demand away from those times and places in which overdemand creates inefficient resource use and to those times and places in which underdemand aggravates the overhead costs of unused capacity. Some electric utilities meet this second requirement by measuring electrical use by individual consumers at peak and at slack times and billing customers at two different rates, one higher and one lower than the original rate.

It is important to see that practices like such billing systems are not "really equivalent" to fining customers for peak time use. For, first, the off-hour rate represents a reduction. But, more importantly, if the same amount of electricity is consumed on the new billing system, a smaller amount of fuel is used to generate the electricity. Coercion may reduce resource use, but it does not motivate efficiency of resource use. By making unused capacity attractive, "as-if altruism" promotes resource use efficiency. Thus, because the two-tiered pricing system is resource efficient, the average price of electricity can fall while utility company profits remain steady.

None of these solutions can be applied unless the Tragedy of the Commons is *visible* with respect to a particular resource or pollution problem. So let us hereafter assume that we are dealing with fully visible (implying "recognizable") TCs. What then tends to make "mutual coercion mutually agreed upon" a more or less desirable solution than a solution which provides an incentive rather than a coercion? (I think of as-if altruistic solutions as non-coercive because they add no external political cost to resource use while reducing total cost of resource use.) Two continua seem most important. First is the "expense" involved in making a coercive solution enforceable. (It would be arbitrary to limit "expense" to dollar values here.) At least two sources of expenses are worth mentioning. The greater the restrictions of personal liberties, the greater the resentment, resistance and rebellion is likely to be. This disturbs the stable functioning of the state and increases the cost of police action. Second, characteristics of the group of agents whose dominant choices are being coercively changed are important. Voluntary solutions will have to rely more and more exclusively on the power of the incentives to the extent that the agents involved are *many, anonymous, non-reciprocally interacting,* and *transient,* and to the extent that their acts are *private* and hence *unknown by others.* Put conversely, the power of "small is beautiful" solutions is in situations of repeated interaction among stable groups of recognizable individuals.

The second important continuum concerns the *diversity of goals,* values or principles within the population of agents. To the extent that this diversity translates into diversities of behavior under different conditions, devising an adequate *incentive* system becomes difficult. It becomes difficult because different motivators then work for different agents, the agents are motivated to different extents, and perceived inequalities tend to rise.

In summary, the interest I find in characterizing the advantages and disadvantages of the three solutions to Tragedies of the Commons is to notice how different is the focus of each. What makes small is beautiful solutions practicable is the *repeated* interactions among *interdependent* individuals who *know* each other. What makes these solutions attractive is both the *intrinsic* and the *instrumental social values* of *trust and friendship.* What makes as-if altruistic solutions practicable is *structurally-harnessable unused resource capacity.* What makes these solutions attractive is their *promotion of autonomy.* What makes coercive solutions practicable is their ability to be *enforced unobtrusively.* What makes these solutions attractive is the *ideal of equality before the law, which they embody.* The divergence of conditions which make these three kinds of solutions practicable and attractive makes manifest the complexity of judging the comparative merits of alternative environmental policies.

I have called the Tragedy of the Commons a losing game. Thus, any player's goal must be to avoid having to play the game. To avoid playing the game, players, perhaps individually, perhaps through social or political representatives, must be ready to play a much better game, which I call the game of games. The game of games addresses the question, "What game do we prefer to play in order to avoid having to play the Tragedy of the Commons?" I have tried to indicate many of the central considerations involved in making that decision.

BIBLIOGRAPHY

1. HARDIN, GARRETT. "Tragedy of the Commons," *Science* (1968): 1243–48.
2. HARDIN, GARRETT, AND BADEN, JOHN. *Managing the Commons* (San Francisco, Freeman, 1977).
3. HOBBES, THOMAS. *Leviathan,* chaps. 13–21, 27.
4. ILLICH, IVAN. *Tools for Conviviality* (New York: Harper & Row, 1973), chap. III.

5. SAGOFF, MARK. "On Preserving the Natural Environment," *Yale Law Review*, 1974.
6. SCHELLING, THOMAS. "The Ecology of Micromotives," in *The Corporate Society*, ed. Robin Marris (New York: Wiley, 1974).
7. SCHELLING, THOMAS. *Micromotives and Macrobehavior* (New York: Norton, 1978).
8. SCHUMACHER, E. F. "Buddhist Economics," *Small Is Beautiful* (New York: Harper & Row, 1973).
9. SMITH, ADAM. *The Wealth of Nations.*

Thermostats, Lemons, and Other Families of Models

Thomas Schelling

SELF-ENFORCING CONVENTIONS

If everybody expects everybody to pass on the right, that's the side to pass on. If everybody expects nobody to applaud between the movements of a quartet, hardly anybody will.

Most one-way street signs need no enforcing by the police. The command—or suggestion—is self-enforcing. A feature of many rules is that, good rules or bad, they are better than no rules at all; and these conventions that coerce via expectations can be exceedingly helpful. (Imagine trying to get along without an alphabetical order!) But people can be trapped into self-enforcing rules that misdirect behavior. A bad system of one-way street signs is likely to be as self-enforcing as a good one. And a tradition that separates the women from the men or the whites from the blacks, the students from the faculty or the officers from the enlisted men, may be strongly self-enforcing even though one or both of the two groups deplore the tradition, and it may continue as long as conspicuous exceptions are an embarrassment.

The man who invented traffic signals had a genius for simplicity.[1] He saw that where two streets intersected there was confusion and lost time

---

[1]In this country credit goes to Garrett A. Morgan, who created an "automatic stop-sign" in 1923 and sold the rights to General Electric for $40,000, according to the biographical note in Russell L. Adams, *Great Negroes, Past and Present*, California State Department of Education, Sacramento, 1973.

because people got in each other's way; and he discovered, probably by personal experience, that self-discipline and good will among travelers was not enough to straighten them out. Even the courteous lost time waiting for each other. And some who mistakenly thought it was their turn suffered collision.

With magnificent simplicity he divided all travelers into two groups, those moving east-west and those moving north-south. He put the traffic into an alternating pattern. Nobody needed tickets, or schedules, or reservations to cross the intersection. All necessary instructions could be reduced to a binary code in red and green lights; all travelers within the scope of the plan could see the signals; and a single alternating mechanism could activate both sets of lights. There was no need to plan the day in advance; neither the lights nor the travelers needed to be synchronized with any other activity. Nor was there need for enforcement: once travelers got used to the lights, they learned that it was dangerous to cross against a flow of traffic that was proceeding with confidence. The lights created the kind of order in which non-compliance carried its own penalty. And there was impartial justice in the way the lights worked: unable to recognize individual travelers, the lights could hurt no one's feelings by not granting favoritism.

A social planner can usefully contemplate traffic signals. They remind us that, though planning is often associated with control, the crucial element is often coordination. People need to do the right things at the right time in relation to what others are doing. In fact, the most ingenious piece of planning ever introduced into society may have been our common scheme for synchronizing clocks and calendars. I do not set my watch at zero every morning on arising and let it run through the day on the decimal system; I have a watch just like yours, one that I coordinate with everybody else's at remarkably little cost. And I know nobody who cheats.

There is a great annual celebration of this accomplishment in early summer when, together, we set our watches ahead for daylight saving. For the government to order us to do everything an hour earlier would be an interference; it would confront everybody with discretionary decisions; we'd all have to check who had actually changed his schedule and who had not. But if we just set our watches ahead on the same night it all goes smoothly. And we haven't much choice.

Daylight saving itself is sweetly arbitrary. Why exactly one hour? When the ancients in the Middle East divided the day into an awkward twenty-four parts, by a duodecimal system that corresponds to the Zodiac and the pence in an old shilling (obstinately disregarding the ten fingers that most of us count by), was it because they looked forward a millennium or two and realized that urban industrial society would want to shift the phase of its daily activities by exactly one twenty-fourth? Like the chickens that conveniently lay eggs of just the size that goes with a cup of flour, did some teleological principle make the unit for counting time exactly equivalent to the nine holes of golf that have to be squeezed in before summer darkness?

I know a man who has calculated that clocks should be set ahead one hour and thirty-five minutes, and another whose habits make a forty-minute shift bring the sun over the yardarm at the right moment during his August vacation. I don't think they'll ever get a bill through the legislature—for the same reason that the sprinter who can do the fastest eighty-seven yards ever stop-watched cannot get a modest adjustment accepted by the Olympic Committee.

Traffic signals and daylight saving both reflect the compelling forces toward convergence in many social decisions. Weights and measures, the pitches of screws, decimal coinage, and right-hand drive are beyond the power of individual influence. Even for governments, few such decisions are as easily manipulated as the one about what time we get up in the summer. Clock technology makes daylight saving markedly easier than switching steering posts and road signs to get all those cars on the other side of the road at the same moment. Coins circulate much more rapidly than screws and bolts; we'll be years working off the non-metric thread angles that we inherited in all of our durable hardware.

Decimal coinage and right-hand drive may be worth the collective effort. Calendar reform would probably work. Spelling reform has been successfully organized. But switching nationally to another language would require the authority of a despot, the fervor of a religious cause, or a confusion of tongues that leaves the focus of a new convergence open to manipulation.

The inertia of some of these social decisions is impressive and sometimes exasperating. The familiar English typewriter keyboard was determined before people learned to play the machine with both hands. Anyone who types could recommend improvements, and experiments have shown that there are superior keyboards that can be quickly learned. The cost of changing keys or even replacing machines would entail no great outlay, especially as typists on different floors of a building can type on different keyboards without disturbing each other. My children, though, apparently as long as they live, will use their ring fingers for letters more appropriate to the index.

Consider a problem akin to daylight saving but more complex, one that may be as far in the future as the design of the standard keyboard is in the past, but which we might wisely anticipate in view of the inertia displayed by some of these social choices. The five-day workweek is common in America, but people may elect to take more of our increased productivity in leisure and less in the things that money buys. The four-day workweek may then become attractive. There is no assurance that it will—the demand for material goods may prove to be elastic rather than inelastic—but there is no compelling reason to suppose that the trend toward shorter workweeks has reached its secular limit. (And if it has, the nine-hour day can still make the four-day workweek popular.) Which day of the week do you want off? . . .

* * *

. . . The day you'd prefer to have off may depend on what days other people have off. A weekday is great for going to the dentist unless the dentist takes the same day off. Friday is a great day to head for the country, avoiding Saturday traffic, unless everyone has Friday off. Tuesday is no good for going to the beach if Wednesday is the day the children have no school; but Tuesday is no good for getting away from the kids if that's the day they don't go to school. Staggered days are great for relieving the golf courses and the shopping centers; but it may demoralize teachers and classes to have a fifth of the children officially absent from school each day of the week, and may confuse families if the fourth-grader is home on Tuesday and the fifth-grader on Wednesday. And the children cannot very well go to school the day that the teacher isn't there, nor can the teacher go to the dentist on the day the dentist takes off to go to the beach with his children.

An important possibility is that we collectively like staggered work-weeks, to relieve congestion and rush hours everywhere, but that we all slightly prefer to be among the 20 percent who choose Friday so that we can go to the dentist if we need to or get away for the long weekend if our teeth need no repair. If everyone feels that way, we shall not end up dispersing ourselves among the days of the week; instead, we shall all pick Friday—up to the point where Friday has become so congested that, all things considered, it is no better than Wednesday. The roads are jammed, the queues are long at the golf tees or the ski lifts, not enough stores are open to make shopping worthwhile; and we have collectively spoiled Friday with congestion. We have overcrowded Friday like a common grazing ground, by freely exercising our separate choices.

One can always hope for some ecological balance, some higher collective rationality, some goal-seeking evolutionary process. But it has not worked for staggered rush hours, which are substantially uninfluenced by government. And we seem legislatively unable to distribute Washington's Birthday town-by-town among the different weeks of February to smooth the peak loads for airlines and highway travel and ski-lift operation.

Meanwhile we can give thanks for small blessings, like our ability to synchronize daylight saving.

THE SOCIAL CONTRACT

A strange phenomenon on Boston's Southeast Expressway is reported by the traffic helicopter. If a freak accident, or a severe one, occurs in the southbound lane in the morning, it slows the northbound rush-hour traffic more than on the side where the obstruction occurs. People slow down to enjoy a look at the wreckage on the other side of the divider. Curiosity has the same effect as a bottleneck. Even the driver who, when he arrives at the site, is ten minutes behind schedule is likely to feel that he's paid the price of admission and, though the highway is at last clear in front of him, will not resume speed until he's had his look, too.

Eventually large numbers of commuters have spent an extra ten minutes driving for a ten-second look. (Ironically, the wreckage may have been cleared away, but they spend their ten seconds looking for it, induced by the people ahead of them who seemed to be looking at something.) What kind of a bargain is it? A few of them, offered a speedy bypass, might have stayed in line out of curiosity; most of them, after years of driving, know that when they get there what they're likely to see is worth about ten seconds' driving time. When they get to the scene, the ten minutes' delay is a sunk cost; their own sightseeing costs them only the ten seconds. It also costs ten seconds apiece to the three score motorists crawling along behind them.

Everybody pays his ten minutes and gets his look. But he pays ten seconds for his own look and nine minutes, fifty seconds for the curiosity of the drivers ahead of him.

It is a bad bargain.

More correctly, it is a bad result because there is no bargain. As a collective body, the drivers might overwhelmingly vote to maintain speed, each foregoing a ten-second look and each saving himself ten minutes on the freeway. Unorganized, they are at the mercy of a decentralized accounting system according to which no driver suffers the losses that he imposes on the people behind him.

Returning from Cape Cod on a Sunday afternoon, motorists were held up for a mile or more, at a creeping pace, by a mattress that had fallen off the top of some returning vacationer's station wagon. Nobody knows how many hundreds of cars slowed down a mile in advance, arrived at the mattress five minutes later, waited for the oncoming traffic, and swerved around before resuming speed. Somebody may eventually have halted on the shoulder just beyond the mattress and walked back to remove it from the traffic lane. If not, it may still have been there the following Sunday.

Again there was no bargain. Failing the appearance of a driver in a mood to do good—not a common mood on a hot highway with hungry children in the back seat—somebody would have had to be elected to the duty or compensated for performing it. Nobody gains by removing the mattress after he has passed it, and nobody can remove it until he has passed it.

Had the traffic helicopter been there, it might have proposed that each among the next hundred motorists flip a dime out the right-hand window to the person who removed the mattress as they went by. This would have given the road clearer a property right in the path he had opened, yielding a return on his investment and a benefit to the consumers behind him. But a long string of automobiles united only by a common journey, without voice communication or any way to organize a mobile town meeting as they approach the mattress, is unlikely to get organized. So we give thanks for the occasional occurrence of individual accounting systems that give a positive score for anonymous good turns.

Both the curiosity on the Southeast Expressway and the urge to get home once the mattress has been passed illustrate universal situations of individual decision and collective interest. People do things, or abstain from doing things, that affect others, beneficially or adversely. Without appropriate organization, the results may be pretty unsatisfactory. "Human nature" is easily blamed; but, accepting that most people are more concerned with their own affairs than with the affairs of others, and more aware of their own concerns than of the concerns of others, we may find human nature less pertinent than social organization. These problems often do have solutions. The solutions depend on some kind of social organization, whether that organization is contrived or spontaneous, permanent or ad hoc, voluntary or disciplined.

In the one case—pausing to look at the wreck—the problem is to get people to *abstain* from something that imposes costs on others. In the second case—yanking the mattress off the cement—the problem is to get somebody to take the trouble to *do* something that benefits himself not at all but will benefit others greatly.

Another distinction is that the first case involves *everybody*, the second *somebody*. We can easily turn the mattress case around and make it an act of carelessness that hurts others, not an act of good will for their benefit. Whoever tied the mattress carelessly may have considered the loss of the mattress in case the knot came loose, but not the risk that a thousand families would be late getting home behind him. So, also, on the Expressway we can drop our prejudices against morbid sightseeing and just suppose that people are driving comfortably along minding their business. They are in no great hurry but somebody behind them is, in fact a lot of people. It is worth a lot of time collectively, and maybe even money, to get the unhurried driver to bestir himself or to pick another route. He needn't feel guilty; he may even want something in return for giving up his right of way to people who like to drive faster. Without organized communication, he may know nothing about the hurry they are in behind him, and care even less.

A good part of social organization—of what we call society—consists of institutional arrangements to overcome these divergences between perceived individual interest and some larger collective bargain. Some of it is market-oriented—ownership, contracts, damage suits, patents and copyrights, promissory notes, rental agreements, and a variety of communications and information systems. Some have to do with government—taxes to cover public services, protection of persons, a weather bureau if weather information is not otherwise marketable, one-way streets, laws against littering, wrecking crews to clear away that car in the southbound lane and policemen to wave us on in the northbound lane. More selective groupings—the union, the club, the neighborhood—can organize incentive systems or regulations to try to help people do what individually they wouldn't but collectively they may wish to do. Our morals can substitute for markets and regulations, in getting us sometimes to do from conscience the things that in the long run we might elect to do only if assured of reciprocation.

What we are dealing with is the frequent divergence between what people are individually motivated to do and what they might like to accomplish together. Consider the summer brown-out. We are warned ominously that unless we all cut our use of electricity in midsummer we may overload the system and suffer drastic consequences, sudden black-outs or prolonged power failures, unpredictable in their consequences. In other years we are warned of water shortages; leaky faucets account for a remarkable amount of waste, and we are urged to fit them with new washers. There just cannot be any question but what, for most of us if not all of us, we are far better off if we all switch off the lights more assiduously, cut down a little on the air-conditioning, repair the leaky faucets, let the lawns get a little browner and the cars a little dirtier, and otherwise reduce our claims on the common pool of water and electric power. For if we do not, we suffer worse and less predictably—the air-conditioner may be out altogether on the hottest day, and all lights out just when we need them, when overload occurs or some awkward emergency rationing system goes into effect.

But turning down my air-conditioner, or turning the lights out for five minutes when I leave the room, or fixing my leaky faucet, can't do me any good. Mine is an infinitesimal part of the demand for water and electricity, and while the minute difference that I can make is multiplied by the number of people to whom it can make a difference, the effect on me of what I do is truly negligible.

Within the family we can save hot water on Friday night by taking brief showers, rather than racing to be first in the shower and use it all up. But that may be because within the family we care about each other, or have to pretend we do, or can watch each other and have to account for the time we stand enjoying the hot water. It is harder to care about, or to be brought to account by, the people who can wash their cars more effectively if I let my lawn burn, or who can keep their lawns greener if I leave my car dirty.

What we need in these circumstances is an enforceable social contract. I'll cooperate if you and everybody else will. I'm better off if we all cooperate than if we go our separate ways. In matters of great virtue and symbolism, especially in emergencies, we can become imbued with a sense of solidarity and abide by a golden rule. We identify with the group, and we act as we hope everybody will act. We enjoy rising to the occasion, rewarded by a sense of virtue and community. And indeed a good deal of social ethics is concerned with rules of behavior that are collectively rewarding if collectively obeyed (even though the individual may not benefit from his own participation). But if there is nothing heroic in the occasion; if what is required is a protracted nuisance; if one feels no particular community with great numbers of people who have nothing in common but connected water pipes; if one must continually decide what air-conditioned temperature to allow himself in his own bedroom, or whether to go outdoors and check the faucet once again; and especially if one suspects that large numbers of people just are not playing the game—most people may cooperate only halfheartedly, and many not at all. And then when they see the dribbling faucet from which the pressure is gone, or read that the electrical shortage is undiminished in spite of exhortations to turn off the air-conditioners, even that grudging participation is likely to be abandoned.

The frustration is complete when a homeowner, stepping onto his back porch at night, cocks his head and hears the swish of invisible lawn sprinklers in the darkness up and down the block. He damns the lack of enforcement and turns the handle on his own sprinkler, making the violation unanimous.

There is no inconsistency in what he damned and what he did. He wants the ban enforced; but if it is not enforced he intends to water his lawn, especially if everybody else is doing it. He's not interested in doing minute favors for a multitude of individuals, most of whom he doesn't know, letting his lawn go to ruin; he *is* willing to enter a bargain, letting his lawn go to ruin if they will let theirs go the same way, so that they can all have unrestricted use of their showers, washing machines, toilets, and sinks.

The trouble is often in making the bargain stick. Water meters capable of shifting gears at peak-load times of day, with weekly water rates or water rations publicized through the summer, would undoubtedly take care of the problem. But fancy meters are expensive; fluctuating rates are a nuisance and hard to monitor; large families with lots of dirty clothes to wash will complain at the rates while a childless couple can afford to wash its new car. Moreover, long before an acceptable "solution" has been devised and publicized, a wet, cold autumn ensues and the problem now is to devise a scheme of mandatory snow tires on select roads in time for that unexpected early snowstorm that snarls everything up because my car, skidding sideways on a hill, blocks your car and all the cars behind you. In waiting to get my snow tires at the after-Christmas sales, I was gambling your dinner hour against the price of my tires.

Sometimes it takes only a fraction of us to solve the worst of the problem. If the electrical overload that threatens is only a few percent, half of us may find a way to enforce a voluntary restriction, and thus avoid the breakdown. It infuriates us that the other half don't do their share. It especially infuriates us if the other half, relieved of whatever anxiety might have made them a little more conscious of wasted electricity, now relax and leave their lights on in the comfortable knowledge that, to prevent blackout, we have turned off our electric fans. Still, if we don't charge too much for spite, it can be a good bargain even for the half of us that carry the whole load. The "free riders" are better off than we are, but as the cooperative half we may be better off for having found a way to make ourselves cut back in unison.

Sometimes it won't work unless nearly everybody plays the game. Trashcans in our nation's capital say that "Every Litter Bit Hurts," but it is really the first litter bits that spoil a park or sidewalk. Ten times as much makes it worse, but not ten times worse. It takes only one power mower to turn a quiet Sunday morning into the neighborhood equivalent of a stamping mill; indeed, the speed with which a few timid homeowners light up their machines, once the first brazen neighbor has shattered the quiet with his own three-and-a-half horsepower, suggests that they expect no reproach once it's clear that it's beyond their power to provide a quiet Sunday by merely turning off one machine among several.

Morality and virtue probably work this way. Whatever the technology of cooperative action—whether every litter bit hurts, or the first few bits just about spoil everything—people who are willing to do their part as long as everybody else does, living by a commonly shared golden rule, enjoying perhaps the sheer participation in a common preference for selflessness, may have a limited tolerance to the evidence or to the mere suspicion that others are cheating on the social contract, bending the golden rule, making fools of those who carefully minimize the detergent they send into the local river or who carry away the leaves they could so easily have burned.

There are the cases, though, in which not everybody gains under the social contract. Some gain more than others, and some not enough to compensate for what they give up. An agreement to turn off air-conditioners, to make sure that electric lights and the more essential appliances can keep functioning, may be a bad bargain for the man or woman with hay fever, who'd rather have a dry nose in darkness than sneeze with the lights on. A ban on outdoor uses of water may be a crude but acceptable bargain for most people, but not for the couple whose joy and pride is their garden. A sudden police order to go full speed past that accident on the Expressway is a welcome relief to the people who still have a mile or so to crawl before they get to the scene of the accident; drivers who have been crawling for ten minutes and are just at the point of having a good look will be annoyed. Ten minutes ago they would not have been; but ten minutes ago somebody ahead of them would have been.

If participation requires unanimous consent, it may be necessary and it may be possible to compensate, for their participation, those to whom the advantages do not cover the costs. Compensation does complicate the arrangements, though, and when that couple who love their garden get paid for seeing it wither, their neighbors will suddenly discover how much they loved their own gardens.

In economics the most familiar cases of this general phenomenon involve some resource or commodity that is scarce, inelastic in supply, but freely available to all comers until the supply has run out. The most striking case was the buffalo, twenty or thirty million of whom roamed the plains west of the Mississippi at the end of the Civil War. As meat they were not marketable; rail transport of live animals had not reached the west. Their tongues were delicious and drew a high price, and for several years there was a thriving business in buffalo tongues, each of which left behind a thousand pounds of rotting meat. Then the hides became marketable and that was the end; twenty billion pounds of live meat was turned to rotting carcasses in the course of half a dozen years. Wagon trains detoured to avoid the stench of decaying buffaloes; and, roughly, for every five pounds of buffalo meat left on the ground, somebody got a penny for the hide. At any plausible interest rate the buffalo would have been worth more as live meat fifteen years later, when marketing became feasible, but to the hunter who killed fifty a day for their hides, it was that or nothing. There was no way that he could claim a cow and market his property right in her offspring fifteen years later.

Whales and electricity, buffaloes and the water supply: scarce to the community but "free" to the individual as long as they last. In the small, the same phenomenon occurs when half a dozen businessmen tell the waiter to put it all on a single check; why save $6 for the group by having hamburger, when the steak costs the man who orders it only $1 more? People drink more at a party where the drinks are free and everybody is assessed his fraction of the total cost afterwards; it's a great way to get people to drink more than they can afford, and conviviality may recommend it. The manager of a club would have to be out of his mind, however, to propose that each month's total dining room budget be merely divided equally among all the members.

At the Shrine of Our Lady of Fàtima, or Why Political Questions Are Not All Economic

Mark Sagoff

Lewiston, New York, a well-to-do community near Buffalo, is the site of the Lake Ontario Ordinance Works, where the federal government, years ago, disposed of the residues of the Manhattan Project. These radioactive wastes are buried but are not forgotten by the residents, who say that when the wind is southerly radon gas blows through the town. Several parents at a recent conference I attended there described their terror on learning that cases of leukemia had been found among area children. They feared for their own lives as well. At the other sides of the table, officials from New York State and from local corporations replied that these fears were ungrounded. People who smoke, they said, take greater risks than people who live close to waste disposal sites. One speaker talked in terms of "rational methodologies of decisionmaking." This aggravated the parents' rage and frustration.

The speaker suggested that the townspeople, were they to make their decision in a free market, would choose to live near the hazardous waste facility, if they knew the scientific facts. He told me later they were irrational—he said, "neurotic"—because they refused to recognize or to act upon their own interests. The residents of Lewiston were unimpressed with his analysis of their "willingness to pay" to avoid this risk or that. They did not see what risk-benefit analysis had to do with the issues they raised.

If you take the Military Highway (as I did) from Buffalo to Lewiston, you will pass through a formidable wasteland. Landfills stretch in all directions, where enormous trucks—tiny in that landscape—incessantly deposit sludge which great bulldozers, like yellow ants, then push into the ground. These machines are the only signs of life, for in the miasma that hangs in the air, no birds, not even scavengers, are seen. Along colossal power lines which criss-cross this dismal land, the dynamos at Niagra send electric power south, where factories have fled, leaving their remains to decay. To

Source: From 23 *Ariz. L. Rev.* 1283 (1982). Copyright © 1982 by the Arizona Board of Regents. Reprinted by permission.

drive along this road is to feel, oddly, the mystery and awe one experiences in the presence of so much power and decadence.

Henry Adams had a similar response to the dynamos on display at the Paris Exposition of 1900. To him "the dynamo became a symbol of infinity."[1] To Adams, the dynamo functioned as the modern equivalent of the Virgin, that is, as the center and focus of power. "Before the end, one began to pray to it; inherited instinct taught the natural expression of man before silent and infinite force."[2]

Adams asks in his essay "The Dynamo and the Virgin" how the products of modern industrial civilization will compare with those of the religious culture of the Middle Ages. If he could see the landfills and hazardous waste facilities bordering the power stations and honeymoon hotels of Niagra Falls he would know the answer. He would understand what happens when efficiency replaces infinity as the central conception of value. The dynamos at Niagra will not produce another Mont-Saint-Michel. "All the steam in the world," Adams wrote, "could not, like the Virgin, build Chartres."[3]

At the Shrine of Our Lady of Fàtima, on a plateau north of the Military Highway, a larger than life sculpture of Mary looks into the chemical air. The original of this shrine stands in central Portugal, where in May, 1917, three children said they saw a Lady, brighter than the sun, raised on a cloud in an evergreen tree.[4] Five months later, on a wet and chilly October day, the Lady again appeared, this time before a large crowd. Some who were skeptical did not see the miracle. Others in the crowd reported, however, that "the sun appeared and seemed to tremble, rotate violently and fall, dancing over the heads of the throng. . . ."[5]

The Shrine was empty when I visited it. The cult of Our Lady of Fàtima, I imagine, has only a few devotees. The cult of Pareto optimality, however, has many. Where some people see only environmental devastation, its devotees perceive efficiency, utility, and the maximization of wealth. They see the satisfaction of wants. They envision the good life. As I looked over the smudged and ruined terrain I tried to share that vision. I hoped that Our Lady of Fàtima, worker of miracles, might serve, at least for the moment, as the Patroness of cost-benefit analysis. I thought of all the wants and needs that are satisfied in a landscape of honeymoon cottages, commercial strips, and dumps for hazardous waste. I saw the miracle of efficiency. The prospect, however, looked only darker in that light.

I

This essay concerns the economic decisions we make about the environment. It also concerns our political decisions about the environment. Some

---

[1] H. Adams, *The Education of Henry Adams* 380 (1970, 1961).
[2] *Id.*
[3] *Id.* at 388.
[4] For an account, see J. Pelletier, *The Sun Danced At Fatima* (1951).
[5] 5 *New Catholic Encyclopedia* 856 (1967).

people have suggested that ideally these should be the same, that all environmental problems are problems in distribution. According to this view there is an environmental problem only when some resource is not allocated in equitable and efficient ways.[6]

This approach to environmental policy is pitched entirely at the level of the consumer. It is his or her values that count, and the measure of these values is the individual's willingness to pay. The problem of justice or fairness in society becomes, then, the problem of distributing goods and services so that more people get more of what they want to buy. A condo on the beach. A snowmobile for the mountains. A tank full of gas. A day of labor. The only values we have, on this view, are those which a market can price.[7]

How much do you value open space, a stand of trees, an "unspoiled" landscape? Fifty dollars? A hundred? A thousand? This is one way to measure value. You could compare the amount consumers would pay for a townhouse or coal or a landfill and the amount they would pay to preserve an area in its "natural" state. If users would pay more for the land with the house, the coal mine, or the landfill, than without—less construction and other costs of development—then the efficient thing to do is to improve the land and thus increase its value. That is why we have so many tract developments. And pizza stands. And gas stations. And strip mines. And landfills. How much did you spend last year to preserve open space? How much for pizza and gas? "In principle, the ultimate measure of environmental quality," as one basic text assures us, "is the value people place on these . . . services or their *willingness to pay*."[8]

Willingness to pay. What is wrong with that? The rub is this: not all of us think of ourselves simply as *consumers*. Many of us regard ourselves *as citizens* as well. We act as consumers to get what we want *for ourselves*. We act as citizens to achieve what we think is right or best *for the community*. The question arises, then, whether what we want for ourselves individually as consumers is consistent with the goals we would set for ourselves collectively as citizens. Would I vote for the sort of things I shop for? Are my preferences as a consumer consistent with my judgments as a citizen?

They are not. I am schizophrenic. Last year, I fixed a couple of tickets and was happy to do so since I saved fifty dollars. Yet, at election time, I helped to vote the corrupt judge out of office. I speed on the highway; yet I want the police to enforce laws against speeding. I used to buy mixers in returnable bottles—but who can bother to return them? I buy only disposables now, but, to soothe my conscience, I urge my state senator to outlaw one-way containers. I love my car; I hate the bus. Yet I vote for candidates

---

[6]See, e.g., W. Baxter, *People or Penguins: The Case For Optimal Pollution* chap. 1 (1974). See generally A. Freeman III, R. Haveman, A. Kneese, *The Economics of Environmental Policy* (1973).

[7]R. Posner puts this point well in discussing wealth maximization as an ethical concept. "The only kind of preference that counts in a system of wealth-maximization," he writes, "is . . . one that is backed up by money—in other words, that is registered in a market." Posner, "Utilitarianism, Economics, and Legal Theory," 8 *J. Legal Stud.* 119 (1979).

[8]Freeman et al., note 6 *supra* at 23.

who promise to tax gasoline to pay for public transportation. I send my dues to the Sierra Club to protect areas in Alaska I shall never visit. And I support the work of the American League to Abolish Capital Punishment although, personally, I have nothing to gain one way or the other. (When I hang, I will hang myself.) And of course I applaud the Endangered Species Act, although I have no earthly use for the Colorado squawfish or the Indiana bat. I support almost any political cause that I think will defeat my consumer interests. This is because I have contempt for—although I act upon—those interests. I have an "Ecology Now" sticker on a car that leaks oil everywhere it's parked.

The distinction between consumer and citizen preferences has long vexed the theory of public finance. Should the public economy serve the same goals as the household economy? May it serve, instead, goals emerging from our association as citizens? The question asks if we may collectively strive for and achieve only those items we individually compete for and consume. Should we aspire, instead, to public goals we may legislate as a nation?

The problem, insofar as it concerns public finance, is stated as follows by R. A. Musgrave, who reports a conversation he had with Gerhard Colm.

> He [Colm] holds that the individual voter dealing with political issues has a frame of reference quite distinct from that which underlies his allocation of income as a consumer. In the latter situation the voter acts as a private individual determined by self-interest and deals with his personal wants; in the former, he acts as a political being guided by his image of a good society. The two, Colm holds, are different things.[9]

Are these two different things? Stephen Marglin suggests that they are. He writes:

> The preferences that govern one's unilateral market actions no longer govern his actions when the form of reference is shifted from the market to the political arena. The Economic Man and the Citizen are for all intents and purposes two different individuals. It is not a question, therefore, of rejecting individual . . . preference maps; it is, rather, that market and political preference maps are inconsistent.[10]

Marglin observes that if this is true, social choices optimal under one set of preferences will not be optimal under another. What, then, is the meaning of "optimality?" He notices that if we take a person's true preferences to be those expressed in the market, we may, then, neglect or reject the preferences that person reveals in advocating a political cause or position. "One might argue on welfare grounds," Marglin speculates, "for authoritarian rejection of individuals' politically revealed preferences in favor of their market revealed preferences!"

[9]R. Musgrave, *The Theory of Public Finance* 87–88 (1959).
[10]Marglin, "The Social Rate of Discount and the Optimal Rate of Investment," 77 *Q. J. of Econ.* 98 (1963).

II

On February 19, 1981, President Reagan published Executive Order 12,291 requiring all administrative agencies and departments to support every new major regulation with a cost-benefit analysis establishing that the benefits of the regulation to society outweigh its costs.[11] The Order directs the Office of Management and Budget (OMB) to review every such regulation on the basis of the adequacy of the cost-benefit analysis supporting it. This is a departure from tradition. Traditionally, regulations have been reviewed not by OMB but by the courts on the basis of their relation not to cost-benefit analysis but to authorizing legislation.

A month earlier, in January 1981, the Supreme Court heard lawyers for the American Textile Manufacturers Institute argue against a proposed Occupational Safety and Health Administration (OSHA) regulation which would have severely restricted the acceptable levels of cotton dust in textile plants.[12] The lawyers for industry argued that the benefits of the regulation would not equal the costs. The lawyers for the government contended that the law required the tough standard. OSHA, acting consistently with Executive Order 12,291, asked the Court not to decide the cotton dust case, in order to give the agency time to complete the cost-benefit analysis required by the textile industry. The Court declined to accept OSHA's request and handed down its opinion on June 17, 1981.[13]

The Supreme Court, in a 5–3 decision, found that the actions of regulatory agencies which conform to the OSHA law need not be supported by cost-benefit analysis. In addition, the Court asserted that Congress in writing a statute, rather than the agencies in applying it, has the primary responsibility for balancing benefits and costs. The Court said:

> When Congress passed the Occupational Health and Safety Act in 1970, it chose to place pre-eminent value on assuring employees a safe and healthful working environment, limited only by the feasibility of achieving such an environment. We must measure the validity of the Secretary's actions against the requirements of that Act.[14]

The opinion upheld the finding of the Appeals Court that "Congress itself struck the balance between costs and benefits in the mandate to the agency."[15]

The Appeals Court opinion in *American Textile Manufacturers* vs. *Donovan* supports the principle that legislatures are not necessarily bound to a particular conception of regulatory policy. Agencies that apply the law, therefore, may not need to justify on cost-benefit grounds the standards

[11]See 46 *Fed. Reg.* 13193 (February 19, 1981). The Order specifies that the cost-benefit requirement shall apply "to the extent permitted by law."

[12]*American Textile Mfgrs. Inst.* v. *Bingham*, 617 F.2d 636 (D. C. Cir. 1979) *cert.* granted *sub nom.* [1980]; *American Textile Mfgrs.* v. *Marshall*, 49 U.S.L.W. 3208.

[13]*Textile Mfgrs.* v. *Donovan*, 101 S.Ct. 2478 (1981).

[14]*Id.* U.S.L.W. (1981), 4733–34.

[15]*Ibid.*, 4726–29.

they set. These standards may conflict with the goal of efficiency and still express our political will as a nation. That is, they may reflect not the personal choices of self-interested individuals, but the collective judgments we make on historical, cultural, aesthetic, moral, and ideological grounds.

The appeal of the Reagan Administration to cost-benefit analysis, however, may arise more from political than economic considerations. The intention, seen in the most favorable light, may not be to replace political or ideological goals with economic ones but to make economic goals more apparent in regulation. This is not to say that Congress should function to reveal a collective willingness-to-pay just as markets reveal an individual willingness-to-pay. It is to suggest that Congress should do more to balance economic with ideological, aesthetic, and moral goals. To think that environmental or worker safety policy can be based exclusively on aspiration for a "natural" and "safe" world is as foolish as to hold that environmental law can be reduced to cost-benefit accounting. The more we move to one extreme, as I found in Lewiston, the more likely we are to hear from the other.

III

The labor unions won an important political victory when Congress passed the Occupational Safety and Health Act of 1970.[16] That Act, among other things, severely restricts worker exposure to toxic substances. It instructs the Secretary of Labor to set "the standard which most adequately assures, to the extent feasible . . . that no employee will suffer material impairment of health or functional capacity even if such employee has regular exposure to the hazard . . . for the period of his working life."[17]

Pursuant to this law, the Secretary of Labor, in 1977, reduced from ten to one part per million (ppm) the permissible ambient exposure level for benzene, a carcinogen for which no safe threshold is known. The American Petroleum Institute thereupon challenged the new standard in court.[18] It argued, with much evidence in its favor, that the benefits (to workers) of the one ppm standard did not equal the costs (to industry). The standard, therefore, did not appear to be a rational response to a market failure in that it did not strike an efficient balance between the interests of workers in safety and the interests of industry and consumers in keeping prices down.

The Secretary of Labor defended the tough safety standard on the ground that the law demanded it. An efficient standard might have required safety until it cost industry more to prevent a risk than it cost workers to accept it. Had Congress adopted this vision of public policy—

[16]Pub. L. No. 91-596, 84 Stat. 1596 (codified at 29 U.S.C. 651–78) (1970).

[17]29 U.S.C., 655(b) (5).

[18]*American Petroleum Institute* v. *Marshall*, 581 F.2d 493 (1978) (5th Cir.), aff'd 100 S. Ct. 2844 (1980).

one which can be found in many economics texts[19]—it would have treated workers not as ends-in-themselves but as means for the production of overall utility. And this, as the Secretary saw it, was what Congress refused to do.

The United States Court of Appeals for the Fifth Circuit agreed with the American Petroleum Institute and invalidated the one ppm benzene standard.[20] On July 2, 1980, the Supreme Court affirmed remanding the benzene standard back to OSHA for revision.[21] The narrowly based Supreme Court decision was divided over the role economic considerations should play in judicial review. Justice Marshall, joined in dissent by three other justices, argued that the Court had undone on the basis of its own theory of regulatory policy an act of Congress inconsistent with that theory. He concluded that the plurality decision of the Court "requires the American worker to return to the political arena to win a victory that he won before in 1970."[22]

To reject cost-benefit analysis, as Justice Marshall would, as a basis for public policy making is not necessarily to reject cost-effectiveness analysis, which is an altogether different thing. *"Cost-benefit analysis,"* one commentator points out, "is used by the decision maker to establish societal goals as well as the means for achieving these goals, whereas *cost effectiveness analysis* only compares alternative means for achieving 'given' goals."[23] Justice Marshall's dissent objects to those who would make efficiency the goal of public policy. It does not necessarily object to those who would accomplish as efficiently as possible the goals Congress sets.[24]

IV

When efficiency is the criterion of public safety and health one tends to conceive of social relations on the model of a market, ignoring competing visions of what we as a society should be like. Yet it is obvious that there are competing conceptions of how we should relate to one other. There are some who believe, on principle, that worker safety and environmental quality ought to be protected only insofar as the benefits of protection balance the costs. On the other hand, people argue, also on principle, that neither worker safety nor environmental quality should be treated merely as a commodity, to be traded at the margin for other commodities, but should

---

[19]See, e.g., R. Posner, *Economic Analysis of Law,* parts I, II (1972, 1973). In *The Costs of Accidents* (1970), G. Calabresi argues that accident law balances two goals, "efficiency" and "equality" or "justice."

[20]581 F.2d 493 (1978).

[21]100 S.Ct. 2844 (1980).

[22]*Id.* at 2903.

[23]M. Baram, "Cost-Benefit Analysis: An Inadequate Basis for Health, Safety and Environmental Regulatory Decision Making" 8 *Ecological Law Quarterly* 473 (1980).

[24]See 49 U.S.L.W. 4724–29 for this reasoning applied in the cotton dust case.

be valued for its own sake. The conflict between these two principles is logical or moral, to be resolved by argument or debate. The question whether cost-benefit analysis should play a decisive role in policymaking is not to be decided by cost-benefit analysis. A contradiction between principles—between contending visions of the good society—cannot be settled by asking how much partisans are willing to pay for their beliefs.

The role of the *legislator,* the political role, may be more important to the individual than the role of *consumer.* The person, in other words, is not to be treated as merely a bundle of preferences to be juggled in cost-benefit analyses. The individual is to be respected as an advocate of ideas which are to be judged in relation to the reasons for them. If health and environmental statutes reflect a vision of society as something other than a market by requiring protections beyond what are efficient, then this may express not legislative ineptitude but legislative responsiveness to public values. To deny this vision because it is economically inefficient is simply to replace it with another vision. It is to insist that the ideas of the citizen be sacrificed to the psychology of the consumer.

We hear on all sides that government is routinized, mechanical, entrenched, and bureaucratized; the jargon alone is enough to dissuade the most mettlesome meddler. Who can make a difference? It is plain that for many of us the idea of a national political community has an abstract and suppositious quality. We have only our private conceptions of the good, if no way exists to arrive at a public one. This is only to note the continuation, in our time, of the trend Benjamin Constant described in the essay, *De La Liberte des Anciens Comparee a Celle des Modernes.*[25] Constant observes that the modern world, as opposed to the ancient, emphasizes civil over political liberties, the rights of privacy and property over those of community and participation. "Lost in the multitude," Constant writes, "the individual rarely perceives the influence that he exercises," and, therefore, must be content with "the peaceful enjoyment of private independence."[26] The individual asks only to be protected by laws common to all in his pursuit of his own self-interest. The citizen has been replaced by the consumer; the tradition of Rousseau has been supplanted by that of Locke and Mill.

Nowhere are the rights of the moderns, particularly the rights of privacy and property, less helpful than in the area of the natural environment. Here the values we wish to protect—cultural, historical, aesthetic, and moral—are public values; they depend not so much upon what each person wants individually as upon what he or she believes we stand for collectively. We refuse to regard worker health and safety as commodities; we regulate hazards as a matter of right. Likewise, we refuse to treat environmental resources simply as public goods in the economist's sense. Instead, we prevent significant deterioration of air quality not only as a matter of individual self-interest but also as a matter of collective self-respect. How shall we balance efficiency against moral, cultural, and aes-

---

[25]*De la Liberte des Anciens Comparee a Celle des Modernes* (1819).

[26]*Oeuvres Politiques de Benjamin Constant,* ed. C. Luandre 269 (Paris, 1874); quoted in S. Wolin, *Politics and Vision* 281 (1960).

thetic values in policy for the workplace and the environment? No better way has been devised to do this than by legislative debate ending in a vote. This is not the same thing as a cost-benefit analysis terminating in a bottom line.

V

It is the characteristic of cost-benefit analysis that it treats all value judgments other than those made on its behalf as nothing but statements of preference, attitude, or emotion, insofar as they are value judgments. The cost-benefit analyst regards as true the judgment that we should maximize efficiency or wealth. The analyst believes that this view can be backed by reasons;[27] the analyst does not regard it as a preference or want for which he or she must be willing to pay. The cost-benefit analyst, however, tends to treat all other normative views and recommendations as if they were nothing but subjective reports of mental states. The analyst supposes in all such cases that "this is right" and "this is what we ought to do" are equivalent to "I want this" and "this is what I prefer." Value judgments are beyond criticism if, indeed, they are nothing but expressions of personal preference; they are incorrigible since every person is in the best position to know what he or she wants. All valuation, according to this approach, happens *in foro interno*; debate *in foro publico* has no point. On this approach, the reasons that people give for their views, unless these people are welfare economists, do not count; what counts is how much they are willing to pay to satisfy their wants. Those who are willing to pay the most, for all intents and purposes, have the right view; theirs is the more informed opinion, the better aesthetic judgment, and the deeper moral insight.

The assumption that valuation is subjective, that judgments of good and evil are nothing but expressions of desire and aversion, is not unique to economic theory.[28] There are psychotherapists—Carl Rogers is an example—who likewise deny the objectivity or cognitivity of valuation.[29] For

[27]There are arguments that whatever reasons may be given are no good. See, e.g., Dworkin, "Why Efficiency?" 8 *Hofstra L. Rev.* 563 (1980); Dworkin, "Is Wealth a Value?" 9 *J. Legal Stud.* 191 (1980); Kennedy, "Cost-Benefit Analysis of Entitlement Problems: A Critique" 33 *Stan L. Rev.* 387 (1980); Rizzo, "The Mirage of Efficiency" 8 *Hofstra L. Rev.* 641 (1980); Sagoff, "Economic Theory and Environmental Law" 79 *Mich L. Rev.* 1393 (1981).

[28]This is the emotive theory of value. For the classic statement, see C. Stevenson, *Ethics and Language* chaps. 1, 2 (1944). For criticism, see Blanshard, "The New Subjectivism in Ethics" 9 *Philosophy and Phenomenological Research* 504 (1949). For a statement of the related interest theory of value, see E. Westermarck, *Ethical Relativity* chaps. 3, 4, 5 (1932); R. Perry, *General Theory of Value* (1926). For criticisms of subjectivism in ethics and a case for the objective theory presupposed here, see generally, P. Edwards, *The Logic of Moral Discourse* (1955) and W. Ross, *The Right and the Good* (1930).

[29]My account is based on C. Rogers, *On Becoming a Person* (1961); C. Rogers, *Client Centered Therapy* (1965); and Rogers, "A Theory of Therapy, Personality, and Interpersonal Relationships, as Developed in the Client Centered Framework" 3 *Psychology: A Study of a Science* 184 (S. Koch ed., 1959). For a similar account used as a critique of the lawyer-client relation, see Simon, "Homo Psychologious: Notes on a New Legal Formalism" 32 *Stan. L. Rev.* 487 (1980).

Rogers, there is only one criterion of worth: it lies in "the subjective world of the individual. Only he knows it fully."[30] The therapist shows his or her client that a "value system is not necessarily something imposed from without, but is something experienced."[31] Therapy succeeds when the client "perceives himself in such a way that no self-experience can be discriminated as more or less worthy of positive self-regard than any other. . . ."[32] The client then "tends to place the basis of standards within himself, recognizing that the 'goodness' or 'badness' of any experience or perceptual object is not something inherent in that object, but is a value placed in it by himself."[33]

Rogers points out that "some clients make strenuous efforts to have the therapist exercise the valuing function, so as to provide them with guides for action."[34] The therapist, however, "consistently keeps the locus of evaluation with the client."[35] As long as the therapist refuses to "exercise the valuing function" and as long as he or she practices an "unconditional positive regard"[36] for all the affective states of the client, then the therapist remains neutral among the client's values or "sensory and visceral experiences."[37] The role of the therapist is legitimate, Rogers suggests, because of this value neutrality. The therapist accepts all felt preferences as valid and imposes none on the client.

Economists likewise argue that their role as policymakers is legitimate because they are neutral among competing values in the client society. The political economist, according to James Buchanan, "is or should be ethically neutral: the indicated results are influenced by his own value scale only insofar as this reflects his membership in a larger group."[38] The economist might be most confident of the impartiality of his or her policy recommendations if he or she could derive them formally or mathematically from individual preferences. If theoretical difficulties make such a social welfare function impossible,[39] however, the next best thing, to preserve neutrality, is to let markets function to transform individual preference orderings into a collective ordering of social states. The analyst is able then to base policy on preferences that exist in society and are not necessarily his own.

Economists have used this impartial approach to offer solutions to many outstanding social problems, for example, the controversy over abortion. An economist argues that "there is an optimal number of abortions, just as there is an optimal level of pollution, or purity. . . . Those who

[30]Rogers, note 29 *supra* at 210.

[31]C. Rogers, *Client Centered Therapy* 150 (1965).

[32]Rogers, note 29 *supra* at 208.

[33]Rogers, note 31 *supra* at 139.

[34]*Id.* at 150.

[35]*Id.*

[36]Rogers, note 29 *supra* at 208.

[37]*Id.* at 523–24.

[38]Buchanan, "Positive Economics, Welfare Economics, and Political Economy" 2 *J. L. and Econ.* 124, 127 (1959).

[39]K. Arrow, *Social Choice and Individual Values* i–v (2d ed., 1963).

oppose abortion could eliminate it entirely, if their intensity of feeling were so strong as to lead to payments that were greater at the margin than the price anyone would pay to have an abortion."[40] Likewise economists, in order to determine whether the war in Vietnam was justified, have estimated the willingness to pay of those who demonstrated against it.[41] Likewise it should be possible, following the same line of reasoning, to decide whether Creationism should be taught in the public schools, whether black and white people should be segregated, whether the death penalty should be enforced, and whether the square root of six is three. All of these questions depend upon how much people are willing to pay for their subjective preferences or wants—or none of them do. This is the beauty of cost-benefit analysis: no matter how relevant or irrelevant, wise or stupid, informed or uninformed, responsible or silly, defensible or indefensible wants may be, the analyst is able to derive a policy from them—a policy which is legitimate because, in theory, it treats all of these preferences as equally valid and good.

VI

Consider, by way of contrast, a Kantian conception of value.[42] The individual, for Kant, is a judge of values, not a mere haver of wants, and the individual judges not for himself or herself merely, but as a member of a relevant community or group. The central idea in a Kantian approach to ethics is that some values are more reasonable than others and therefore have a better claim upon the assent of members of the community as such.[43] The world of obligation, like the world of mathematics or the world of empirical fact, is intersubjective, it is public not private, so that objective standards of argument and criticism apply. Kant recognizes that values, like beliefs, are subjective states of mind, but he points out that like beliefs they have an objective content as well; therefore they are either correct or mistaken. Thus Kant discusses valuation in the context not of psychology but of cognition. He believes that a person who makes a value judgment— or a policy recommendation—claims to know what is *right* and not just what is *preferred*. A value judgment is like an empirical or theoretical judgment in that it claims to be *true*, not merely to be *felt*.

We have, then, two approaches to public policy before us. The first, the approach associated with normative versions of welfare economics, asserts that the only policy recommendation that can or need be defended

---

[40]H. Macaulay and B. Yandle, *Environmental Use and the Market* 120–21 (1978).

[41]Cicchetti, Freeman, Haveman, and Knetsch, "On the Economics of Mass Demonstrations: A Case Study of the November 1969 March on Washington, 61 *Am. Econ. Rev.* 719 (1971).

[42]I. Kant, *Foundations of the Metaphysics of Morals* (R. Wolff, ed., L. Beck trans., 1969). I follow the interpretation of Kantian ethics of W. Sellars, *Science and Metaphysics* chap. VII (1968) and Sellars, "On Reasoning about Values" 17 *Am. Phil. Q.* 81 (1980).

[43]See A. Macintyre, *After Virtue* 22 (1981).

on objective grounds is efficiency or wealth-maximization. Every policy decision after that depends only on the preponderance of feeling or preference, as expressed in willingness to pay. The Kantian approach, on the other hand, assumes that many policy recommendations other than that one may be justified or refuted on objective grounds. It would concede that the approach of welfare economics applies adequately to some questions, e.g., those which ordinary consumer markets typically settle. How many yo-yos should be produced as compared to how many frisbees? Shall pens have black ink or blue? Matters such as these are so trivial it is plain that markets should handle them. It does not follow, however, that we should adopt a market or quasi-market approach to every public question.

A market or quasi-market approach to arithmetic, for example, is plainly inadequate. No matter how much people are willing to pay, three will never be the square root of six. Similarly, segregation is a national curse and the fact that we are willing to pay for it does not make it better but only makes us worse. Similarly, the case for abortion must stand on the merits; it cannot be priced at the margin. Similarly, the war in Vietnam was a moral debacle and this can be determined without shadow-pricing the willingness to pay of those who demonstrated against it. Similarly, we do not decide to execute murderers by asking how much bleeding hearts are willing to pay to see a person pardoned and how much hard hearts are willing to pay to see him hanged. Our failures to make the right decisions in these matters are failures in arithmetic, failures in wisdom, failures in taste, failures in morality—but not market failures. There are no relevant markets to have failed. What separates these questions from those for which markets are appropriate is this. They involve matters of knowledge, wisdom, morality, and taste that admit of better or worse, right or wrong, true or false—and these concepts differ from that of economic optimality. Surely environmental questions—the protection of wilderness, habitats, water, land, and air as well as policy toward environmental safety and health—involve moral and aesthetic principles and not just economic ones. This is consistent, of course, with cost-effectiveness and with a sensible recognition of economic constraints.

The neutrality of the economist, like the neutrality of Rogers' therapist, is legitimate if private preferences or subjective wants are the only values in question. A person should be left free to choose the color of his or her necktie or necklace—but we cannot justify a theory of public policy or private therapy on that basis. If the patient seeks moral advice or tries to find reasons to justify a choice, the therapist, according to Rogers' model, would remind him or her to trust his visceral and sensory experiences. The result of this is to deny the individual status as a cognitive being capable of responding intelligently to reasons; it reduces him or her to a bundle of affective states. What Rogers' therapist does to the patient the cost-benefit analyst does to society as a whole. The analyst is neutral among our "values"—having first imposed a theory of what value is. This is a theory that is impartial among values and for that reason fails to treat the persons who have them with respect or concern. It does not treat them even as persons but only as locations at which wants may be found. And thus we may conclude that the neutrality of economics is not a basis for its legitimacy. We recognize it as an indifference toward value—an indifference so deep, so studied, and so assured that at first one hesitates to call it by its right name.

VII

The residents of Lewiston at the conference I attended demanded to know the truth about the dangers that confronted them and the reasons for these dangers. They wanted to be convinced that the sacrifice asked of them was legitimate even if it served interests other than their own. One official from a large chemical company dumping wastes in the area told them, in reply, that corporations were people and that people could talk to people about their feelings, interests, and needs. This sent a shiver through the audience. Like Joseph K. in *The Trial*,[44] the residents of Lewiston asked for an explanation, justice, and truth, and they were told that their wants would be taken care of. They demanded to know the reasons for what was continually happening to them. They were given a personalized response instead.

This response, that corporations are "just people serving people" is consistent with a particular view of power. This is the view that identified power with the ability to get what one wants as an individual, that is, to satisfy one's personal preferences. When people in official positions in corporations or in the government put aside their personal interests, it would follow that they put aside their power as well. Their neutrality then justifies them in directing the resources of society in ways they determine to be best. This managerial role serves not their own interests but those of their clients. Cost-benefit analysis may be seen as a pervasive form of this paternalism. Behind this paternalism, as William Simon observes of the lawyer-client relationship, lies a theory of value that tends to personalize power. "It resists understanding power as a product of class, property, or institutions and collapses power into the personal needs and dispositions of the individuals who command and obey."[45] Once the economist, the therapist, the lawyer, or the manager abjures his own interests and acts wholly on behalf of client individuals, he appears to have no power of his own and thus justifiably manipulates and controls everything. "From this perspective it becomes difficult to distinguish the powerful from the powerless. In every case, both the exercise of power and submission to it are portrayed as a matter of personal accommodation and adjustment."[46]

The key to the personal interest or emotive theory of value, as one commentator has rightly said, "is the fact that emotivism entails the obliteration of any genuine distinction between manipulative and non-mani   '

---

[44]F. Kafka, *The Trial* (rev. ed. trans. 1957). Simon (note 29 *supra*) at 524 applie analogy to the lawyer-client relationship.

[45]Simon, note 29 *supra* at 495.

[46]*Id.*

tive social relations."[47] The reason is that once the effective self is made the source of all value, the public self cannot participate in the exercise of power. As Philip Reiff remarks, "the public world is constituted as one vast stranger who appears at inconvenient times and makes demands viewed as purely external and therefore with no power to elicit a moral response."[48] There is no way to distinguish tyranny from the legitimate authority that public values and public law create.[49]

"At the rate of progress since 1900," Henry Adams speculates in his *Education*, "every American who lived into the year 2000 would know how to control unlimited power."[50] Adams thought that the Dynamo would organize and release as much energy as the Virgin. Yet in the 1980s, the citizens of Lewiston, surrounded by dynamos, high tension lines, and nuclear wastes, are powerless. They do not know how to criticize power, resist power, or justify power—for to do so depends on making distinctions between good and evil, right and wrong, innocence and guilt, justice and injustice, truth and lies. These distinctions cannot be made out and have no significance within an emotive or psychological theory of value. To adopt this theory is to imagine society as a market in which individuals trade voluntarily and without coercion. No individual, no belief, no faith has authority over them. To have power to act as a nation, however, we must be able to act, at least at times, on a public philosophy, conviction, or faith. We cannot replace with economic analysis the moral function of public law. The antinomianism of cost-benefit analysis is not enough.

[47]Macintyre, note 43 *supra* at 22.

[48]P. Reiff, *The Triumph of the Therapeutic: Uses of Faith after Freud* 52 (1966).

[49]That public law regimes inevitably lead to tyranny seems to be the conclusion of H. Arendt, *The Human Condition* (1958); K. Popper, *The Open Society and Its Enemies* (1966); L. Strauss, *Natural Right and History* (1953). For an important criticism of this conclusion in these authors, see Holmes, "Aristippus In and Out of Athens" 73 *Am. Pol. Sci. Rev.* 113 (1979).

[50]H. Adams, note 1 *supra* at 476.

SELECTED
BIBLIOGRAPHY

ACKERMAN, BRUCE. *Private Property and the Constitution*. Yale University Press, 1977.
_____. *The Uncertain Search for Environmental Quality*. Free Press, 1974.
BAXTER, WILLIAM. *People or Penguins: The Case for Optimal Pollution*. Columbia University Press, 1974.
BECKER, LAWRENCE. *Property Rights*. Routledge and Kegan Paul, 1977.
BLACKSTONE, WILLIAM, ED. *Philosophy and the Environmental Crisis*. University of Georgia Press, 1974.
BOSSELMAN, FRED ET AL., EDS. *The Taking Issue*. Washington, D.C.. Government Printing Office, 1973.
BOULDING, KENNETH. "Fun and Games with the Gross National Product." In H. W. Helfrich, Jr., ed., *The Environmental Crisis*. Yale University Press, 1970.
BOWIE, NORMAN. "Value Theory in Economics." In *Philosophy in Context* 7 (1978): 30–50.
CALDWELL, LYNTON. "Rights of Ownership or Rights of Use?—The Need for a New Conceptual Basis for Land Use Policy." *William and Mary Law Review*, 1974.
CALLICOTT, BAIRD. "Elements of an Environmental Ethic: Moral Considerability and the Biotic Community." *Environmental Ethics*, 1979.
CARSON, RACHEL. *Silent Spring*. Houghton Mifflin, 1962.
COLWELL, THOMAS. "The Ecological Basis of Human Community." *Educational Theory*, 1971.
DALY, HERMAN. *Steady State Economics*. W. H. Freeman, 1977.
_____, ed. *Toward a Steady-State Economy*. W. H. Freeman, 1973.
DORFMAN, ROBERT. *Economics of the Environment*. Norton, 1972.
DRENGSON, ALAN. "Environmental Problems and Shifting Paradigms." *Environmental Ethics*, 1980.

FEIVESON, HAROLD. ET AL., EDS. *Boundaries of Analysis.* Ballinger, 1976.
GOODPASTER, KENNETH, AND KENNETH SAYRE, EDS. *Ethics and Problems of the 21st Century.* University of Notre Dame Press, 1979.
HARDIN, GARRETT, AND J. BADEN, EDS. *Managing the Commons.* W. H. Freeman, 1977.
HARDIN, GARRETT. "The Tragedy of the Commons." *Science,* 1968.
HARGROVE, EUGENE. "The Historical Foundations of American Environmental Attitudes." *Environmental Ethics,* 1979.
HELD, VIRGINIA, ED. *Property, Profits and Economic Justice.* Wadsworth, 1980.
HIRSCH, FRED. *Social Limits to Growth.* Harvard University Press, 1976.
LEMONS, JOHN. "Cooperation and Stability as a Basis for Environmental Ethics." *Environmental Ethics,* 1981.
LOWRANCE, WILLIAM. *Of Acceptable Risk.* William Kaufman, 1976.
MARX, LEO. *The Machine in the Garden.* Oxford University Press, 1973.
————. "Pastoral Ideals and City Troubles." *The Fitness of Man's Environment,* Smithsonian Annual II, 1968.
MCHARG, IAN. "The Place of Nature in the City of Man." *Annals of the American Academy of Political Science,* 1964.
MONCRIEF, LEWIS. "The Cultural Basis of Our Environmental Crisis." *Science* 170 (October 30, 1970): 508–12.
NAESS, ARNE. "The Shallow and the Deep, Long-Range Ecological Movement." *Inquiry,* 1973.
NASH, RODERICK, ED. *The American Environment.* Addison-Wesley, 1976.
————, ED. *Wilderness and the American Mind,* rev. ed. Yale University Press, 1973.
OPIE, JOHN, ED. *Americans and the Environment: The Controversy over Ecology.* D. C. Heath, 1971.
PASSMORE, JOHN. *Man's Responsibility for Nature.* Scribner's, 1974.
REGAN, THOMAS. "The Nature and Possibility of an Environmental Ethic." *Environmental Ethics,* 1981.
ROLSTON, HOLMES III. "Can and Ought We to Follow Nature?" *Environmental Ethics,* 1979.
SANTMIRE, H. PAUL. "Historical Dimensions of the American Crisis." *Dialog,* summer 1970.
SAYRE, KENNETH. "Morality, Energy and the Environment." *Environmental Ethics,* 1981.
SCHUMACHER, ERNST. *Small is Beautiful: Economics As If People Mattered.* Harper and Row, 1977.
SESSIONS, GEORGE. "Anthropocentrism and the Environmental Crisis." *Humboldt Journal of Social Relations,* 1974.
SHEPARD, PAUL. *The Tender Carnivore and the Sacred Game.* Scribner's, 1973.
SIMON, ANNE. *The Thin Edge.* Harper and Row, 1978.
SNYDER, GARY. *The Old Ways.* City Lights, 1977.
STONE, CHRISTOPHER. *Should Trees Have Standing?* William Kaufman, 1974.
TAYLOR, PAUL. "The Ethics of Respect for Nature." *Environmental Ethics,* 1981.
TRIBE, LAWRENCE ET AL., EDS. *When Values Conflict.* Ballinger, 1976.
————, AND L. JAFFE, EDS. *Environmental Protection.* Bracton, 1971.
WHITE, LYNN. "The Historical Roots of Our Ecological Crisis." *Science* 155 (March 10, 1967): 1203–07.